Louis Nazaire Bégin

The Bible and the Rule of Faith

Louis Nazaire Bégin

The Bible and the Rule of Faith

ISBN/EAN: 9783337098674

Printed in Europe, USA, Canada, Australia, Japan

Cover: Foto ©Lupo / pixelio.de

More available books at **www.hansebooks.com**

THE

Bible and the Rule of Faith.

BY THE

ABBÉ LOUIS NAZAIRE BÉGIN,

DOCTOR OF THEOLOGY, THEOLOGICAL PROFESSOR
IN THE UNIVERSITY OF LAVAL.

TRANSLATED FROM THE FRENCH

BY

G. M. WARD.

LONDON: BURNS AND OATES,
Portman Street and Paternoster Row.
QUEBEC: JOHN BARROW, 16 JOHN STREET.
1875.

Imprimatur.

✠ E. A. ARCHPUS. QUEBECEN.

Quebeci, die 26 Martii 1874.

Quum ex Seminarii Quebecensis præscripto recognitum fuerit opus cui titulus est *La Sainte Ecriture et la Règle de Foi, par l'Abbé L. N. Bégin*, nihil obstat quin typis mandetur.

THOS. S. HAMEL, PTER.,
R. U. L.

Quebeci, die 28 Martii 1874.

Imprimatur.

HENRICUS EDUARDUS,
Card. Archiep. Westmonast.

Westmonasterii, die 7 Augusti 1875.

CONTENTS.

TRANSLATOR'S PREFACE . . . . p. ix
INTRODUCTION xi

Part the First.
OF THE RULE OF FAITH IN GENERAL.

CHAPTER I.
Human reason left to itself—Lights of revelation—Reason and faith show us the obligation of believing revealed truths, and not altering their real meaning—Divine mission of the Church; anathemas pronounced on those who corrupt the true doctrine . . p. 1

CHAPTER II.
Necessity of a rule of faith—Its characteristics; it should be adapted to all classes of society; it should be sure, efficient to put an end to controversies, and perpetual . . . . . . p. 7

CHAPTER III.
What is the rule of faith which was established by our Lord Jesus Christ; or what means did He choose to communicate His doctrine to us?—The Bible—Tradition . . . . . p. 10

Part the Second.
THE PROTESTANT RULE OF FAITH.

CHAPTER I.
The Protestant remote rule of faith, or the book of the Holy Scriptures . . . . p. 14

FIRST ARTICLE.

It is impossible for a Protestant to know whether the Sacred Scriptures are an inspired book—Examination of the characteristics by means of which Protestants assert that they establish the inspiration of the Sacred Books . . . . . . p. 15

SECOND ARTICLE.

It is impossible for a Protestant to know what books compose the canon of Scripture or the Bible—Incessant variations of Protestantism on the subject . . . . p. 19

THIRD ARTICLE.

It is impossible for a Protestant to establish the authenticity of all the texts of the Bible by means of Scripture; in point of fact such proof is very difficult, and above the capacity of minds of ordinary intelligence or but little cultivation—Acknowledgment of Protestantism on this important subject . . . p. 25

FOURTH ARTICLE.

It is impossible for a Protestant to establish as *articles of faith* the authenticity and integrity of the Sacred Writings—Nature of the decision pronounced by the Church on the Scriptures—In the Catholic proofs there is no defective reasoning—Wiseman, Perrone . . . . p. 32

FIFTH ARTICLE.

It is impossible for a Protestant to prove that the Bible contains all the truths revealed by God—Answer to some difficulties—In what sense the Bible is perfect . . . . p. 40

CHAPTER II.

The Protestant proximate rule of faith . . . . . p. 48

FIRST ARTICLE.

Inadequacy of individual reason to know the truths revealed in the holy books—The obscurity of the Scriptures is mentioned by the inspired writers themselves, by the Fathers of the Church, by the Protestants at least practically—The Bible is clear on all fundamental articles : reply to this objection—Private examination of the Bible can never be the rule of faith instituted by Jesus Christ, because this means never has been and never will be applicable to all—The first Christians had no Bible—The Evangelical Alliance is not unity of faith, and is not capable of producing it—Whatever Dr. Burns may say, the Bible, interpreted by each individual, is not a principle of unity—Free examination has only led and can only lead to divisions and subdivisions ; it can justify any preconceived ideas . . . . p. 48

SECOND ARTICLE.

Illusion of those who think that each one of the faithful who piously reads the Holy Scriptures receives from the Holy Ghost a special help, a supernatural enlightenment, enabling him to understand the real sense of it—This system is not founded on the Word of God ; it infers the actual reading of the Bible, and consequently cannot be applicable to every one ; it is calculated to give rise to illusions and religious fanaticism . . . . . p. 77

THIRD ARTICLE.

The authority of a fallible Church, such as admitted by Anglicans, cannot be the real rule of faith—It cannot put an end to religious controversies ; it offers no guarantee of orthodoxy—Anglicanism and Puseyism bring us back ultimately to the private examination of the Scriptures—The Gorham affair . . . p. 85

CHAPTER III.

The contradictions existing between the Protestant rule of faith and those who profess it—Bible colportage—Results obtained . p. 92

CHAPTER IV.

What Catholics think about reading the Bible—Their respect for this divine book is greater and more sincere than that of Protestants —There is no precept about reading the Bible—The Church and reading the Bible in the vulgar tongue—Necessity of an infallible interpreter of the Bible—Wiseman—What the Catholic Church has done to preserve the Bible intact . . . . p. 99

CHAPTER V.

Unity of faith is radically impossible in Protestantism—Unity the peculiar characteristic of truth—Jesus Christ and the Apostles recommend unity—It is impossible without an infallible authority—Unity of faith and of communion between individual Churches among Catholics, under the supreme and infallible authority of the Popes—Protestantism perceives its own disorganisation and divisions—The Protestant rainbow . . . . . p. 112

CHAPTER VI.

The results of Protestantism—The civil authority substituted for the religious authority of the Holy See, or subjection of the Church to the State—Religious scepticism—Rationalism . . p. 123

Part the Third.

THE CATHOLIC RULE OF FAITH.

CHAPTER I.

THE REMOTE RULE OF FAITH—HOLY SCRIPTURE AND TRADITION.

FIRST ARTICLE.

Of the Holy Scriptures— The collection of the books of the Old Testament looked on as divine by the Saviour and the Apostles—The canon of the Council of Trent is conformable to Christian antiquity—Authenticity and origin of the Vulgate—Protestantism recognises its exactness . . . . p. 141

SECOND ARTICLE.

Of tradition: its nature—*Objective* tradition—Protestants must necessarily admit tradition, under pain of losing all foundation for their rule of faith and several of their articles of belief—The Scripture and the Fathers of the Church admit *objective* tradition as a part of Revelation—St. Vincent de Lérins—Testimony favourable to tradition of several Protestant writers—Jesus Christ only rejects vain and false traditions—Revealed truth is written everywhere in ineffaceable characters—Christian monuments—*Active* tradition—Transformations undergone by Catholic churches that have been taken possession of by Protestantism—The Anglican Liturgy has only preserved the accessories of worship . . . p. 151

CHAPTER II.

THE PROXIMATE RULE OF FAITH, OR THE TEACHING CHURCH.

FIRST ARTICLE.

Necessity of a doctrinal authority proclaimed by reason—Jesus proves His divinity; He preaches, but does not write—He gives a mission to His Apostles to preach His doctrine, but none to write it—He constitutes St. Peter head of the Apostolical College and of His whole Church, and pastor of His whole flock—He gives supreme authority to the teaching body, and the obligation to believe and obey to the faithful—The inspired writings of some of the Apostles in nothing change the primitive constitution of the Church of Christ; error of Protestantism on this subject—The Church is invested with infallible authority by Jesus Christ Himself; proofs taken from Scripture; promises of the Saviour; assistance of the Holy Ghost—It is the Catholic Church alone which lays claim to this infallibility, and that until the end of time—The Church of England proclaims herself fallible . . . . p. 170

ARTICLE SECOND.

Distinctive characteristics of the only Church of Christ: unity, sanctity, catholicity, and apostolicity—Peter dies at Rome; his successors on the throne of that city claim and exercise the same authority as Peter over the Universal Church; testimony of the earliest centuries on this question—The Roman Church the guardian and propagator of the whole Word of God, written and unwritten — Protestantism, by rejecting the supremacy of Peter and his successors, by denying the existence of an infallible authority, and by making the Bible its only rule of faith, has changed the constitution of the Church of Christ—Protestantism possesses neither unity (avowals of the Reformers on this subject, Synod of Lausanne), nor sanctity (the heads judged by themselves), nor catholicity, nor apostolicity—The Catholic or Roman Church is no other than the Church of Christ; she is founded on Peter; she is infallible; she is one; answer to objections concerning the dogmas of the Immaculate Conception of Mary and Papal Infallibility; concerning the disputes between the Thomists and Scotists, between the Jesuits and Jansenists; she is Holy, Catholic, and Apostolic . . . . p. 188

CONCLUSION.

Some remarks on the Real Presence, on Transubstantiation, on confession, on the worship of the Blessed Virgin and the Saints— Answer to an objection . . . . p. 238

TRANSLATOR'S PREFACE.

ABBÉ BÉGIN'S work, *La Sainte Écriture et la Règle de Foi*, was published in Quebec rather more than a year ago, and was pronounced by competent critics to be an exhaustive, though succinct, reply to the many assertions made by the members of the Bible Society and the Evangelical Alliance. Since the publication of the work in French there has been another convocation of the Evangelical Alliance at Montreal; and of the many errors there broached, I think there is not one of which the refutation may not be found in the following pages.

I have ventured to translate the book into my own tongue, and thus introduce it to a larger class of my own countrymen and countrywomen than would have perused it in the original. My share of the work is therefore very small, and, I cannot but fear, very imperfectly performed. I have aimed at accurate translation rather than at elegant writing. Such as it is, I offer it to all interested in the vital subjects of which it treats, with the ardent hope that in reading they may be convinced of the truth of all herein contained; and, as Abbé Bégin himself says, be confirmed in the truth, or won over to it.

Some parts of this work certainly seem to apply more particularly to the locality where it first appeared; but as the Evangelical Alliance must, from its very nature, propagate the same doctrine (or absence of doctrine) wherever it holds its meetings, so the same replies to objections made by them will hold good all over the world, even in that Eternal City where they so confidently anticipate meeting together at some not very remote period, perhaps even with the coöperation of our Holy Father Pope Pius IX. himself, whom they are not without hopes of winning over to their views!

G. M. WARD (MRS. PENNÉE).

Quebec, July 1st, 1875.

INTRODUCTION.

CARDINAL WISEMAN, whose death was so irreparable a loss to science and religion, on terminating his first conference (preached at St. Mary's, Moorfields, London, in 1836), remarked as follows: 'We do not wish to think that we have adversaries or enemies to attack, for we are willing to consider all who are separated from us as in a state of error indeed, but of *involuntary* error. We hope that, having been educated in certain principles and opinions, and not having taken leisure to examine sufficiently into the grounds of their faith, or having had their first impressions so far strengthened by the subsequent efforts of their instructors, that it is almost impossible for any contrary impression to be made, they are rather separated from us than armed against us—rather wanderers from the city of God than enemies to its peace. Hence it is not in the way of controversy, it is not as attacking others.'[1]

In this present work, the object of which is the examination of the fundamental principles on which Protestantism is based, and the refutation of the principal errors which have crept into the discourses delivered by

[1] *Lectures on the Principal Doctrines and Practices of the Catholic Church*, by Cardinal Wiseman, p. 29, 3d American edition, Baltimore, 1851.

the speakers of the Bible Society and Evangelical Alliance, I think I cannot do better than take the same view as the illustrious Cardinal, and, as far as lies in my power, imitate his spirit of moderation towards those who do not belong to the Church of Rome. The strength of religious conviction doubtless inspires the greatest energy in combating the sophisms of error. On this matter any compromise would be culpable, but there is no necessity for failing in that courtesy due to others.

I do not aim at awaking religious antipathies, creating agitation, sowing the seeds of discord in our hitherto peaceful country; God forbid I should contribute to such an end! I only wish to show on what a fragile basis Protestantism is founded; to reply indirectly to a considerable number of objections, so peremptorily made as to appear unanswerable; at the same time, I wish to strengthen the faith of the weak, to arm them against the seductions of error, and to present the sweet light of Catholic truth to those who are not yet in our ranks. How many poor souls in the bosom of Protestantism are a prey to the anguish of doubt! They are more numerous than is generally believed; they feel the need of some solid basis on which to found their belief, and they find it not. One resource remains open to them, there is one infallible means of their finding that calm after which they sigh; they can enter the Catholic Church, and cling to the immovable rock which Jesus Christ Himself has given it as a foundation.

My greatest desire is to contribute to bringing to a knowledge of the truth some of these souls, who are more unfortunate than guilty, who are more weary of the darkness around them than affected by their own moral shortcomings. May it be granted me to show them the way leading to the ark of salvation! May these pages receive the dew of heavenly blessing, without which nothing can bear fruit; and may they be of use to all those who will give them a few moments' serious attention!

The subject in hand is no new one; many Catholic writers have treated it with a skill and logical vigour which cannot be surpassed. It will be sufficient to recall the names of Cardinal Wiseman;[2] Rev. Father Perrone, S.J.;[3] Monsignor Malou,[4] formerly a professor at Louvain, subsequently Bishop of Bruges; the learned Milner,[5] Smarius,[6] and a number of others, to show that learning and talent have not been wanting in the manifestation and defence of the truth in this fundamental question. Their works, however, are, generally speaking, lengthy, little known to the greater number of readers, and often treat of many other subjects, which, although of vital interest, do not affect the present question.

It is to remedy this inconvenience that I have thought of offering the present work to the public, hoping thereby to combat errors which are incessantly spreading, and at the same time to develop a matter which must always be of the greatest importance to every Christian, because it concerns the very foundations of our faith.

[2] In the work already cited.
[3] *Il Protestantismo e la Regola di Fede*.
[4] *De la Lecture de la Bible en Langue Vulgaire*.
[5] *End of Controversy*.
[6] *Points of Controversy*.

Introduction.

It is by drawing on the profound science and enlightened orthodoxy of my former professors of the Roman College, and also by consulting the works of the eminent men whose memory I have just recalled, that I have undertaken to speak of the Rule of Faith. The object of this work is to show the necessity and characteristics of such a rule, to prove that it is not to be found in Protestantism, but only in the Catholic Church. I have tried to proceed methodically and with all the clearness possible, so as to be easily understood by persons not familiar with theological studies. God grant that I may attain the end I have in view, and dissipating the doubts which beset many minds, confirm them in the truth, or lead them into the bosom of the Catholic Church!

More than the word of man is necessary to make faith take root in a soul; God's grace alone can work such a marvel; it is that alone which can enlighten the understanding and touch the heart sufficiently to cause truth to be loved, to gain it adherents, to raise man above his own prejudices, habits, and even those temporal interests which so often keep him in the path of error. Happily God never refuses His aid to such upright souls as seek Him in all sincerity. His tender forethought for such is unbounded; His grace is around them like an atmosphere of heaven, lucid and life-giving, aiding them to perceive the truth more easily, and profess it with a firm and immovable conviction. For the last eighteen centuries many persecuting Sauls have been arrested in their course by Jesus, and transformed into courageous apostles of His religion. At His all-powerful word more than one Lazarus has started from his tomb of error and sin, and given glory to the infinite goodness of the Divine Master. These resurrections, which our own days have so frequently witnessed, reveal to us, in a striking manner, the continual action of God in His Church, and His constant wish to save all men, provided they present no obstacles to His grace. Let us, then, pray that the Saviour's most ardent desire may be realised, and that soon there may be 'but one fold and one Shepherd.'[7]

Quebec, March 25th, 1875.

[7] St. John x. 16.

THE

BIBLE AND THE RULE OF FAITH.

Part the First.

OF THE RULE OF FAITH IN GENERAL.

CHAPTER I.

Human reason left to itself—Lights of revelation—Reason and faith show us the obligation of believing revealed truths, and not altering their real meaning—Divine mission of the Church; anathemas pronounced on those who corrupt the true doctrine.

HUMAN reason, in its present state, cannot of its own strength arrive at a just and perfect knowledge of God and of the worship we owe Him. It only throws an uncertain light on many religious truths; sometimes even it seems itself to be plunged into the deepest obscurity. Like a ship sailing in the darkness of the night, and running the risk of being dashed against the rocks which lie in its course, so reason, left to itself, is often exposed to wander from the right path and lose itself in fathomless depths, before it has been able to descry that clear light of truth which it is seeking so ardently. Facts have already abundantly proved this: how many errors do we not find scattered through the different works of the old philosophers? In what uncertainty have they not left the most serious questions, even those of the most vital interest? They were, however, neither deficient in genius nor in the sincere desire of arriving at the knowledge of truth. Who, then, can say into what strange aberrations commonplace and uncultivated minds might allow themselves to be led?

But, in His infinite mercy, it has pleased God to add to that natural revelation which is contained in the great book of nature, in the mind and heart of man, another manifestation of a higher order, a solemn exterior, positive, supernatural revelation. Of this revelation there have been three phases, three more memorable and distinct epochs. The first, which is its dawn, as it were, extends from the time of Adam to that of Moses. The second, more brilliant and more fully developed, comprises the prophecies and other truths revealed by God from the time of Moses to that of the coming of the Messiah. The other, which extends from the days of Jesus Christ to the present time, and which is to last to the end of ages, is the noonday as it were, the perfection, the full and perfect light. It is that eternal and uncreated Truth which, manifesting itself to the world, shines brighter than the noonday sun, and bathes the whole universe in its beneficent beams. Numerous proofs, irrefragable motives of credibility, attest the existence of these divine manifestations, convincing every reasonable and docile mind, and imperatively demanding from each one of us a most sincere and hearty adhesion.

All Christians, whether Protestants or Catholics, admit the fact of this supernatural revelation, and give thanks to God for so signal a favour.

Reason itself proclaims that if a God, who is perfect Wisdom and Truth, infinite in all His perfections, deigns to speak to us and communicate His divine teachings, we, who owe Him all we are and all we have, are strictly obliged to receive His slightest words with faith, respect, and love, and to take all possible care to preserve them intact. If so much pains are taken to record the maxims, witty sayings, and even table-talk of certain men whom history looks on as great, how much the more should we not attach a high price to the Word of God, that inexhaustible treasure of science and virtue! The sublimity and importance of this revelation are so stupendous. The rays of the sun of eternal justice manifest so clearly to us the ineffable grandeur of God and His goodness towards men. How could we do otherwise than carefully gather up, like precious pearls, the very least of the words which God Himself deigns to address us?

Besides, the infinite truthfulness of God compels us to believe not only what it pleases us to admit, or what a narrow understanding considers as important and fundamental, but everything which He teaches us: to accuse God of being a liar, even in a thing of itself insignificant, would be a horrible blasphemy; to pay no attention to His teachings would be a revolting insult, an act of impiety.

Therefore, in considering the infinite majesty of God, the importance of revealed truth, and the absolute obligation all men are under of accepting such truth as divine, human reason sees clearly that there is a supreme necessity for purity in doctrine, and consequently unity of faith. Is not a glance at the life and doctrine of Jesus Christ and the Apostles sufficient to convince us of this fact? For what purpose those numerous miracles of the Saviour which astonished all Judea? For what purpose those prophecies fulfilled in His person, if it were not to prove the divinity of His mission on earth? And why place these proofs before our eyes, if not to convince us of the infallible truth of His teachings, and to engage us to give them our complete adhesion and to believe in them entirely?

Each book of the Sacred Writings shows us how ardently our Saviour Jesus Christ desired that the true doctrine should be kept intact, and how He held in horror those who distorted His divine words.

This is why He sent His Apostles with the same authority which He had received from His Heavenly Father: He enjoined them to preach the Gospel to all nations, teaching them all that He commanded them to teach; He promised to be with them to the end of time.[1] He sent unto them the Spirit of truth, which was to abide with them, and guard them from every error. The power He conferred on them was such that whosoever listens to them listens to Him, and whosoever scorneth them scorneth Him.

It is very evident that Jesus Christ, by promising to His Apostles, and to their successors, His perpetual assistance, by giving them the Spirit of truth, by ordering all nations to listen to them and to respect their

---

[1] St. Matt. xxviii. 19, 20; St. Mark xvi. 15, 16; Acts of the Apostles i. 8; St. John xiv. 26, xvi. 13.

teaching, by adding even that whosoever does not believe shall be condemned,—it is, I say, very evident that thereby He established His teaching Church, and that He gave it the necessary guarantees for preserving in its perfect integrity that doctrine which He had just revealed to the world.

On the other hand, those who abandon or corrupt the faith are called false prophets, ravening wolves, liars, children of malediction, dried-up fountains, clouds blown about by every wind, antichrists, seducers, trees twice dead and plucked up by the roots, wandering stars, &c.[2]

All these false teachers are to be carefully avoided; they are wolves in sheep's clothing. St. Paul even tells us to flee from a heretic after a first and second warning.[3] St. John[1] goes so far as to say that we are not to receive into our houses nor even salute those who do not keep the doctrine of Jesus Christ, because it is to communicate with their wicked works. By this may be seen how important Jesus Christ and His Apostles considered it that the divine teachings which they had just given to the world should not be in any way altered, or left a prey to the caprices and passions of men.

Reason and faith therefore agree in proclaiming aloud that if God, who is infallible in His very essence, vouchsafes to reveal to us truths which are beyond our understanding, we are obliged to believe them all without reserve or distinction. Now all the Christian world admits the fact of divine revelation. Therefore it must

---

[2] St. Matt. vii. 15 ; Acts xx. 29 ; 2 Peter ii. 17 ; 1 John ii. 18 ; Jude 12, 13, &c.   [3] Titus iii. 10.   [4] 2 John 10, 11.

necessarily admit all which is contained in that revelation, the smallest things equally with the most important. What is more, we have seen that Jesus Christ has made use of the most efficacious means, His special protection and the aid of the Holy Ghost, to maintain the integrity of His teachings in His Church, and that He has stigmatised in the most terrible manner those who propagate false doctrine. Hence it is of extreme importance, it is even necessary, according to the express will of our Saviour, that we should seek to know all the truths which it has pleased Him to manifest to us, and the true sense in which He has vouchsafed to reveal them to us.

CHAPTER II.

Necessity of a rule of faith—Its characteristics ; it should be adapted to all classes of society ; it should be sure, efficient to put an end to controversies, and perpetual.

THERE are none amongst the Protestants (if we except Socinians and Unitarians, of whom we shall not speak) who do not acknowledge that Jesus Christ is true God ; consequently all ought to admit the truth of His teachings, and make them the object of their faith.

This faith is so highly necessary, that Jesus Christ Himself declares that 'he that believeth not shall be condemned;' that 'without faith it is impossible to please God.'

If it be thus, 'God, who will have all men to be saved, and to come to the knowledge of the truth,' must have given to all an easy way of knowing the object of their faith, the truths which He has revealed to them. In fact it is in essential opposition to the infinite goodness of God that He should exact from men faith in His teachings, that He should exact it even under pain of damnation, without giving them, meanwhile, sure, easy, infallible means of knowing what is His doctrine ; this would be willing the salvation of men, and at the same time not willing it; this would be imposing an obligation of arriving at a certain end without giving the means of doing so.

It is evident to every one that the means of arriving at the necessary knowledge of the truths revealed by God should not be suited only to the capacity of superior minds—minds cultivated by long and serious study; but they should be *adapted to all classes of society*, suited to the capacity of the poor and ignorant, who also have souls to save, and a happy eternity to strive for.

They should also be *certain* and *sure*, for doubt and uncertainty are incompatible with an act of divine faith; a fallible testimony, unless it bears its confirmation in itself, cannot produce so firm and unchangeable an assent as such an act of faith would exact; and under these circumstances hesitation would be permissible. Any soul desirous of working out its eternal salvation might exclaim with fear, Who knows whether the doctrines I am professing, or which are being taught me, have really God for their author? Who knows whether I am not far advanced in the paths of error? And yet, how impossible for me, amidst the tumult and confusion of thousands of different opinions, to distinguish what is true from what is false! how impossible for me to know whether I am not on the brink of a precipice! What an ever-fruitful source of uneasiness, of ceaseless alarm, of interminable anguish! How can it be believed that a God who is infinitely good can have left His creature a prey to agitation and doubt, and with no possibility of finding rest on the solid ground of certainty? No, indeed; such an assumption is entirely inadmissible.

These means of ascertaining what doctrine is revealed should be *efficient*, to put an end to controversy;

otherwise the innumerable difficulties which have been raised on all the points of divine revelation would always remain unsolved, and would at one blow annihilate the Christian creed, all those truths which Jesus Christ has given to the human race. At the same time they ought to be *perpetual* and *indefectible;* for they should extend to all men, and hence embrace all ages. The rule of faith must last as long as the true faith itself. Now the true faith must last to the end of time. The rule of faith therefore will likewise have the same duration. It is, besides, evident that in our day men have no less need of this compass than those of past ages had if they wish to follow in the path of truth, that narrow path which leads to God, their true end, and consequently to the heavenly land.

Such are the requisite conditions for the sacred deposit of revelation remaining intact in the midst of humanity, and shedding abroad on it that bright light of which it is the burning centre. Otherwise there can never be anything but dissensions, all kinds of opinions, pernicious scepticism, the darkness of error. If I do not mistake, this is a conclusion which every one will readily admit, and which experience is incessantly confirming.

CHAPTER III.

What is the rule of faith which was established by our Lord Jesus Christ; or what means did He choose to communicate His doctrine to us?—The Bible—Tradition.

ALL vie with one another in proclaiming that the *revealed Word of God* is the rule of faith. On this point also there is unanimity of feeling.

But where is this word of God, this supernatural revelation, to be found? Protestants answer: '*In the Bible, and only in the Bible.*'[1] Catholics, on the contrary, unanimously reply: '*In the Bible and in Tradition.*' Here is the first divergence. According to Protest-

[1] 'We may well assert, that the rejection of tradition as a rule of faith was the *vital principle of the Reformation.*' Herbert Marsh, *Comparative View of the Churches of England and Rome*, p. 83, 1841.

'What I have always conceived to be the great leading principle of Protestantism is, namely, the entire sufficiency of Scripture, independently of tradition, as a rule of faith and doctrine.' P. N. Shuttleworth, *Not Tradition but Scripture*, p. 21-2, 1839.

'With the doctrine of the supremacy of the Holy Scriptures to the consciences of individuals, and the right of private judgment in contradistinction to the authority of the Church, she (the reformed Church of England) stands or falls.' Goode, *Regula Fidei Divina*, vol. i. præf. p. xlii.

'The grand fundamental distinction between the Roman Catholic and the Protestant religion consists in this very point, that whilst Protestants maintain that a full and perfect rule of faith is contained in the Scriptures, and that, consequently, these furnish in and by themselves a sufficient basis for all doctrines necessary to salvation, the Church of Rome holds that the Holy Scriptures are insufficient by themselves, and that we must admit, in addition to them, a second source, from which some essential articles of faith are derived, namely, tradition; and that this second source is of equal authority with the first, and independent of it.' Gayer, *Catholic Layman*, vol. i. p. 61.

Of the Rule of Faith in general.

ants, there is not any revealed truth outside the Sacred Writings.

According to Catholic doctrine, there is the written and the unwritten word of God; the whole preserved to us by means of tradition, *i.e.* by the divinely-instituted teaching body, the Apostles and their successors, whom Jesus Christ has commanded to preach His doctrine; and in this case the Sacred Writings are, to speak truly, only a part of objective tradition.

It would not, perhaps, be out of place here to give the argument which Schurft made use of against Luther, and which wounded the Saxon reformer to the quick: 'What is the Bible other than a tradition? How prove its divinity, except by oral tradition, the tradition of past ages, which assures us that the inspiration of God is spread over its pages? The New Testament is not *like the heavens*, where each star speaks in a language understood by all. Who handed to us this book of good tidings? Men. Who transmitted it to us from age to age? Men. Therefore it is by tradition you know that the name of Christian which you bear comes from Christ. It is the stream of tradition which has borne to you the two Testaments, the Sinai and Thabor, the Old and the New Law, God and Jesus.' Scripture, then, is in reality only tradition; it is by men that it has been transmitted and preserved until our times.

But let us for a moment leave aside tradition properly so called, or the unwritten word of God, and let us fix our eyes only on the Scripture, which is the rule of faith for all Protestants. They acknowledge and openly profess that the Bible contains the word of God to man;

on this point also are they in perfect harmony with Catholics, whose doctrine is laid down in the Fourth Session of the Council of Trent. In fact, that Council declares that God is the author of the Old and of the New Testament, and that all the books therein contained, and each part of them, should be received with piety and veneration. All Christians, then, profess profound respect for the written word of God.

Now how can we appropriate to ourselves this word of God, this revelation contained in a book? How enable the intelligence of each one to lay hold of the object of our faith? By what means is the word of God to reach our souls? In other terms, what is the *proximate* rule of our faith?

Catholics reply: It is the infallible Church, established by Jesus Christ to teach all nations what it has pleased Him to reveal; it is to her that He has confided the whole sacred deposit of His doctrine, to be preserved and propagated in its integrity until the end of time. It is true that a part of this revelation has been, by the special providence of God, consigned to the Sacred Books, but this fact has in no way destroyed the mission committed by Christ to His Church to teach His doctrine orally, nor the obligation of the faithful to follow and obey these teachings. It is, then, from the teaching and divinely-constituted Church that we should receive the revealed truth, whether contained in the Holy Scriptures or only in tradition.

Protestants are not all agreed on this important question. Some hold, as the right means of arriving at the knowledge of written revelation, the exercise of *in-*

Of the Rule of Faith in general.

dividual reason, which can and ought to study the word of God in the Bible, penetrate its meaning, and deduce from it a creed or assemblage of truths which it is bound to believe. Others assert that every reader of the sacred text, in so far as he is a prayerful man, animated by pious feelings, a fervent Christian, may rely on the *light of the Holy Ghost*, which will enlighten his understanding, making him comprehend biblical obscurities in their true sense; that is to say, by the light of a heavenly flame, which can only be extinguished through the want of a right intention on the part of each individual. Others, again, receive the doctrine contained in the Scriptures by the medium of their *Church;* but this Church is not infallible, it can err, and nobody is obliged to submit to its teachings, unless such teachings are found to be conformable with the Bible.

Let us first consider the Protestant rule of faith *objectively*, that is to say, the Scripture itself and in itself; and afterwards *subjectively*, that is to say, in the different ways which our adversaries employ to arrive at a knowledge of written revelation, or of the sense of the Bible. In other terms we will, in the first place, study their *remote*, and in the second place their *proximate*, rule of faith, and we shall see that it is neither *suited to the capacity of all*, nor *efficient to put an end to controversy*, nor *indefectible*, and that consequently it does not possess the characteristics which ought to be inherent in every rule of faith.

Part the Second.

THE PROTESTANT RULE OF FAITH.

CHAPTER I.

The Protestant remote rule of faith, or the book of the Holy Scriptures.

For us Catholics, all questions that may arise with regard to the Holy Scriptures receive an easy and complete answer from the Church. In her we have a living, infallible, supreme tribunal; she speaks, and on that subject, as on all others, every Catholic submits his intelligence and will to hers, yielding her the firm and free adhesion of his faith. Hardly has she pronounced her judgment, when the question is decided; doubt disappears before the splendour of truth; the doctrine just defined takes its place amidst the array of knowledge already gained by the human mind, and no one any longer thinks of contesting it. But our separated brethren remain, and always will remain, in uncertainty on a number of controverted points, precisely because they refuse to recognise the supreme tribunal which Jesus Christ has instituted for teaching all nations. Who will tell them which are the books inspired by God? Who will indicate to them which books compose the canon of the Holy Scriptures? Who can inform them indubitably that their Bible is authentic, that it has not been falsified, that it is indeed the expression of the divine word? No one. These are so many enigmas for them, of which, as we are going to see, they have no solution; they sap the very foundations of the edifice of Protestantism; doubt upon doubt, with all its terrible anguish,—this is the shoreless ocean upon which they are tossed about; this is the fathomless abyss in which all hope of certainty is swallowed up. Some development of this subject will better show the state of this question; the impartial reader will be able to remark a whole series of impossibilities which are inherent in the fundamental principles of Protestantism, and which destroy it completely.

FIRST ARTICLE.

It is impossible for a Protestant to know whether the Sacred Scriptures are an inspired book—Examination of the characteristics by means of which Protestants assert that they establish the inspiration of the Sacred Books.

What is inspiration? Without wishing to give here a strict definition of it, I will say that it is a supernatural process, which passes in the mind of man, and which, like all interior processes, is only known by God and by him who is inspired. Inspiration cannot then be made manifest to other men except by exterior effects, that is to say, by the *book* itself which results from the inspiration, or by some trustworthy *testimony*.

But what exterior marks can be found in the *Book* of the Holy Scriptures to establish the fact that they are inspired by God? Let us first acknowledge that it cannot be proved by the Scriptures that the Scriptures themselves are inspired. This would be proving a thing by means of itself; and besides, there is no text which affirms this inspiration of the Bible in general, nor from which we can deduce it.

Will it be said, as some Protestant writers have affirmed, that the Scriptures are inspired, because they contain the narration of miracles and prophecies which have been faithfully accomplished? Evidently not; for a book whose author is an ordinary man, left to the resources of his own intelligence, might contain a recital of these supernatural manifestations. At the very most, we might conclude that he was relating a doctrine, or revealed facts, such as any profane historian might do; but there is a long distance between that and the inspiration which indicates such a direct influence of God on the sacred writer, as makes that writer express just what God wills to be revealed to the world, and nothing farther; so that one might exclaim, This book is God's Book, this word is God's Word.

Will it be affirmed that the sanctity, sublimity, and harmony of the doctrine contained in the Scriptures prove them to be inspired? No, I would unhesitatingly reply; such cannot be constituted a proof, for all these qualities are certainly to be found united, and to an equally high degree, in the magnificent letters of St. Clement Romanus, St. Ignatius the Martyr, St. Polycarp, and even in the *Imitation of Jesus Christ*, as in the books of Paralipomenon (Chronicles), or in the Epistles of St. John, St. Jude, St. Peter, or St. Paul to Titus and to Philemon. If among the inspired books we are to range all those which bear the impress of a holy, sublime, and ever-logical doctrine, we should have to count them by thousands; and the writings of the fathers and doctors of the Church would certainly not occupy the lowest place.

Will the inspiration of the Scriptures be maintained, because those who read them are moved by them to great feelings of piety, and experience marvellous effects as regards their spiritual advancement? Again, no; for books of piety, ascetic works, such as those of St. Bonaventure, of the Blessed Louis of Grenada, of St. Ignatius of Loyola, of St. Francis de Sales, would certainly produce an equally consoling effect as reading the Book of Numbers or the Apocalypse of St. John. It is therefore impossible to draw from the book of the Bible itself any convincing proof of its inspiration.

To know, therefore, whether God is really the principal Author of the Scripture, no other way remains than that of testimony extrinsic to the Sacred Book, and trustworthy. This testimony must be either *human* or *divine*. If it is human, it must necessarily take its origin from the inspired writer, for he alone and God are, in an immediate manner, aware of the fact of inspiration.

But if this testimony is human—in other words, if the authority on which I lean is that of a man—I could only believe the fact of inspiration with a *human and fallible faith*. Consequently, it is as clear as noonday that it is only with a *human faith* that I can believe what is contained in the Bible—all the truths which God may have there inspired and revealed. In fact, in that case human testimony is the basis of my faith, of my belief in the fact of inspiration. Now a faith which reposes on purely human testimony is not and cannot be other than a human and fallible faith; and if we can only believe the fact of inspiration with a human and fallible faith, we can only believe the truths contained in Scripture with a human and fallible faith also. Still, as is acknowledged by all, Catholics and Protestants, we ought to believe everything contained in the Bible with *divine faith*. Human testimony, then, is entirely insufficient to establish the fact of inspiration; *divine* testimony is the only basis on which the edifice of our faith can solidly repose.

There is evidently no necessity that God Himself should render this testimony in an immediate manner; it is sufficient that He should do so by an authentic organ, by a legitimate ambassador, to whom He would have directly revealed the fact of the inspiration of such and such a book. For us Catholics this divinely-constituted organ is the teaching Church, which can show all the titles of her heavenly mission. But as Protestants do not admit her divine authority, it results, as an inevitable consequence, that they are unable to prove the inspiration of the Bible, and of each of the books composing it.

This demonstration, the substance of which I have borrowed from the Rev. Father Franzelin, my former teacher, and one of the glories of the Gregorian University, appears to me conclusive and unanswerable.[1]

---
[1] See Franzelin, *De Divinâ Traditione et Scripturâ*, p. 331.

SECOND ARTICLE.

It is impossible for a Protestant to know what books compose the canon of Scripture or the Bible—Incessant variations of Protestantism on the subject.

I interrogate any Protestant whatever who professes to believe in the Word of God contained in *the Bible,* and in *the Bible alone,* and I put to him this question : Which are the books composing the Bible? How many are there? He will doubtless, in the first place, cite me all the Protocanonical books of the Old Testament.[2]

But why do you not admit the Deuterocanonical books into your Bible?[3] What reasons have you for excluding them from it? Because, he will say, the Protocanonical, which form the canon of the Jews, were comprised in the collection of the Scriptures in the time of Jesus Christ and the Apostles, whilst thus much cannot be said for the Deuterocanonical. Now it may be seen in many places of the New Testament that our Saviour

---

[2] The name of *Protocanonical* is given to those books which have always been looked on as inspired, and about which there has never been any difficulty regarding their admission into the canon of the Scriptures. The Jews, who looked on these books as divine, reckoned the number of them as twenty-two, the same in number as the letters of their alphabet. They are the following : Genesis, Exodus, Leviticus, Numbers, Deuteronomy, Josue, Judges, Ruth, two books of Samuel, two books of Kings, two books of Paralipomenon, Esdras and Nehemiah, Esther, Isaias, Jeremias and the Lamentations, Ezechiel, Daniel, the twelve lesser Prophets, Job, the Psalms, the Proverbs of Solomon, Ecclesiastes, the Canticle of Canticles.

[3] The *Deuterocanonical* books are those concerning which there have been doubts as to their inspiration at certain times and in certain places. In the Old Testament they are : Tobias, Judith, Wisdom, Ecclesiasticus, first and second book of Machabees, Baruch. To these complete books are added some portions of Daniel (iii. 24-90, xiii. and xiv.) and the last seven chapters of Esther (x. 4 to xvi. 24).

and the Apostles have approved this collection as being composed of inspired books; we have therefore divine testimony to the inspiration of the Protocanonical Books.

Admitting such to be the case, I will remark that this testimony is purely *affirmative*, and not *exclusive*. We may conclude from it, if you will, that these books are inspired; but it would be illogical to deduce from it that these books *alone* are inspired, to the exclusion of all others, and that the Jewish canon was complete.

The reasoning of Protestantism appears to be all the more false, since all Christians acknowledge that the Apostles transmitted to the Churches other books, which are part of the New Testament, and are looked on as inspired; that the Jews had in their possession other books with regard to which there was a doubt, that is to say, as to whether they had the same authority as the Protocanonical; that probably the Hellenist Jews had Bibles containing other books besides those enumerated. It is, then, impossible for Protestants to prove whether their canon of the Old Testament is complete or incomplete.[4]

Perhaps I may be told that the Protocanonical books are quoted in the New Testament to confirm and prove certain dogmas, and that consequently Jesus Christ and the Apostles looked on them as divine and inspired.

To this I reply that it is false to say there are quotations from all the books, even the Protocanonical, of the

---

[4] See the discourse of the Rev. Mr. Doudiet, pronounced at the assembly of the Bible Society, held at Quebec, February 14, 1872, and reported in the *Morning Chronicle* of the following day.

Old Testament; for no vestige is to be found of the book of Judges, of Ecclesiastes, of the Canticle of Canticles, of Esther, of the first and second books of Esdras. Moreover, even supposing they were all quoted in the New Testament, that would not prove they were the *only* inspired ones; for no testimony can be brought forward to support such an assertion. Besides, quotations from profane authors even may be met with, such as Epimenides and Aratus, and also from works which certainly form no part of the canon of Scripture, and which have not even reached us, such as the *Book of the Wars of the Lord*.[5]

But let us come to the books of the New Testament,[6] the inspiration of which can only be proved by *tradition alone*, or at the same time by the apostolic writings. Except St. Peter[7] no one makes mention of St. Paul's Epistles as belonging to *Scripture*. He says they 'contain things hard to be understood, which the unlearned and unstable wrest, *as they do also the other Scriptures*, to their own destruction.'

Here it will not be without utility to make some short remarks on this subject. The *first* is, that St. Paul had not yet written the second Epistle to Timothy when St. Peter wrote that of which we have spoken; an evident

[5] Perrone, *Regola di Fede*, vol. i. p. 145.
[6] A great number of Protestant communions now admit into their Bibles all those books of the New Testament which we ourselves admit. However, on this subject, as on many others, there are nearly infinite variations. The parts more generally considered as *Deuterocanonical* are the Epistle of St. Paul to the Hebrews, that of St. James, the second of St. Peter, the second and third of St. John, that of St. Jude, and the Apocalypse of St. John. In this capricious condemnation are included some fragments of the Gospels, such as St. Mark xvi. 9-20, St. Luke xxii. 43-44, St. John viii. 2-12.   [7] 2 Peter iii. 16.

proof that the Prince of the Apostles could not have reckoned this Epistle to Timothy among the inspired books, since it did not then exist. The *second* is, that neither the Gospel nor the Apocalypse of St. John were yet composed, and that none of the other Gospels are mentioned in this text by St. Peter. Nevertheless, Protestants admit these books into their Bible. On what ground do they so? Only on that of Catholic tradition: there is no other possible basis. The *third* is, that this second Epistle of St. Peter is precisely one of those books whose authenticity and apostolic origin can only be proved by means of tradition. The *fourth* is, that those Protestants who do not admit the canonicity of this second Epistle of St. Peter have absolutely no other means of establishing the inspiration of the books of the New Testament than the authority and testimony of the Catholic Church. Now they reject this testimony. It is therefore absolutely impossible for them to show why they admit such and such books into their Bible.

The evident conclusion to be drawn from the preceding remarks is, that Protestants are not able to give any reason for the choice they make of their Bible, which contains only Protocanonical books, over the Catholic Bible, which also contains the Deuterocanonical. In no part of the Scriptures is there to be found a ready-prepared catalogue of the Sacred Books. Here and there only are there some short quotations from the books of the Old Testament, or a somewhat vague confirmation of what is contained in the *Law*, the *Prophets*, and the *Psalms*. But what is designated by these general appellations? Tradition may guide us up to a certain point, but it cannot indicate this precisely; and as to several books of the New Testament a certain proof is radically impossible. I sum up by saying to them: You lay down as a principle that only the books contained in your Bible, your canon, contain the Word of God and are divinely inspired, and that tradition can have no authority of itself except in so far as it agrees with the Scriptures. Now the Scriptures contain no positive testimony concerning the number and the canon of the books of the Old and New Testament, which all Protestants look on, however, as inspired. If, then, the silence of Scripture suffices for considering a tradition as false or doubtful, it necessarily ensues that historical tradition is of no value in proving the inspiration of the books of the Old and New Testament. It is therefore absolutely essential either to renounce the fundamental principle of *the Bible alone*, or else to renounce all hopes of showing which are the inspired books composing the Scriptures or the Bible.

Now let us look a little at the variations of Protestantism with regard to the canon and number of the Sacred Books. 'Luther rejected from the canon of the Scriptures Job, Ecclesiastes, the Epistle to the Hebrews, the second Epistle of St. Peter, the second and third of St. John, that of St. Jude, and the Apocalypse. Calvin removed also from it the books of Esther, Tobias, Judith, Wisdom, Ecclesiasticus, and the two books of Machabees. Spinosa and other critics cast a doubt on the authenticity of the Pentateuch, the Judges, Kings, the two books of Paralipomenon, Isaias, Jeremias, Ezechiel, Daniel, and the twelve lesser Prophets; Hobbes that of

Ruth; Péreyre that of Josue. Grotius asserts that the Canticle of Canticles, the Book of Wisdom, and the two last Epistles of St. John are not inspired. The Socinians denied the divinity of the book of Proverbs; the Anabaptists that of the Psalms and the books of Esdras. Strauss contests the authenticity of the Gospel of St. Matthew; Griesbach that of St. Mark; Evanson and Wette that of St. John, which Theodore Beza had already mutilated; Semler, March, and Collins, those of the four Evangelists at once. Sleimacher denies the divine inspiration of the first Epistle to Timothy; Eichorn, that of the second, as well as of the Epistle to Titus; Breitschneider, that of the two last of St. John; Balten, that of St. Jude; Cludius, that of the first of St. Peter; and the mythologists, as well as the rationalists, neither believe in the epistles of the Apostles, nor in any books whatever of the Old and New Testament; so that a Protestant bookseller who wished to publish a Bible containing only books whose authority would be recognised by all his co-religionists would have nothing to print. The Reformation has no Word of God. Luther tampered with this sacred deposit; his disciples have entirely dispersed it. A thousand times blessed be the wisdom of the Popes, who have kept it intact for us!"[8]

Besides, who does not know that from the days shortly after the Apostles the heretics denied the authenticity of a great number of our Sacred Books, and substituted others in their place, such as the Gospel *according to the Hebrews*, *according to the Egyptians*, *of the Childhood*, *of Nicodemus*, &c.? On the other hand, do we not know

[8] Constant, *Infaill. des Papes*, vol. ii. p. 451, &c.

that certain individual Churches for a time looked on sundry books as canonical and inspired, which books have since been rejected as apocryphal or as purely human, such as the Letters of St. Clement, the *Pastor* of Hermas, the Epistle of St. Barnabas? Now take away the infallible authority of the Church and try to get out of this chaos; choose among all these writings those animated by the divine Spirit; discriminate those which are inspired from those which are not; prove the authenticity, the divinity, the integrity of some, and at the same time the apocryphal or purely profane character of others; you will be very clever if you discriminate to the entire satisfaction of every one, and in such way as to put an end to all doubt. Whilst waiting for a favourable solution of this question, I must allow myself to believe that it is absolutely impossible to arrive at so magnificent a result. Neither the authority of talent, nor the prestige of science, nor deep and conscientious study, can ever weigh sufficiently with intelligent minds to convince them, and bring them to a state of unity on these fundamental points. There is but one supreme authority, divinely constituted, infallible, and recognised as such, which can decide this controversy and put an end to the incessant fluctuations of human reason, which is always inclined to pride, even in the midst of its most lamentable weaknesses.

THIRD ARTICLE.

It is impossible for a Protestant to establish the authenticity of all the texts of the Bible by means of Scripture; in point of fact such proof is very difficult, and above the capacity of minds of ordinary intelligence or but little cultivation—Acknowledgment of Protestantism on this important subject.

It must not be lost sight of that Protestants find

the word of God only in the Bible; for them there are no revealed truths apart from that volume. Now the Bible is entirely silent as to the authenticity of the books composing it, and also as to the integrity of the text; there is no mention of a great number of these books either in the Old or in the New Testament; and even supposing that there was reference to them in some part, the authenticity of the book and passage wherein they were spoken of would have to be proved, consequently the problem could never be solved. As to several books of the two Testaments, it is impossible to know the authors of them, or to determine the precise epoch at which they were written. 'For,' as the celebrated Father Perrone writes,[*] 'if so many modern critics have not only doubted but even denied the authenticity of the Pentateuch as the work of Moses, although these are some of the least contested books, and are proved to be authentic by the most solid reasoning, what may not be said of the books of Job, Josue, Judges, Ruth, Kings, Paralipomenon, and others?'

Perhaps some basis or proof, apart from the Scripture, will be sought to prove the authenticity and integrity of them—perhaps recourse will be had to the authority of the Synagogue and the Jewish people. This is well; but then why persistently refuse to the Catholic Church, to its legions of saints and learned men, an authority so easily acknowledged in so many other persons?

Again, how can they prove that the books of the New Testament are indeed the work of those whose

[*] *Regola di Fede*, vol. i. p. 158.

names they bear? Not very easily. Indeed, many modern critics have not hesitated to consider as apocryphal the second Epistle of St. Peter, the Epistles of St. James and St. Jude, as well as the Apocalypse. A writer need not necessarily be the author of a book because his name is placed at the beginning of it; the name may have been added afterwards. Nearly every one admits now that it was not the Evangelists themselves who entitled their writings *Gospel according to St. Matthew, St. Mark, St. Luke, or St. John*. How prove they are really authentic? This is not so easy a thing as is generally supposed; to be personally assured of it a man must devote himself to such serious study, to such infinite research, as not one in a thousand of the human race is capable of. How prove with that clearness which springs from certainty, which compels conviction, and which is absolutely necessary in such a matter—how prove that there has been neither interpolation nor corruption of the primitive text during a period of eighteen centuries? This point offers still greater difficulties to solve than the preceding one; and I even do not hesitate to say that it is impossible to prove clearly the integrity of all the texts of Scripture by applying only the rules of ordinary criticism. For us Catholics, who believe that all the Word of God, even the written, has been confided to the care of the infallible Church of Jesus Christ, to be by her preserved and propagated in all places and throughout all ages, we remain perfectly secure, for our faith is founded on the immovable rock of the divine promises. But I openly declare that were I a member of some Protestant sect my tranquillity would be far less perfect; I would ask both myself and of my ministers whether this Book, this Bible which they present to me, be indeed inspired by God, and whether it is in reality the Word of God. I would ask them whether this volume contains the whole of the Word of God, or only a part; whether the books they reject as Deuterocanonical and uninspired may not, by chance, be as divine as the Protocanonical; whether this Bible which they give me may not have been falsified in many parts; if many texts may not have been omitted, altered, or invented. These are fundamental questions for all who admit 'the Bible only' as their rule of faith; questions excessively difficult to answer, and of which the solution, if left to the feeble resources of historical criticism, must necessarily leave doubts and anxieties in the minds of all those interested. How, indeed, could a Protestant remain tranquil, how could he possess a shadow of certainty, when he reflects that his personal opinion is in direct contradiction with that of thousands of learned Catholics, who, humanly speaking, are all as capable as learned Protestants to decide this question? If, at any rate, there was perfect agreement among these latter with regard to the constituent parts of the Bible, as to the books and texts which should be contained in it, it would be a surer human guarantee. But we have seen what nearly infinite diversity of opinion reigns on these vital questions, which concern the very basis of the famous Reformation in the sixteenth century; it is sufficient to discuss them, to examine them for a moment, to perceive the fragility of the foundations on which Protestantism rests.

Besides, I ask any man of good faith, is it credible that many Methodists, Lutherans, Calvinists, Quakers, Baptists, and others, have convinced themselves by their own researches, by conscientious and certainly painful study, that all the books, and those books alone, of their Bible, that all the texts, and such texts only, of these books, are authentic, and contain the pure Word of God just as the Holy Spirit dictated it to the inspired writers? Without wishing in any way to make light of the labour and acquirements of the members of the different Protestant denominations, I do not hesitate to say that there are few, very few, of them who have made these fundamental researches, and explored ground so thickly sown with difficulties; perhaps there are still fewer who, having seriously set themselves to this study, have reaped from it a firm conviction of the integrity, authenticity, exactness of the version and of the inspiration of each of the books of the Bible. I leave it to the conscience of each among them to decide as to the truth of what I now affirm. But as I may be accused of undervaluing Protestant learning and exaggerating the difficulties of these questions, I borrow the words of Protestants themselves. Here is what the celebrated Richard Baxter has written on this subject:[10] 'Are the most highly-instructed and intelligent Christians capable of proving the truth of the Scriptures? Still further, are the lower members of the clergy able to do so?' And a little further on he adds that he finds it strange that some have such a horror of that part of Popery which consists in giving the authority of the Church as a basis for our faith; and yet,

[10] *The Saints' Everlasting Rest.*

he says, we, like the greater number of professors, content ourselves with the same sort of faith; the only difference consists in the Catholics believing that the Bible is the Word of God because such is the teaching of their Church, whilst we believe the same thing because our Church or our leaders affirm it.

The Rev. Jeremiah Jones,[11] speaking of the same question, says: first, that the task of establishing the canonical authority of the books of the New Testament is full of difficulties; secondly, that it is of great importance; thirdly, that a great number of Christians are not in a position to give one single reason to justify the belief they hold that the books of the New Testament are canonical; fourthly, that very few works on this subject exist.

M. Scherer, a celebrated Protestant Genevan doctor, does not shrink from admitting that there is but one infallible Church, which is able to present the canon of the Scriptures to the faith of the Christian. Here are his very words: 'Unless with Catholicism we attribute supernatural infallibility to the Church, we are forced to acknowledge that she may have made a mistake in the constitution of the canon, admitting books which should have been excluded, and excluding others which should have been admitted. The consequence is that every Protestant Christian has the right, not to say is bound by duty, to challenge the authority of the Church in this matter; to examine into its decision, and, where there is room for doubt, to substitute his own. Now what are the

---

[11] *New and Full Method of Settling the Canonical Authority of the New Testament.* First edition, Oxford, 1827.

results of this liberty which Protestantism implicitly concedes to the faithful? That the question of canonicity, which forms one of the elements of Protestant authority in matters of faith, is a question left to individual decision; that the rule of authority does not exist in an objective and certain manner; that we may differ in this respect without ceasing to be Christian; that each individual is called upon to pronounce on matters concerning which learned men doubt and differ; that the humblest of the faithful, before feeling certain about his faith, must decide questions of authenticity and canonicity, criticism and history; in short, that the cardinal article of Christian faith, the very foundation of authority, itself rests on the quicksands of delicate research, of uncertain literary operations—in a word, of studies rarely favoured by the light of evidence. Here is, in truth, a solid foundation for the faith of the Church! Behold a rule of faith perfectly accessible to the mass of Christian people!"[12] A Catholic would not have spoken differently. That these questions are difficult, very little studied, and above the reach of ordinary intelligence, is a fact which no one will dare to deny, and which is but too well known by all those who interest themselves in these matters.

It is, then, absolutely impossible for Protestants, first, to prove the inspiration of the Scriptures; secondly, to determine which books form the canon of the Scriptures; thirdly, to establish the integrity of these books and of all the texts they contain; fourthly, to place these difficult researches within the reach of ordinary intelligence; they will always be confined to a very small number.

[12] *La Critique et la Foi*, pp. 13, 14.

FOURTH ARTICLE.

It is impossible for a Protestant to establish as *articles of faith* the authenticity and integrity of the Sacred Writings—Nature of the decision pronounced by the Church on the Scriptures—In the Catholic proofs there is no defective reasoning—Wiseman, Perrone.

For Protestants the Bible is the only rule of faith; they reject divine tradition. Nevertheless divine faith must be grounded on the Word of God, either written or traditional.

Now it is impossible, as we have seen, to prove by the Bible the integrity, authenticity, and inspiration of all the Sacred Books and of each part of them; therefore, if these points can and ought to be established as articles of faith, there is no other means left of arriving at this result except seeking for a basis in the traditional Word of God. Now our adversaries, with the exception perhaps of certain sects, only admit this as an authority in so far as it appears to them conformable to Scripture.

Therefore they have no means of establishing the above-named points as *articles of divine faith*. In other words, every article of divine faith ought to rest on the Word of God.

Now Protestants pretend that the Word of God is contained in the Bible alone, and the Bible does not suffice to prove the inspiration, authenticity, and integrity of the books composing it.

Therefore it is impossible for a Protestant to establish these three points as articles of divine faith. But if our adversaries cannot prove that the Scriptures are inspired and authentic, it is impossible for them to make an act of divine faith as to that which is contained in them; impossible to deduce an article of faith from them. This would be giving more extension to the consequence than to the premises. During the first ages of Christianity certain doctors, and even certain individual churches, admitted into the canon of the Scriptures the Pastor of Hermas, the Epistle of St. Barnabas, &c.; still they had some doubts as to their canonicity. Could they have deduced articles of faith from these doubtfully inspired writings? Assuredly not; for to draw a certain irrefutable conclusion, we must have certain irrefutable premises; if the foundation is in ruins, the edifice will be so likewise.

But, our adversaries reply, if it belongs to the Church alone to determine the canonicity and inspiration of the Scriptures, it ensues that the Church has greater authority than the Scriptures. In point of fact, the authority of the judge is greater than that of the individual who is judged. Now the Church in this case gives judgment on the Scriptures, and by so doing gives them authority; therefore, in the Catholic system, the Church has greater authority than the Scriptures.

To this I reply, that the Church has never pretended to possess more intrinsic authority than the Scripture, nor to confer divine authority on it; for the Scripture itself is divine. It contains the Word of God independently of the judgment of the Church, and prior to that judgment. The Church's part is confined to making known which are the inspired books which contain the Word of God, and which consequently possess divine authority. The Church, by any declaration she may make, cannot cause a book which has been written without divine inspiration to become inspired, or to be considered as such. No; she verifies, but she neither bestows nor causes inspiration. In other words, the decision of the Church as to the Scriptures is not intended to give *them* inspiration, but only to make known to *us* that authority which they already possess.

Very well, is replied; but then the basis on which you build is no less fragile than ours. You prove the divine authority of your Church by Scripture, and then you demonstrate the divine authority of Scripture by that of the Church. This is evidently a vicious circle.

The answer is easy enough. To constitute a vicious circle the two propositions should be equally uncertain and controverted. Now this is not the case in the question at present under discussion. In point of fact, when we prove the infallibility and authority of the Church by the Bible, we are on common ground with the Protestants. We build on a basis of which they, equally with ourselves, admit the solidity, *i.e.* the infallible truth of the Scriptures; whence it follows that we can deduce from them conclusive arguments against our adversaries. The texts we bring forward to prove the infallibility of the Church are clear— the clearest in the Bible. Still further, every man not imbued with prejudices, who is searching for religious truth in all the sincerity of his soul, can and must necessarily give the Catholic meaning to these texts, without needing for that either an infallible interpreter or the special assistance of the Holy Ghost. In fact, although we may require an infallible Church in order to thoroughly understand all the Scriptures; in order to repress the boldness of error, and put an end to the controversies which so often arise about the meaning of the divine words; still we freely admit that many texts are clear enough to be understood without this particular help. Therefore, in controversy against the Protestants, we can, without making use of any vicious circle, prove the infallibility of the Church by texts from the Holy Scriptures, and thence show them that if they read the Bible without prepossession, without prejudices, and with an ardent desire to arrive at the truth, they would themselves find there the institution of a teaching and infallible Church, and the condemnation of their own fundamental principle, of their rule of faith.

We do not believe the Church on the authority of the Scripture, properly so called; we believe it on the authority of *Christ;* and if His commands, in her regard, were recorded in any other book which we felt ourselves bound to believe, although uninspired, we should receive them, and consequently the authority of the Church, equally as now.

We consider the Scriptures therefore, in the first instance, as a book manifesting to us One furnished with divine authority to lay down the law; we take it in this view, and examine what He tells us, and we discover that, supported by all the evidence of His divine mission, He has appointed an authority to teach; and then this authority not merely advises, but obliges, us, by that power which Christ has invested in it, to receive this sacred book as His inspired word.

As regards the chain of reasoning we make for ourselves to enable us to give an account of the faith that is in us, it in no way entails any vicious circle. For a perfect answer, I will content myself with asking our adversaries whether the faithful Christians in the first ages of the Church believed in the divine and infallible mission of Jesus Christ, His Apostles, and their successors, by means of reading a Bible which certainly was not all written, or at any rate was very little known among the Christians. How did they come to join the teaching Church? Whence did they draw their reasons, their motives, for obeying the Church? If they did not possess the brilliant and divine light of the Scriptures, apparently they must have had some other which showed them the right way, and attracted them by its brilliancy. Yes, they did possess another, in the miracles which the Apostles and their successors performed, and which were as striking as those of their Divine Master; in the prophecies of the Old Testament and of Jesus Christ, which were realised in the Catholic Church; in her unity of faith, in the sanctity of her faithful, in her rapid spread despite all obstacles; in those numerous motives of credibility which have always accompanied the Church, rendering her visible to the eyes of all nations, and pointing her out through all ages as the work of Jesus Christ, as the only and true heir of the promises which God made to man. The Church proved her heavenly mission as Jesus Christ and His Apostles had done; and the faithful believed in her as they had believed in them. The Bible had nothing to do with their conversion from paganism to Christianity.

Let us listen to the voice, always so sure and authoritative, of an eminent theologian, of a man who has grown old amidst serious study—of the Rev. Father Perrone, one of the glories of the Roman College and of the Company of Jesus.[13]

'Our starting-point,' he says, 'is the establishment of the Church, first promised by our Divine Saviour, then solemnly inaugurated by the visible descent of the Holy Ghost on the Apostles assembled in the guest-chamber. Hardly was the Church thus established than she commenced her career by preaching, by the administration of sacraments, by the exercise of worship, only to end it when time itself shall be no more. Like an electric current which passes from one to another of an assembled circle, she spreads with a lightning-like rapidity among the neighbouring people, and even to far-off nations. From her very commencement we see her divided into two classes; the one class charged with teaching, the other compelled to receive the teaching of the former class. Now, as to teaching, this Church must first of all have obtained from those whom she wished to draw out of Judaism, or from the ranks of the Gentiles into her own bosom, faith in her divine mission; that is to say, the mission confided to her by God of converting the world, which she fulfilled by miracles, by prophecies, and by all sorts of supernatural deeds, called motives of credibility. Without manifest proofs of this divine mission, her preaching, however august its source, would not have gained faith, nor would the articles of belief which were the object of it have been admitted with certainty.

[13] Perrone, *Regola di Fede*, t. ii. pp. 85-89.

'Faith in the divinity of the mission of the Apostles and the teaching Church was, as is evident, the first step, the first condition, lacking which it would have been useless to enter into the details of the truths taught; and this condition fulfilled, this faith established in a manner to put an end to all doubt, the rest all followed and resulted from it. For from the moment when it was proved, and clearly proved, that he who presented himself to the various people to teach them a new doctrine had indeed received his mission from God, it necessarily followed that those people must have an unbounded confidence in this divine messenger, and admit with entire faith all that he announced to them with such a recommendation. Now this confidence, this full and entire faith, is only possible in so far as any one remains convinced that this divine messenger, in what he proposes for belief as coming from God and revealed by God, as a means of salvation, can neither deceive himself nor others in delivering what is false as a truth revealed by God. And it is thus that the gift or privilege of infallibility in matters of faith is inherent, intrinsic, and identical, as it were, with the divine mission solemnly delivered to His Church by God Himself.

'Strong in this divine mission, and in the prerogative of infallible teaching consequent thereon, the Church, after having given convincing proofs of her power to the Jews and Gentiles, to whom she had to teach the Gospel, placed before them methodically a belief in all she had learnt from her Divine Founder; and the people, aided by divine grace, interiorly fortified by its celestial light, without any difficulty formed their act of supernatural faith by believing each and all of the truths which had been preached to them.

'Now, all this was done and accomplished many years before any of the books of the New Testament had been composed; and consequently the existence of the Church and her divine prerogatives, as well as all the other truths constituting the sacred deposit of the faith, are altogether independent of the Scriptures. Could any one be found capable of believing that, in proportion as the sacred books were being written under the influence of divine inspiration, the Church had to lose some portion of those prerogatives to which those very books bear testimony, or of the right of proclaiming the truths that were to be read therein henceforth, and which until then she had taught by word of mouth, and kept alive by means of oral tradition? I think no one could be senseless enough even to suspect such a thing. But the prerogatives of the Church and the truths she taught remained what they were, with this only difference, that besides their continuing to be kept alive by tradition, they had another means of preservation, in the monumental existence of these divine books. So far from the appearance of these books putting an end to the authority which the Church had until then enjoyed to instruct the people, this authority became more than ever necessary in order to give a sanction to these same books as they appeared. For, although these books were divine in themselves and contained divine teachings, those into whose hands they fell had no certainty of the fact. It was necessary therefore that the Church, which, as I have just said, was looked on by all the faithful as infallible in its teachings, should assure them by her testimony that these books contained the same truth as she was preaching, that the authors of them were really those whose names were borne by them, and that God had dictated them—that is to say, that their authors had been divinely inspired. A similar testimony could only be given by a Church which was enlightened by the Holy Spirit, and which Jesus Christ had established to serve all nations as mistress, as a guide in the way of truth.'

FIFTH ARTICLE.

It is impossible for a Protestant to prove that the Bible contains all the truths revealed by God—Answer to some difficulties—In what sense the Bible is perfect.

It is not sufficient for our adversaries to prove by texts that the Holy Scriptures are profitable to teach, to reprove, to correct;[14] Catholics admit this as well as Protestants, since they make use of it in their theological theses and in their preachings; but they must prove that they *alone* and *exclusively* are profitable.

Neither is it sufficient to show that in many cases the sacred books throw light on questions now under consideration; that is an incontestable fact which we most willingly admit; but it must be demonstrated that they contain *all* the light of which we have need.

It is not sufficient to prove that the Bible contains revealed truths, the Word of God, a part of the remote rule of faith—this every Catholic would concede without the slightest hesitation; but it ought to be clearly established that the Bible contains *all* the Word of God, *all* the revealed truths, and is the *only* rule of faith.

[14] 2 Tim. iii. 16, &c.

All the texts of Scripture which Protestants bring to bear always to prove their thesis do not prove enough, for they only logically establish what all Catholics have likewise universally recognised.

Thus, for example, when Jesus Christ says: 'Search the Scriptures, for you think in them to have life everlasting; and the same are they that give testimony of Me,'[15]—does He mean thereby to say that the Scriptures contain the whole Word of God, and are the only rule of faith? Evidently not; such a conclusion is by no means to be drawn from our Saviour's words. In fact, Jesus Christ addresses Himself in these terms to the Jews who were not yet converted; He wishes to convince them of the truth of His divine mission, and as they admit the testimony of the writings of the Old Testament, He refers them to it so as to allow them to identify the Messiah, who had been promised and so clearly announced for centuries, with Him who was now in their midst, and thus to verify in Himself the accomplishment of the numerous prophecies concerning Him. Besides, it is very clear that He could not counsel them to read all the Bible, since the books of the New Testament did not then exist. All that we can deduce from this passage is that our Lord wished to prove His divine mission to the Jews, by giving it a basis which they must necessarily admit; just the same as Catholics act towards Protestants, when they make use of clear and decisive texts of the New Testament to prove to them the divinity and infallibility of the Church. This was *one* of the proofs of His mission, but it was not the only

[15] St. John v. 39.

one, since a little before (v. 36) He had brought forward His works or His *miracles*, in order to prove the same truth in a decisive manner.

These remarks may and ought to apply to the passage in the Acts of the Apostles,[16] where it is said *that the Jews of Berea received the Word with all eagerness, daily searching the Scriptures whether these things were so.* Here again it is of the Old Testament that St. Paul speaks to the Jews whom he is wishing to convert, by showing them that Jesus Christ was indeed the Messiah announced by the prophets, and in whom all the predictions were fulfilled. These Jews compare the words of the Apostle with those of the prophecies, in order to make themselves sure of the truth of His teaching. In their so doing, while there is nothing but what is most laudable, there is also nothing to show that the Bible contains *all* revealed truths.

In like manner, whenever, in certain places of the holy writings,[17] it is a question of the *Law of the Lord* which converts souls, or the *Word of God* which enlightens our footsteps, the application is attempted to be made to Scripture *alone;* the reasoning is bad, since the *Law* and the *Word* of God may be written or unwritten, and at the same time be also left in the hands of the infallible Church to be taught by her, and by her to be preserved and propagated.

The same remark applies to the famous text in Deuteronomy[18] where God expressly says: 'You shall not

---

[16] Acts xvii. 11.
[17] Psalm xviii. 8; Isaias lv. 10, &c.; Jeremias xxxiii. 24.
[18] Deut. iv. 2.

add to the word that I speak to you, neither shall you take away from it.' Whilst we have no proof that the Word of God can only be contained in the Bible and can only mean the Scriptures, whilst we have no proof that God is compelled to speak to man only in a book, absolutely nothing will have been proved; the question will not even have been approached, for it consists in proving that Scripture *alone* contains the Word of God, and that it is the *only* source of revealed doctrine, the *only* rule of faith.

It is easy to remark also that all these last texts of the Old Testament, which concern the ancient law, could evidently never make us come to any conclusion which regards only the new law, the constitution of the Christian Church.

But, it will be said, can Jesus Christ then, the wisest of legislators, have omitted to place a part of His laws in His code? Is it not an impiety to suspect that our Saviour could leave His work incomplete?

Such a conclusion could only bear the stamp of truth under the supposition that Jesus Christ had wished to make a code of laws of the Scriptures, a code which was to be the sole organ of His commands, as human legislators do; but this is what can *never* be proved. No, it is *absolutely impossible* to prove that God has wished to make of the Bible a sole rule of faith, the only deposit of revealed truths; and this explains, perhaps, why the Scripture contains certain little details, apparently of minor importance, and passes over more essential truths in silence: it is because the former might have been lost without the sacred books, whilst, in respect of fundamental truths, God had provided for their preservation by the oral and traditional teaching of the body of pastors.

But then, our adversaries reply, the Bible is only an *imperfect* work.

I make a distinction; it is imperfect, if considered with regard to tradition, of which it is but a part, and in the sense that it does not contain all which is comprised in tradition; but it is perfect in the sense that it contains all which God willed to be inserted there. In the same way, although each book has its own and absolute perfection, because nothing is wanting which ought to be included, there is, however, in the Bible a relative want of perfection, because it does not contain all that is to be found elsewhere. It is therefore no more matter of astonishment that the Bible has, in a certain way, its *supplement* in tradition, than that each sacred book requires and has received *its supplement* in the other books which were written at different epochs. Thus, then, the reasoning of Protestants is altogether false, because it supposes that God has chosen to give us the Bible as the only rule of our faith, as a complete code of the truths He has given to man.

This last supposition, which the Protestants admit without any proof, is, however, in evident opposition to the teaching of the Church. Let us listen, again, on this subject to the remarks, so full of wisdom and science, which fall from the pen of Rev. Fr. Perrone; they will show us another weak side of the fundamental principle of Protestantism.

'That is a famous passage in which the Apostle recommends the faithful of Thessalonica to hold fast to the traditions which they had received from him, both by word of mouth and by writing. It has been justly remarked on this passage, that not only the Apostle distinguishes between oral and written tradition, but also that he attributes to one and the other the like authority, the like value. There is a well-known text in which the same Apostle recommends Timothy to guard the deposit which he had confided to him; and there is no doubt that in speaking thus he made no allusion to the Bible, which at that period was not even finished, but only to the doctrine he had taught him, by warning him, immediately after the words we have just quoted, that some have turned away from him, of whom were Phigellus and Hermogenes; and immediately before he had recommended him to hold the form of sound words which he had heard from him in faith. There are well-known passages in St. John, where that Apostle declares he will not commit some of his instructions to paper, reserving them to deliver by word of mouth. Let it not be said that at least the necessary truths are to be found in the Bible; for that, again, would be an allegation which the Protestants could not justify with their rule limited to the Bible *alone*, since the Bible does not speak thereon. And then it would be after all but a miserable piece of equivocation, since, if we are to understand by these truths necessary to be known and believed only those which are indispensable to salvation, and of which we cannot without guilt be ignorant, we might take out of the Protestant creed many truths whereof we might, indeed, remain in ignorance without prejudice to our salvation, and which for this very reason we are not obliged to believe explicitly. If by these truths necessary to be known and believed may be understood all those which it has pleased God to reveal to us, and to propose to our belief when they come to our knowledge, there is not one single article in the whole of revelation which it is not necessary to believe in this last sense.

'If, then, revealed truths are not all contained in the Bible alone, but are also to be found in tradition; still further, if all truths are contained in tradition, and there is only a part of them contained in the Bible, it is evident that the true rule of faith is that founded both on the Scriptures and on tradition; and such, to the exclusion of all others, is the rule of the Catholic Church, founded on the whole of the Word of God, written and traditional. I have said, *the rule of the Catholic Church to the exclusion of all others*, because this is the only Church which can have such a rule, being the only one that has had no interruption in her course, nor consequently in her teaching, since there is an unbroken chain of her pastors from the times of the Apostles: an advantage that no communion separated from her can possess, since of no other can the commencement be fixed nor the origin indicated. And this is the true motive of the really *native* aversion in which all sects hold tradition. There is not one of them which does not abhor it, because each of them knows and feels that it is deprived of it like those streams of water which, cut off and separated from their fountain-head, change into putrid and muddy water, no longer being fed by the living water, which continues to flow in the principal channel.'[19]

Later on the question of the Church and tradition will again present itself; we will then enter into further details.

[19] *Il Protestantismo e la Regola di Fede*, t. ii. p. 61, &c.

CHAPTER II.

The Protestant proximate Rule of Faith.

AFTER having rapidly sketched the impossibilities which result from the Protestant system *concerning the Bible,* or the *remote* rule of faith; after having pointed out that, without the aid of that Catholic tradition which our adversaries reject, neither the inspiration of the Bible, nor even the authenticity and integrity of all its books, can ever be proved in a manner suited to the capacity of ordinary intelligences,—it remains to be considered how Protestantism interprets this dead letter of the Scripture, what means it employs to make itself master of the revealed truths contained in the Bible. In other words, we have now to make a serious study of the *proximate* rule of faith of Protestants. I have already mentioned cursorily that the different Christian sects separated from the Roman Church place this rule of faith, some in *individual reason,* others in the *inspiration of the Holy Ghost,* others again in the *fallible authority of their Church.* It is easy to show the insufficiency of each of these means to discover the veritable doctrine contained in the Holy Scriptures.

FIRST ARTICLE.

Inadequacy of individual reason to know the truths revealed in the holy books—The obscurity of the Scriptures is mentioned by the inspired writers themselves, by the Fathers of the Church, by the

Protestants at least practically—The Bible is clear on all fundamental articles: reply to this objection—Private examination of the Bible can never be the rule of faith instituted by Jesus Christ, because this means never has been and never will be applicable to all—The first Christians had no Bible—The Evangelical Alliance is not unity of faith, and is not capable of producing it—Whatever Dr. Burns may say, the Bible, interpreted by each individual, is not a principle of unity—Free examination has only led and can only lead to divisions and subdivisions; it can justify any preconceived ideas.

It is not difficult to become convinced of the inadequacy of individual reason thoroughly to understand the sense of the doctrine contained in the Holy Scriptures. It is sufficient for this purpose to consider, first, the obscurity in which the greater part of the holy books are wrapped; secondly, the feeble light of human intelligence.

I. It is very easy to understand that Protestants have proclaimed in every key the extreme clearness of the Bible; they had an interest in so doing; in fact, without their so doing, their system would at once have collapsed and become radically impossible. Also Luther did not fail to affirm that 'Scripture is its own surest and clearest, and at the same time most intelligible, interpreter; it proves everything to everybody, and it judges all and enlightens all.' In another place he says, 'Here is what I affirm of the whole Scripture. I do not approve its being called obscure in any of its parts.'[1] Farther on he adds again, 'Christians should above all hold as certain and indubitable that the Holy Scriptures are a spiritual light much brighter than the sun itself.' Let us compare these most explicit words with those others by the same Luther,[2] and we shall see that, like a

[1] *Præf. assert. art. a Leone Pontifice damnati.*
[2] See Audin, *Histoire de la Vie de Luther*, t. ii. p. 339.

real chameleon in point of doctrine, he knew how to modify his opinions from day to day. 'To fathom,' he said, 'the sense of the Holy Scriptures is *an impossible thing*; we can but skim the surface; to understand the sense thereof would be a wonder. Hardly is it given to us to know the alphabet. Let theologians say and do what they will, to penetrate the mystery of the divine words will always be an enterprise above our intelligence.'[3]

These avowals, which, from time to time, were extorted from Luther and other heads of the reform by the force of their very obviousness, are fully confirmed by the Scripture itself and by all subsequent writers.

St. Peter, the Prince of the Apostles, declares plainly that in St. Paul's letters there are '*certain things hard to be understood*, which the unlearned and unstable wrest, as they do also *the other Scriptures*, to their own destruction.'[4]

The eunuch of the Ethiopian queen, who was reading the prophet Isaias on his journey, acknowledged to the deacon Philip that he could not understand the sense of these predictions unless some one explained them to him.[5] Our Lord Himself is obliged to explain the Scriptures to His disciples on their way to Emmaus; He tells them they have not understood the prophets.[6]

All the fathers of the Church, those indefatigable defenders of revealed truth, those faithful guardians, those apostles of sacred science, have recognised the same difficulties in the interpretation of the Holy Scriptures; those even who have commented on the sacred books in the

---

[3] See Perrone, *Regola di Fede*, t. i. p. 249.
[4] 2 Peter iii. 16. [5] Acts viii. 31. [6] St. Luke xxiv. 25-27.

most learned manner have been the first to proclaim that they are obscure in many places.

Thus Clement of Alexandria affirms that 'neither the prophets nor the Saviour Himself have spoken of the holy mysteries in so ordinary and common a manner that the first comer can easily understand them;' and he adds, 'the explanation of them must be asked of those who have received it from Jesus Christ and who preserve it.'[7]

Origen writes that 'many men filled with zeal have arrived, by dint of study, at understanding the Scriptures, although in many places they are obscure.'[8]

St. Jerome complains that the Holy Scriptures are interwoven with difficulties, and especially the prophets, which are filled with enigmas.[9]

In his epistle to Algas he again writes: 'The whole Epistle of St. Paul to the Romans is enveloped in extreme obscurity, and can only be understood by the help of the Holy Ghost, who dictated it to the Apostle.'

In his fifth epistle to St. Paula he adds: 'The Apostles Peter, James, John, and Jude have written seven epistles, which are so mystical, that rarely can any one be found who can interpret them without committing some error. The Apocalypse of St. John contains as many mysteries as words.'

After this testimony of a doctor so erudite as was St. Jerome, so familiar as he was with Greek and Hebrew, so well versed in the knowledge of the Holy Scriptures, consuming his whole life in studying and commentating on them, how could we, with the audacity of a Luther, of a Mosheim, and others, affirm that the Scriptures are

[7] Strom. i. 6.   [8] Cont. Cels. i. 4, n. 2.   [9] In cap. iii. Nahum.

as clear as the sun, and that each one of the faithful can and ought to read them and extract a creed from them? Really this is pushing the spirit of system too far. In fact, whoever has studied the Bible somewhat seriously must be convinced a thousand times over of the truth of St. Jerome's words.

St. Augustine[10] is no less explicit on this subject in his work on the *Christian Doctrine*.

But let us listen awhile to the oracle of Lerins, St. Vincent,[11] who attests that, 'seeing the depth of the Scripture, all men cannot draw the same meaning from it. One person interprets the divine oracles in one manner, another in a way so altogether different that it seems as if from the one source as many opinions may be taken as there are heads to form them: one interpretation is that of Novatian, another that of Sabellius; there are, again, those of Donatus, Arius, Eunomius, Macedonius, Photinus, Apollinorus, Priscillian, Jovinian, Pelagius, Celestius, and lastly Nestorius. This is why it is extremely necessary, on account of the numerous variations of error, that the interpretation of the writings of the Prophets and Apostles should be directed by the decisions of ecclesiastical tradition.' This is why he would have 'what has been believed in all times and places, as well as by all the faithful, carefully kept.'

And as if this were not sufficient to express his way of thinking, he adds that 'the peculiar property of the Catholic and faithful son of the Church is taking care to interpret the Scripture conformably to the tradition of the universal Church,' &c.

It would be easy here to accumulate testimony from

[10] De Doct. Christ. l. ii. c. 6. [11] Commonitorium, c. 2.

all ages, but of what use would it be? Do not Protestants recognise, at least practically, that the Scriptures are obscure, when, in order to understand them aright, they call to their help all the rules of the hermeneutic art, strive after making voluminous commentaries, study the Oriental languages and the expressions used by contemporaries? Is not this recognising implicitly that there are numerous and grave difficulties in the Bible? And still every one knows that this immense amount of work produces them no other result than that of an infinite variety of opinions and interpretations. Evidently a very clear book ought to be understood by every one and in the same sense. From the moment that a large number of men, studious, learned, and, at least apparently, lovers of truth, cannot agree as to the right way of interpreting a multitude of passages from the Bible, it is but logical to conclude unhesitatingly that that Bible contains difficulties, ambiguities, obsolete and now almost incomprehensible expressions, passages of which the true meaning could only be fixed by an infallible authority. By means of the infallible authority of the Church which interprets them, the Scriptures become a brilliant light for the faithful; without this authority they can but produce a chaos of different opinions, and increase the darkness of error.

Doubtless, the Apostles, filled with the Holy Ghost, perfectly understood the Scriptures which then existed; they could explain them without danger of mistaking them; and as they were intrusted by Jesus Christ with teaching the people, they must certainly have communicated the true sense of these Scriptures to the faithful.

There is no doubt that it was the Apostles themselves who originated that universal custom prevailing in the first ages of the Church of reading and explaining the sacred books in the public assemblies of the Christians. This authentic interpretation given by the Apostles, but which has not been written down, has been preserved and propagated by Catholic tradition, that is to say, by the teaching body constituted by Jesus Christ and aided by the light of the Holy Ghost.

It is true, our adversaries say, it is true that Scripture is obscure in certain parts, but only in things which are of little importance and fortuitous; in essential things, those necessary to be believed, it is so clear and luminous, that any one can extract from it the dogmas of faith, and make for himself a creed from it.[12]

To this worn-out objection, which, however, is still often employed by Protestant writers, I answer: 1. That this distinction between essential and fortuitous things, in the way our adversaries understand it, or between the fundamental and non-fundamental articles, was always unknown to Christian antiquity. The arguments which have been brought forward to prove the obscurity of the Scriptures in no way indicate this distinction. Still more, St. Peter[13] speaks in no equivocal terms of the obscurity of the Scriptures even on essential points, since he makes reference to articles which the unlearned and unstable wrest to *their own destruction*. It is very evident that destruction and perdition indicate errors in essential matters.

[12] See the discourse of the Rev. Mr. Doudiet, in the Quebec *Morning Chronicle* of Feb. 15, 1872.   [13] 2 Epistle iii. 15.

2. But which, then, are the articles reputed to be fundamental, and which must necessarily be believed, under pain of no longer belonging to the Church of Christ, under pain of damnation? On this point, as on many others, it is again impossible for Protestants to agree. Some would have those cease to be Christians who deny the Trinity, and the Divinity of Jesus Christ; others refuse that title to those who reject baptism, or who will have no Lord's Supper, or who refuse to admit the Apostles' Creed. Others regard as fundamental the articles which are clearly contained in the Bible, or which are considered as necessary to salvation, or which Jesus Christ and the Apostles have the oftenest and most strongly recommended, or such as concern the Divinity of Christ, or which were universally admitted in the first ages, or are now to be found in all the Christian sects. Others even go so far as to think that it is neither necessary nor possible to make this distinction between fundamental and non-fundamental articles, and that the best way is to destroy all creeds as so many causes of division; they not only deny the necessity of *unity of faith*, but even the *necessity of faith*; their *religious* tolerance is so vast that it can embrace the whole world, and make the names even of schism and heresy disappear. Hence it is easy to conclude that, even in things wherein belief is certainly necessary, the Scriptures are not sufficiently clear to produce uniformity of opinion among those who make a serious study of them.

3. Every day's experience marvellously confirms the remarks I have just made. No one is ignorant of the fact that, amongst the different Christian sects who look

upon Scripture as their rule of faith, may be found every shade of opinion, even the most contradictory, on points evidently essential; for example, on the Divinity of Jesus Christ, on the eternity of hell-fire, on the effects of baptism, on the validity of infant baptism, on good works as necessary to salvation, on the Real Presence of Jesus Christ in the Holy Eucharist, &c. How, then, boast of this pretended clearness of the Scriptures in things necessary to salvation?

4. But let us suppose even that some, by dint of labour and by means of the rules of the hermeneutic art, of Oriental tongues, and of archæology, should succeed in elucidating the greater part of the difficulties, could that suffice? No, certainly; for whatever may be the skill of these erudite scholars, their interpretation can never be, in reality, anything more than that of individual writers, to whom no one is bound to submit, nor to yield complete and blind faith; their authority, however great it may be supposed to be, can never, in the eyes of the people, bear the divine mark of infallibility, which alone is capable of producing in their minds that unity of faith which Jesus Christ requires in His Church.

What is more, these learned men themselves, more often than not, differ from one another in the meaning they assign to the same passage of Scripture; the one will find, with Luther, that these perfectly clear words of our Saviour at the Last Supper, 'This is My Body, this is My Blood,' announce the Real Presence of Jesus Christ in the Eucharist; another will maintain, with Calvin, that they express nothing more than a sign, a figure, a remembrance of our Saviour. On whom can the simple faithful, the unlearned man rely under similar circumstances? These men both appear to him of equal learning: which opinion shall he embrace? And if he must make his decision on a purely human authority, why should he not equally well adopt the interpretation of the Catholics, who, even humanly speaking, count amongst their ranks as many learned men of celebrity as the Protestants can? Let no one, then, boast to us of the luminous clearness of the sacred books, since it is impossible to interpret them in a uniform manner elsewhere than in the Infallible Church of Jesus Christ. Outside this ark of salvation there can be but that obscurity, that maddening uncertainty which inevitably leads to the ruin of all religious belief or to pure rationalism.

II. The feebleness of the light of human reason is another proof that the Protestant rule of faith, based on the private interpretation of Scripture, is altogether insufficient.

It is curious to expose another contradiction in Luther's writings. According to him, individual reason can and ought to inquire into the sense of the sacred oracles; it is possible for it to understand them. Having made such an affirmation, having laid down a similar fundamental principle, it might be expected that he was going to exalt the force of human reason, attributing to it a power and a penetration which would guarantee it from all grave errors. Not at all; logic presents no obstacles to him. In his eyes, human reason, free will, all, has in man not only been weakened, but absolutely destroyed by original sin. But, then, how can this human reason, reduced to the most complete powerlessness, and in a state bordering on non-entity, scrutinise the sublime depths and dissipate the undoubted obscurity of Holy Scripture? I leave the solution of this difficulty, if any solution is possible, to those whose glory it is to profess the doctrines of the great Saxon reformer. Now let us approach the question nearer, and demonstrate that *private judgment or free inquiry cannot be the divinely-constituted interpreter of Holy Scripture, to which every one should have recourse in matters of faith:* in other terms, free inquiry cannot be the proximate rule of faith.

Jesus Christ cannot have given, as a rule of faith, a means which never has been, cannot now, and never will be employed by the greater part of the human race, a means which, not only on account of the malice and weakness of men, but by its very nature, must necessarily give rise to the most ridiculous and contradictory opinions, and which has only produced, and is still producing, division and disorder.

Now such are the characteristics of the proximate rule of faith, such are the well-known and inevitable results of private inquiry, of the free interpretation of Scripture. One glance will suffice to prove the truth of this assertion.

1. How could these means have been made use of during the fourteen centuries which preceded the invention of printing? The entire canon of the Holy Scriptures was only completed sixty years after our Saviour's death, and consequently no one could search those books which were not written till then. Can any one dare to

deny that these first faithful were good and perfect Christians, more perfect even than those of our days—they of whom the Scripture affirms that they were of one heart and one soul, that they persevered in prayer, in the breaking of bread, in giving alms, and other works of charity? They were, then, Christians without Scripture, without having ever applied the force of their individual reason to understanding the sense of it. Yes, they were perfect Christians through the preaching of the Apostles and their successors; in other terms, through the teaching Church which Jesus Christ left in substitution for Himself here below, before making His glorious ascension into heaven.

It must not be imagined that, after the death of the Apostles, the Scriptures were at once gathered into one volume, which each one had in his possession; this would be a grave error. Certain individual churches even did not acquire them till long after their publication; others mixed with them various apocryphal or profane writings, such as the different gospels and apocalypses, which are certainly neither divine nor authentic; as well as the epistles of St. Clement Romanus, St. Barnabas, and the Pastor of Hermas, which are very authentic, but not inspired; others, again, admitted into their canon only a part of the sacred books, because they somewhat doubted the inspiration of the others. It was only at the end of the fourth century that the question was clearly decided, when the Council of Hippone (393) and the Third Council of Carthage (397) admitted into their canon all the books which the Council of Trent included in it, and which we still have. Pope Innocent I., St. Augustine, St. Gelasius I., and others also enumerated the same writings as the Councils of Hippone and Carthage. Can it indeed be thought, that during this period of the great persecutions, when so many faithful suffered martyrdom for the faith, —can it be thought that there were no good and fervent Christians? And if there were, had they become so by means of the Bible, which individual churches hardly possessed? Assuredly not; and, as the illustrious Bishop of Châlons, Monseigneur Meignan, so well points out, 'the disciples of Jesus Christ had for a long time been accustomed to recite the *Pater*, before that divine form of prayer was written down; for a long time the Apostles had been baptising "In the name of the Father, the Son, and the Holy Ghost," before those sacramental words were placed in a book; apostolic men had for a long time been preaching and governing in the name of Christ; and, in a word, the Church had been constituted long before our Gospels were arranged and published' (p. 126).

I might add, that for a long time the Church had been filling the entire world with its glory and its triumphs, that her faith had been sealed with the blood of thousands of martyrs, before a perfect understanding was come to as regards the canon of the Scriptures. St. Irenæus, who lived towards the end of the second century, speaks of the Christians scattered among the Gauls in Germany, among the Sarmatians, &c., and he affirms that they had not the sacred books in their possession.

Later, and during the Middle Ages, it continued to be the custom to have extracts from the Old and the

New Testament read aloud in their churches on Sundays and holy days, and to comment on them, as is still the practice in our day. But this is very different from believing that each one of the faithful had his Bible, read it, interpreted it in his own manner, and drew from it his own creed. Besides, what could have been the number of fortunate mortals who would be rich enough to have the whole Bible carefully copied for them? Accustomed as we are to have books at very moderate prices, we are led to fancy there were the same facilities before the fifteenth century; but in that we make a grave mistake. Bibles were to be found in episcopal schools, in churches, particularly in monasteries, where the monks occupied themselves in copying them, and in some rich private houses: elsewhere very few were to be met with.

Let us even suppose that it had been possible for all to have them, how many would have been in a state to profit by them? Doubtless, very few. Elementary and secondary instruction were not as common as in our day; very small was the number of those who had studied sufficiently to be able to read the Bible and understand what was in it.

The historian Macaulay says the same thing when he writes: 'There was then through the greater part of Europe very little knowledge, and that little was confined to the clergy. Not one man in five hundred could have spelled his way through a psalm; books were few and costly; the art of printing was unknown. Copies of the Bible, inferior in beauty and clearness to those which every cottager may now command, sold for prices which many priests could not afford to give. It was obviously impossible that the laity should search the Scriptures for themselves.'[14]

Formerly a knowledge of religion was acquired, not by perusing the sacred books, but by tradition, by oral instruction, absolutely the same as our peasants, who, when they do not know how to read, still learn their prayers and their catechism; and their religious knowledge was perhaps neither less extended nor less solid than that of our modern demi-savants. Probably there is no exaggeration in saying that nine-tenths of the population were not in a position to read the manuscripts of the Bible. According to the Protestant system, we should have to conclude, therefore, that these poor unfortunate beings had no rule of faith, and were out of the path of salvation.

Another rigorous consequence of this doctrine is, that Jesus Christ must have established as a rule of faith, as necessary to salvation, a means which, in the first place, could only be employed by some few fortunate ones of each age—a means which, even after the discovery of printing and all the efforts of biblical societies, is not yet within reach of every one, and which probably never will be. How many children, how many people of every age, how many poor—above all, among certain less-civilised nations—how many will never be able either to read or appreciate for themselves all the divine beauties of written revelation!

Who cannot at once see the radical error of such a system? What! Jesus Christ, God infinitely good, who

---

[14] *History of England*, chapter i.

sacrificed even His life for the salvation of humankind, could He have revealed to His cherished people a certain number of truths necessary to salvation, and then have consigned them to a book which the greater number of men could never either read or understand, or in any manner know? Could He have never even given them masters intrusted with making known to them infallibly all the heavenly treasures of truth, love, and tenderness which this book contains? Could He have threatened them with eternal damnation if they had not the faith, and then have given them no means of acquiring it? Or, again, could He have waited several centuries—that is to say, until the discovery of printing —to make it a little more within their reach? This is simply incredible, and any one must be completely under the reign of prejudice or the spirit of system to maintain such a thesis. Is it not acknowledging, at any rate tacitly, that our Lord has imposed on men an obligation of reaching an end without giving them the means for arriving there? Would not this be accusing Him of injustice towards men, since He would be exacting an impossible thing?

'Let us speak out,' says Monseigneur Douey, Bishop of Montauban, in his *Letters on Protestantism* (p. 107). 'It is frightful to think and to say that the revelation of an infinitely wise and good God could lead to such a result. You commence by making of revelation a religion which can only be directly known and studied by the learned, or at any rate by those who know how to read, provided they have the Word of God in their hands written in a language which they understand.

And thus the ignorant, the immense mass of the human race, are condemned to only knowing religion through the word and teaching of the learned. God has not vouchsafed to communicate with them more immediately and directly. But the learned themselves are condemned to being never certain of having properly understood and fathomed the intentions of God as contained in His Word. God has placed the ignorant either under an impossibility of knowing the religion He has vouchsafed to reveal to us, or under the necessity of only knowing it by the mouth of the learned; and He has placed the learned themselves under an impossibility of making themselves sure as to whether they are teaching properly what He has written in the sacred books, and what He has revealed. There is, I repeat, a frightful derision in saying and thinking that God has acted thus; and if such is not what Jesus Christ Himself has called *a sin against the Holy Ghost*, we must despair of ever understanding the meaning of the clearest words. Jesus Christ said then to the Jews, Do what the Scribes and Pharisees teach you, because they are seated in the chair of Moses; and yet in His own Church He has not established a chair to which Christians can address themselves with the same confidence as the Jews addressed themselves to the synagogue.'

The Protestant system supposes, too, that each person possesses a copy, or rather a translation, of the Bible in a vulgar language which he understands. This is evident; for to give a Hebrew, Greek, or English Bible to some one who only understands Italian or French, is to make him a most useless present. It would be much the same thing as presenting him with a copy of the undecipherable hieroglyphics which cover the old tombs or the obelisks of Egypt. To apply this system of free examination of the Bible, it will either be necessary that each person should learn one of the languages into which the Bible has been translated, or else that there be as many translations as there exist languages and particular idioms on the whole surface of the globe.

No one has ever dared to maintain the first hypothesis.

The second can hardly stand when considered seriously. In fact, in order to translate well, we must have as *perfect* an acquaintance as possible with every existing idiom. I say *perfect;* for otherwise one runs a great risk of employing improper expressions, and distorting the true meaning of the Word of God, or giving it a ridiculous and absurd meaning. It is moreover necessary thoroughly to understand the languages in which the Scripture was first given to the world — Hebrew, Greek, Chaldean. To this must be joined theological studies, a knowledge of manners and customs, a cultivated and ingenuous mind, erudition, prudence, right-mindedness. Without all these it is impossible to obtain the desired result.

Is it really the case that the versions made by Protestants for the different nations of Asia, Africa, and Oceanica are exempt from numerous faults? Doubtless they praise their exactness; but is such really to be found? I will only mention one testimony, that borne by Mr. Marshall in his work on this subject. He maintains that the defective versions of Scripture produce a similar effect on the disciples of Confucius in China to that which is produced in certain parts of Great Britain by the *Book of Mormons and Mormonism;* there is only to be found in them a tissue of absurdities and impious pretensions, which are not worth examining into.[15]

2. It is not even sufficient to have a good version of the Bible and to be able to read it, we must also be in a condition to understand it in its true sense; otherwise this Bible becomes perfectly useless, and even hurtful, since it may become to certain individuals a sadly fruitful source of pernicious errors. Now, it cannot be understood by all, and we have already seen that, in a large number of books and passages containing dogmas, the sense is so obscure, that the greater number of people, if left to themselves, would be absolutely incapable of understanding the sense and extracting the true doctrine from it. I might add, that even the most learned interpreters, with all their treasures of erudition, with all the resources of their science and genius, would never be able, independently of the infallible authority of the teaching Catholic Church, to draw from Scripture a complete creed unspotted by error.

To be convinced of the truth of my assertion, is it not enough to cast a glance on the present state of Protestantism? The facts are as clear as the sun at noonday, and any one must be blind not to perceive both them and the consequences ensuing therefrom. Lutherans, Calvinists, Methodists, Presbyterians Reformed and Un-reformed, Episcopalians, Baptists, Anabaptists,

---

[15] *Christian Missions*, vol. i. p. 53.

Pedobaptists, Free-will Baptists, Seventh-day Baptists, Six-principle Baptists, Quaker Baptists, Anti-pedobaptists, Unitarians, Universalists, Socinians, Emancipators, Quakers, Jumpers, Tumblers, Moravians, Non-resistants, Illuminati, Campbellites, Harmless Christians, Primitive Christians, Puseyites, Free-communion Baptists, Christian Connection, Come-outers, Fighting Quakers, Swedenborgians, &c.; all read the Scriptures, all seek to understand them, and discover in them doctrines often entirely contradictory to one another. The Rev. Mr. Doudiet finds in this pell-mell of antagonistic opinions all the beauty of the variegated colours of the rainbow; he has a horror of uniformity, as if truth could vary with different individuals and different latitudes. What appears beautiful to him, however, is a monstrosity in the eyes of every philosopher; for it is indubitable that the Holy Ghost, who inspired the sacred writers, can never have taught doctrines which are in flagrant contradiction with one another. God, who is the essence of truth, cannot teach error. If it is true that Jesus Christ is God, that He is really present in the Holy Eucharist, that it was He who instituted the Sacraments, that there is an everlasting hell, &c., for that very reason it is false to affirm that Jesus Christ is not God, that He is not really present in the Holy Eucharist, that He did not institute the Sacraments, and that there is no everlasting hell. There is no medium, no possible rainbow; the same thing cannot be both true and false. It must therefore be admitted that a great number of Protestants, who interpret Scripture according to the light of reason, according to their private judgment, fall into grave errors. I will not yet determine who is right or who is wrong; for the moment I content myself with proving the insufficiency of individual reason in arriving at an entire and certain knowledge of the truths revealed in Scripture. Show me amongst Protestants one single dogma, one single doctrine, which has not met with adversaries founding their objections on the Bible, and persuaded that they interpret that Bible rightly, and I will hasten to proclaim the fact everywhere. In the mean while, I maintain that Protestants, with their fundamental principle of individual interpretation, never have had, have not now, and never will have a common symbol of faith, however limited a one it might be. They may speak of *Evangelical Alliance* as much as they please, hold pompous annual assemblies, praise up the spectacle of their unity, the final result will always be the same;[16] unity of faith is radically impossible for them, and *never* will Protestantism verify those words of the Saviour: 'There shall be but one flock and one shepherd.'

But, it will be said, you count among Protestants sects which are not even Christian.

When you will have decided what articles of faith must be absolutely admitted under pain of ceasing to be Christian, then it will be allowable for you to refuse this name to those who do not consent to receive them.

[16] Quebec *Morning Chronicle*, Feb. 27th, 1874. The Rev. Dr. Burns had the courage to make these affirmations: 'Protestantism must be looked on as a great *united whole*, in spite of the prejudice and passion which the discussion of religious principle might evoke. Upon the great points of Christian doctrine they are all one, the sole difference being in matters of government. The Book brought them together and united them.'

But as you have never succeeded in coming to an agreement on this point, and as all sects, founded like you on the Bible, lay claim to being Christian, I do not know why I should credit your word more than theirs, particularly since they take as the basis of their rule of faith your fundamental principle of the free interpretation of Scripture. Either renounce your principle or else cease anathematising these sects when they do nothing further than apply that very principle.

This is also what Abbé Magnin wisely remarked when he wrote the following lines: 'Mr. Bost cannot see the primacy of St. Peter nor that of the Pope in the text *Tu es Petrus;* he rejects the Catholic interpretation of it, and according to his principle he is right. But the Socinian cannot find the divinity of the Word in Holy Scripture; then according to the same principle he is right in denying it. Luther finds in the Scripture that Real Presence which Calvin, on his side, has a right to anathematise, because he does not find it there. The Catholic finds there the supremacy of the Pope: I ask Mr. Bost himself, what does a Catholic's conscience dictate to him when Holy Scripture speaks to him in these terms? Will this author say that all those who do not understand the Bible in the same sense as himself are unfaithful to the Holy Spirit or to the light of reason? He would not dare to say so. Any reproach, too, that he addressed to others, would they not have an equal right to address to him? Who could be judge between them? Scripture? But she is silent; violence is done her without her saying a word in reply. The light of reason? Who is there that does not himself lay claim to possessing it? Either, then, abjure the principle of the Reformation or keep silence on all errors in religion, recognising the right of each to be called the pure word of God: we see no mean between these two extremes.'[17]

It is, then, unquestionable that *de facto* this principle of free interpretation has only led to endless subdivisions, to a whole swarm of sects more or less strange and dissimilar, having no other common bond than the Bible—a dead letter which says nothing and tolerates everything—and hatred of the Catholic Church. Seeing the horrible medley formed by these different separated communions, who could ever believe that they are all founded on the same Bible? Who could even suspect that the Puseyite has the same rule of faith as the Methodist, the Harmless Christian, or the Jumper? They are as different as night and day; indeed, Luther and Calvin were, even in the very midst of the Reformation, frightened at the extent of these disagreements.

Let us now note well that these divisions and subdivisions are not due to accidental circumstances, extrinsic to Protestantism; they are in reality only the natural product of its fundamental principle, free investigation, private interpretation of the Scripture. Protestantism has no authority, and without authority unity is but a dream, a mere chimera.

Poor human reason, although capable of acquiring a certain amount of knowledge, is none the less weak, tottering, exposed to error, and an easy prey to prejudice. If it stumbles so often in proving natural truths, how can it constitute itself queen and judge of supernatural

[17] *La Papauté aux Prises avec le Protestantisme*, p. 309.

things? If uniformity of sentiment in philosophical questions has never been arrived at, how can we ever dare hope to attain it, apart from infallible authority, in a sphere far beyond the reach of human intelligence? How many sublime dogmas, how many abstract doctrines are contained in Holy Scripture, and which the greater number of the faithful are not capable of discerning! How many unfathomable mysteries! How many expressions whose meaning we might completely misunderstand! For example, who, the Bible in their hand, could extract from it the famous Thirty-nine Articles of the English Church, or the Apostles' Creed? Who cannot at once see that such a task is even above intelligences which, although cultivated, have not made an habitual and special study of the Scripture? Theologians well know that there are a multitude of arduous questions very dangerous to orthodoxy; they are like narrow slippery paths on the edge of frightful precipices: the least deviation from the right way may involve you in the gulf. Under such circumstances what would inexperienced and but little instructed Christians do? Each one would take his own course and blindly rush towards the abyss. Or, again, one day we might think we had discerned the truth, but the next day other texts would present themselves and renew hesitation and doubt; then what we had taken for the pure word of God would vanish away like a dream.

How painful it must be to the Protestant desirous of knowing revealed truth not to be able to put an end to this perpetual fluctuation of doctrine, to seek vainly for a more solid foundation than the quicksands of human reason, to be incessantly turning over the pages of the mysterious book, and not be able to derive anything more from it than discouraging silence, to find it only a dead letter! What must not be his anxiety at seeing himself, on a multitude of points, contradicted by millions of Christians as intelligent and learned as himself! Might he not thence conclude that it is not possible Jesus Christ can have left His beloved, whom He bought with His own blood, in all the terrible anguish of uncertainty, that He had given them an impracticable rule of faith, far beyond their comprehension, and which, from its very nature, must necessarily breed innumerable divisions? Why should He have come to bring a holy doctrine to men if, notwithstanding all their efforts, they were only to gather up some miserable fragments of the truth, to see only a weak, uncertain, vacillating light, quite insufficient to guide them to the heavenly country?

'To condemn each one of the faithful to form for himself a faith from the Scripture, to seek for each separate truth of Christianity by the deceiving light of reason, is to place him on the road to error, and forbid him, in his work, the use of the traditional sense; not only exposing him thereto, but condemning him to it inevitably and necessarily; for it is putting him in a labyrinth without the only clue for escaping therefrom. Only look up and see: no child of the Reformation can tell by what characteristics he recognises the Holy Writings, whence comes to him the book containing them, whether it has reached him free from all alteration, and if in its interpretation he does not take error for truth.

Protestantism, in the position it has made for itself, resembles the Wandering Jew, perpetually pursuing an object it can never reach. Like a blind man, it cannot see in the brightest light, and gropes about in the full blaze of noonday. It wished to separate what God had indissolubly united—the Church and the Bible; and, behold, one of those terrible and just judgments has befallen it which we cannot contemplate without horror. The book of the divine Word has become unintelligible to it; it has, so to speak, become a blank: for Protestantism it is like the book sealed with seven seals, before which the prophet of Patmos wept bitterly, because no man could open it.'[13]

Another cause of error and division amongst all these partisans of the *Bible alone* is the numerous prejudices brought to the reading of the inspired Book. The Scriptures are not read after throwing aside all preconceived ideas, and in order to find out what God really has revealed, but only to find there the doctrine with which we have been imbued from infancy; and we always find it there. Children brought up in Presbyterianism, going through the Scriptures with their inherited prejudices, will almost infallibly fancy they discover in the Bible all the doctrines of their sect; it will be the same thing with Quakers, Moravians, Methodists, Baptists, and others; and thus the God of all truth will be made to say the most contradictory and absurd things.

It is thus that 'kings to justify their tyranny have brought forward the words: "You shall rule them with

[13] Magnin, *La Papauté aux Prises avec le Protestantisme*, p. 320.

a rod of iron."[19] And the people to overthrow the kings have quoted this verse: "He hath put down the mighty from their seat."[20] During the Peasants' War an insurgent aspired to the command by applying the following words to himself: "Lifting up the poor out of the dunghill."[21] Add to these that there is no unchasteness which has not been authorised by these words of the Bible: "Increase and multiply."[22] Luther married in spite of his vow of chastity, because he had read in the Sacred Book: "It is not good for man to be alone."

'It has been justly remarked that the English Parliament, when sanctioning Henry VIII.'s divorce from Catherine, in order to justify his marrying Anne Boleyn, ought to have justified its proceedings by saying that it was written in the First Book of Kings: "Because he loved Anne." In a word, every one has sought and found what he wished in the Bible. Erasmus said—so persuaded was he that reading the Bible could not form true faith in souls—that the interpretation of the Scriptures by individual minds had never ended in anything but laming texts which walked perfectly straight.'[23]

Once more, is it credible that the Saviour of the world can have given so ruinous a foundation to His Church, that He can have left His doctrine a prey to human disputes, as well as the perversity and feebleness of our reason? Whence arose all the monstrous heresies which infested the early ages of the Christian Church, and which Protestants repudiate with the same horror as

---

[19] Revelations xix. 15.   [20] St. Luke i. 52.
[21] Psalm cxii. 7.   [22] Genesis i. 28.
[23] Berseaux, *L'Eglise et le Monde*, p. 173.

we do? Only from a false interpretation of the Bible. This is what made St. Augustine remark: 'Heresies have had no other origin than the Scriptures, which, though good in themselves, are not well understood.'[24]

The theologian Eck recognised this same truth when he said to Luther: 'Martin, none of the heresies which have rent the Church have sprung from aught but the interpretation of the Scriptures. The Bible is the arsenal whence each innovator has drawn his arguments.'[25]

'If the world should subsist a long time,' says Luther, 'with all these different interpretations which are given of Scripture, no other means for preserving unity would remain to us than receiving the decrees of the Councils and taking refuge in their authority.' 'Nothing throws so much discredit on our Gospel as our own intestine discord.' 'We know well enough whom to avoid, but not whom to follow.'

'It is of great importance,' wrote Calvin to Melancthon, 'that future ages should have no suspicion of the divisions which reign among us; for it is more ridiculous than can be imagined, that after having broken with every one else, we agree so badly among ourselves from the very commencement of our Reformation.'[26]

'But,' resumes Abbé Constant, 'of what use proving by history a fact which occurs every day before our eyes among Protestants? For example, does the faculty

---

[24] Aug. *Tract.* 18 *in Joan.* 'Non aliunde natæ sunt hæreses nisi dum Scripturæ bonæ intelliguntur non bene.'

[25] See Audin, *Histoire de Luther*, vol. i. c. 20.

[26] See Bishop Charvay of Pignerol's *Le Guide du Catéchumène Vaudois* (Paris, 1840), ii. 9-11.

of Geneva, which does not believe in the divinity of Jesus Christ, interpret in the same way as the faculty of Montauban, which still defends that dogma, the following passage of St. John: "And the Word was God"? The words, "This is My body," do they bear the same meaning for the Lutherans of Alsace, who believe in the Real Presence, as for the Swiss Calvinists, who reject it?

'Do Mr. Gorham and the supreme tribunal of the Church of England, who have decided that the reception of baptism was optional for salvation, take in the same sense as the Bishop of Exeter these words of our Lord: "Go, teach all nations, baptise them," &c.; "If any one be not born again by water," &c.? Do we not find that all the sects which abound by hundreds in England and the United States maintain that the extravagant ideas which form their creed—when they have one—are to be found in the Scripture? and every day do we not see the number of these sects increased by a different interpretation of some biblical text?'[27]

This confusion of religious ideas, this Babel of opinions and systems, so far from diminishing, has gone on increasing, and will fatally result in individualism; from individualism to the complete destruction of all supernatural religion there is but a step, and this step, unhappily, many have already taken. From all that has been said in the preceding pages I draw the conclusion that Jesus Christ cannot have given the Holy Scriptures, as left to the free interpretation of each individual, as a rule of faith to men, first, because this

---

[27] *Histoire de l'Infaillibilité des Papes*, vol. ii. p. 448.

rule of faith would be impossible, materially impracticable for the greater number of men and at all periods; secondly, because even cultivated minds are not capable of deducing from it the dogmatic truths which are the basis of Christianity; thirdly, because this rule of faith can only lead to interminable divisions, to innumerable sects, of whom the greater number cannot be otherwise than entangled in the paths of error and repudiated by Jesus Christ, who is truth itself, and must necessarily therefore detest error.

Individual reason applied to the interpretation of the Holy Scriptures is, then, insufficient to understand them, and cannot be the rule of faith which our Lord has given to men.

SECOND ARTICLE.

Illusion of those who think that each one of the faithful who piously reads the Holy Scriptures receives from the Holy Ghost a special help, a supernatural enlightenment, enabling him to understand the real sense of it—This system is not founded on the Word of God; it infers the actual reading of the Bible, and consequently cannot be applicable to every one; it is calculated to give rise to illusions and religious fanaticism.

Certain Reformers, perceiving that reason, left to its own strength, is powerless to discern the truths revealed in the Scriptures, and, in a word, can only be the grave of all religious belief, conceived the idea of substituting for it a supernatural and interior illumination of the Holy Spirit, communicating itself to individuals prepared to receive it. Luther himself seems neither to have been a stranger nor hostile to this rule of faith.

In this system everything is subordinate to inspiration, even the Holy Scripture. It is in this illumination that they make their proximate rule of faith consist.

However, certain conditions are necessary before the Holy Spirit thus enlightens the readers of the Bible. Here is how the minister Monnot, the 'converter of the Lyonnese,' expresses himself on this subject: "Take then the Bible; read it, but on your knees; the Holy Ghost who wrote it will Himself explain it to your heart. If some persist in maintaining that the Bible is obscure, let them know that it is only obscure for them and by their own fault.' Several other Protestant writers express themselves in a similar manner. Such appears to be the doctrine of the Anabaptists, Quakers, Modern Methodists or Wesleyans, Swedenborgians, Mennonites, Moravian Brothers, &c. According to them the Church, rites, the sacraments, creeds, apostolical tradition, all is human; the Scripture alone is divine.

But this rule of faith has several very grave and even radical faults, among others—first, its not being founded on the Word of God; secondly, being impracticable for the greater number of men; thirdly, producing many illusions and obstinate fanaticism; fourthly, rendering all our holy books useless.

I. This principle or this rule of faith is neither founded on the Word of God preserved by tradition—besides which they do not admit tradition—nor on the written Word of God. When we look into the inspired books we see clearly that the assistance of the Holy Ghost was promised to the Apostles and their successors to enable them to teach all truth, all that Jesus Christ Himself had taught them; but nowhere do we find that this promise has been made to each of the faithful. All the sacred texts they bring forward to prove their strange thesis show that God constantly disposes hearts by His holy grace and renders them docile; that He governs the human race with His benign Providence; that He sometimes gives extraordinary lights to His elect to enable them to arrive at the summit of perfection; but in no manner do these texts prove that God has promised to give to each one direct inspiration or illumination, enabling him to extract the dogmatic sense of Scripture in general, and constituting him a supreme judge of the faith.

Besides, these texts, which serve as a basis to this system, are interpreted in a different sense, not only by Catholics, but also by all Protestants who only admit as a rule of faith that private interpretation of Scripture of which we spoke in the preceding article. This divergence of opinions as to the meaning of texts ought naturally to inspire the partisans of direct illumination with a fear lest they should be themselves in error. If piety and good-will are sufficient to cause the rays of divine light to be shed on the Scriptures, how comes it that the Ethiopian eunuch, St. Jerome, St. Augustine, St. Chrysostom, and so many other personages, illustrious by their pious lives and their sincere love of truth, did not also receive these celestial illuminations, which would have prevented their complaining of the obscurity of the Scriptures? This pretended individual inspiration has, then, no foundation in the written Word of God.

II. This rule of faith is impracticable for the greater number of men. It will be said that this is a strange assertion: if the Holy Ghost vouchsafes Himself to teach men, what easier and surer method could be devised? That is true; but this divine teaching also presupposes the actual reading of the Bible; you are indeed told to read the Scripture, but piously and on your knees.

To such a system, there is no need of giving any very serious reply; I will content myself with saying to these partisans of divine inspiration: 'Yes, read the Bible piously, all of you Protestants who do not know how to read; particularly do not fail to read it on your knees, otherwise the Holy Ghost might perhaps not enlighten you, and the Sacred Book might remain as unintelligible to you and as closely sealed as that which the Apostle St. John wept at not being able to open! You also who do not know whether what is presented to you as the Bible is in reality a book inspired by God you who do not know if the version presented to you is authentic, complete, and faithful, do you keep on reading the Bible piously and on your knees! The Spirit of God will make known to your intelligence whether it be exact and complete or altered and incomplete; it will suggest to you the meaning of each passage; it will give you a course of biblical exegesis.' How many miracles to make everybody understand the Scripture!

But then there can be no more obscurity, no more uncertainty; all becomes clear as the sun at noon-day. Doubtless it is because certain Protestants do not read their Bible on their knees and piously, that their co-religionists often reproach them with understanding it but little or interpreting it so badly; unless, indeed, all these contradictory interpretations by our modern visionaries ought not to be looked on as true and dictated by the Holy Ghost, and that the Holy Ghost—of whom, perhaps, some no longer recognise the divinity—does not suggest the yes or no, the true and the false, according to circumstances. To advance such a proposition is in the eyes of a Catholic to utter a blasphemy.

However, I am far from denying that the Holy Ghost sometimes enlightens men in a more particular manner, provided they sincerely seek the truth, and above all by the means ordained by God, through the ministry of legitimate pastors.

III. This same Protestant rule of faith is calculated to produce many illusions and a blind fanaticism. Who does not know that man may often, particularly when his imagination is lively or a little excited, take for supernatural, for divine inspiration, that which springs from his own self, that which is only a passing enthusiasm, a momentary over-excitement? History is at hand to bear witness to the frequent illusions into which a man of good faith can allow himself to be hurried away under the empire of this pretended illumination. What follies did not the Montanists practise, guided by Montanus and Priscilla?

Did not Montanus declare himself exempt from error, by his doctrine superior to Christ Himself, and did he not believe himself to be the Paraclete promised to the world by Jesus Christ? What can be said of the extravagances of certain Gnostic sects of the early ages of the Church and of the Illuminati of the Middle Ages, who often joined the greatest immorality and the most obstinate fanaticism to their strange wild notions? Perhaps our modern visionaries will refuse to admit beneath their banners the authors of so many eccentricities and crimes; still they ought at least to recognise that, their principle being the same, it may lead to equally sad consequences.

However, let us examine a little into what this system has produced since the Reformation. Whoever has read history is acquainted with the excesses, the violence, the savage brutality of the Anabaptists at Munster and in other towns of Germany and the Low Countries, the fearful delirium of a Thomas Munzer, of a John of Leyden, of a Rattman, of a Knipperdolling, and others. In their moments of inspiration they ravaged towns, committed horrible massacres, proclaimed polygamy, &c. David George went so far as to proclaim himself *the true Son of God*. Let them also recall the frenzied delirium of the shoemaker George Fox, head of the sect of Quakers, and the pretended illuminations, the strange commotions, the agitations, tremblings, sighs of his co-religionists in the midst of their assemblies, when the Spirit of God visits them. What might not be said of the Methodist camp-meetings and of their ministers, who, according to the testimony of the preacher Rauschenbusch,[28] have no real knowledge of the Bible and are without any scientific culture? The same writer adds[29] that, during their divine service, preaching, or prayer, they make such an uproar, by all crying at once, that it is absolutely impossible to understand whoever is preaching or declaiming a prayer. They take all these illusions, these artificial groans and this extraordinary over-excite-

[28] *Die Nachte des Westens*, p. 32, Barmen, 1847.   [29] Ibid. p. 43.

ment, for the supernatural action of the Holy Ghost. Again, what a sensation was created in England by Joanna Southcott, a visionary who, at the end of the last century and commencement of the present, was always acting under the direction of the Spirit of God, giving passports for heaven furnished with three seals, and promising soon to give a new Messiah! She had many followers, and even after her death, which happened in 1814, many continued to believe in her, although her promised Messiah had not made his appearance.

It can easily be understood how, with so elastic a principle as that 'each person is free to follow the interior spirit by which he feels himself inspired,' great lengths may be gone. There are some who have even carried their folly so far as to proclaim that adultery, homicide, and all other crimes do not render man less agreeable to God; that grace abounds there where sin had most abounded, &c.; that from the moment wherein any one believes himself to be under the influence of the Holy Ghost, he can do what seems best to him—give himself up to the greatest disorders, even become dangerous to society; nothing can be said; it is God who is leading him and inspiring him to commit these acts. Hence that frenzy which may be remarked among these sectarians, when they persuade themselves they are acting according to the inspiration of heaven; no obstacle can stop them; advice becomes useless. Some there have been seen who, being condemned to death and conducted to the foot of the scaffold, believed they saw the heavens opened and Jehovah holding out His arms to welcome them to His kingdom. It is an incontestable fact that, if this principle were universally adopted, Christianity would, in certain points of view, become worse than paganism, and would be of a nature to exercise a most disastrous influence over the masses.

Let it not be said that the examples given above are exceptional; they are cases which recur frequently and inevitably among all these sects of enthusiasts. It is easy to become convinced of this by casting a glance at the annals of history, which contain thousands of facts analogous to those of which I have spoken.

IV. This principle of individual inspiration, once admitted, would render the Scriptures useless. For if God had chosen this interior teaching of the Holy Ghost as a means for conducting all men to the truth, doubtless it would have been sufficient in itself, and then there would have been no need of exterior teaching. However, we know that God chose to give us an exterior revelation, and that by so doing He has subjected us to a teaching from without. Doubtless God could have adopted some other means, just as He might have rendered us at once perfect: but it was not His will to do so; it is for us to submit ourselves to His adorable decrees. With this doctrine of inspiration, of what use are the Scriptures? of what use the Apostolate? of what utility can a teaching Church be? This baneful error annihilates the work of Jesus Christ, submitting it to the caprices and mental aberrations of each individual, and allowing of the suppression of man's redemption as a useless work.

THIRD ARTICLE.

The authority of a fallible Church, such as admitted by Anglicans, cannot be the real rule of faith—It cannot put an end to religious controversies; it offers no guarantee of orthodoxy—Anglicanism and Puseyism bring us back ultimately to the private examination of the Scriptures—The Gorham affair.

Anglicans claim to follow an intermediate course between what they call *Romanism*, with its infallible authority, and the endless multitude of *dissentient* sects, whose fundamental principle of private interpretation of the Scriptures tends essentially to further subdivisions among their members. It is, however, manifest that Anglicanism, as we are about to see, is in reality nothing more than one of those sects it affects to look down upon, for its fundamental principle is ultimately the same.

The Thirty-nine Articles which serve as its basis, and which have been borrowed from Catholicism, from Lutheranism, and more particularly from Calvinism, were drawn up in 1562. According to this system Holy Scripture is the *only* source of revelation (Art. 6); the Deuterocanonical books of the Old Testament are rejected as well as tradition. The Apostles' Creed, the Nicæan, and the Athanasian are admitted (Art. 8), but only because they are regarded as conformable to Scripture. For the same reason the hierarchy, consisting of bishops, priests, and deacons, is retained; but the King of England has been arbitrarily substituted for Peter and his successors, whom Jesus Christ chose to be the foundation of His Church (Arts. 23, 26, 32, 36, 37); it is by the king's authority that the bishops, priests, and deacons are ordained and established in their functions (Arts. 33, 36, 37). It is by his order also that universal councils are convoked, which councils are expressly declared and recognised as fallible and subject to error (Art. 21). It is true that in Art. 20 is recognised the Church's right to decide in discussions of faith and to interpret Holy Scripture; but her decisions must be drawn from the Scripture itself, outside of which she has neither right nor power. If the faithful discover that the decisions of their Church are not conformable to the sacred text, they are at liberty to reject them. Any way, it is the king who ultimately pronounces dogmatic decisions; no higher authority than his can be appealed to; and thus that *infallibility* which is refused to the Church is implicitly acknowledged in him.

This, then, is the curious mixture of doctrines which constitutes the basis, the rule of faith, of the Anglican Church, of the High Church of England: on the one side a fallible Church, intrusted with putting an end to controversies by the examination of Holy Scripture; on the other, the faithful, who are not obliged to submit to its decisions, except in so far as they find them conformable to the Bible.

It is very evident that everything is eventually reduced to the free examination, the private judgment, of the Bible. The authority of the Church can, then, only be that of a body of learned men, who throw more or less light on the complicated questions of theology, on the difficult texts of the Bible, but whom nobody is bound to obey, from the moment they are believed to be entangled in error. Such a Church may well say: 'I *think* that such or such a doctrine is revealed; *it seems to me* that it is contained in the teachings of Jesus Christ;' but never will she be able to say: ' Such or such a truth is certainly revealed; it must *necessarily* be believed on pain of losing all hopes of salvation; it is an article of faith *binding on all.*' Such a way of expressing themselves as this can only be found among those who have a perfect conviction that they are not deceiving themselves, and who are absolutely certain of having the perpetual assistance of the Holy Ghost, as is the case with the Catholic Church.

Let us suppose for an instant that a member of the Anglican Church should compare with the Holy Scriptures that doctrine contained in the Thirty-nine Articles which only admits the Sacraments of Baptism and the Lord's Supper, which contains the Creeds of the early ages, which proclaims justification by faith *alone* without works, and that he should become intimately convinced that the Bible also contains the doctrine of the Sacrament of Penance (which Henry VIII. always looked on as necessary), that it (the Bible) occasionally contradicted the early Creeds, that it recognises the necessity of good works besides faith for salvation: could he not, ought he not even to abandon that fallible Church, which has in reality taught him error, or kept back a part of revealed doctrine? If he has any doubts as to the orthodoxy of the teaching imparted by his Church —and who would not have in a Church which proclaims itself liable to error?—is he not strictly obliged to inquire into whatever is the object of his doubts? Now all may be and ought to be uneasy about knowing if the way they are in is the right or the wrong, the good or the bad, way; the question is a most important one, since it concerns eternal salvation or reprobation; all these ought to satisfy themselves whether the Thirty-nine Articles, and the subsequent decisions of their Church, be in perfect harmony with the Scriptures. But who are those who are in a state to engage in such a study, even supposing they have a faithful version of the inspired books? How many are there whose mind is sufficiently cultivated and who have sufficient leisure to undertake such a difficult work and succeed in it? I do not hesitate to say that the number must be excessively limited.

We see, then, first, that this authority, held by a fallible Church, cannot put an end to religious controversies; secondly, that it cannot offer any guarantee of orthodoxy or certainty to those who profess to recognise it; thirdly, that it brings them back eventually to the private examination of the Scriptures. Therefore it is easy to conclude that this system is insufficient, impossible, and opposed to revelation, as we have already shown.

The Puseyite system, which aims at a nearer approach to the Catholic rule of faith, is subject to the same disadvantages as the preceding. It is not founded on Scripture, for the very reason that it declares the Church could err, and did err after the first four or five centuries, thereby proclaiming the Church of Jesus Christ to be fallible, and that each individual should verify its definitions by examining whether they are conformable to Scripture. Here we arrive again at private examination, individual interpretation of the Bible.

Let us see whether facts do not confirm what we have just said. Dr. Marsh, the Anglican Bishop of Peterborough, affirms that the Church of England extends her authority no farther than a concern for her own preservation rigorously exacts; he adds, that no one is obliged to accept an interpretation given by the Church if he thinks it false, and that, in the latter case, he is altogether free to separate himself from Anglicanism.[30] The Rev. Father Perrone has cleverly treated the same question. In the following terms[31] he draws up an historical statement of the animated discussions which took place in the English Parliament in 1840: 'In the heat of the contest which took place on the subject of the Thirty-nine Articles, and which the new Oxford school only rendered still more animated by seeking to give these articles an interpretation approaching nearer to Roman doctrines, the petitions of a great number of Anglican ministers were presented to the Parliament but a few years ago, with a view of obtaining some modification in these articles, as well as in the Book of Common Prayer. Hence arose that stormy debate which took place in the Parliament, March 26th, 1840, when the Anglican bishops showed themselves to be divided on the question of the authority of their Church. On the one side, the Bishop of Norwich claimed that the English Church was founded on *liberty of conscience* and on the *right of private judgment*, and that a refusal to admit certain doctrinal points of the Liturgy or of the Athanasian Creed ought not to prevent any one from being admitted to Holy Orders. On the other side, the Bishop of London protested that such a claim was an injury done to the Established Church, and that the only means of maintaining this latter was to keep the *needle of the theological compass* steady: upon which some other person observed, the compass was *twisted*

---

[30] *Comparative View of the Churches of England and Rome*, ch. viii.
[31] *Regola di Fede*, vol. i. p. 542.

round, and that nobody was any longer able to put it straight again.'

And this same truth the Anglican Archbishop of Dublin had proclaimed some few years previously (August 7th, 1833) in that same House of Peers, saying 'that there was neither any individual nor body of individuals, in the Anglican Church, to whom any doubt or difficulty whatever could be referred for solution; in a word, no constituted authority to which recourse might be had for the decision of questions of this sort.'[32]

There was a case that occurred in England but a few years ago, which shows in the clearest manner that the Anglican Church has no authority in doctrinal matters, that its Creed is a nullity, and that a man may deny anything and yet not cease to be a member of it. This was the recent Gorham case. 'Nominated by the government to be minister of a church in the diocese of Exeter, he met with a refusal of investiture to his cure from Bishop Philpotts, on account of his denying the dogma of baptismal regeneration. This refusal made a great sensation, and the Anglican Church was divided into two parties, the one for Gorham, the other for the Bishop of Exeter. Gorham appealed against his bishop's sentence before the Queen's Privy Council, which is considered the supreme authority in matters of religious controversy. In the mean while the Bishop of Exeter, fearing perhaps a sentence unfavourable to the step he had taken, wrote the energetic letter we reproduce here:

'Very serious doubts have arisen in the minds *of a great number* on the point of knowing whether the Anglican Church, by accepting this judgment in a passive

[32] *Dublin Review*, no. xxii. November 1840.

manner, would not lose its rights to be regarded as a portion of the Church of Jesus Christ. This is why there are strong reasons for fearing that the sole effect of such a judgment would be to drive away from our Church a large number of its members, who would, perhaps, submit themselves to Rome—to that Church which promises repose as the price of having sought after the truth. Lastly, I declare *that I can neither remain without sin, nor will I any longer remain, should God vouchsafe me the grace, in communion* with him [the Archbishop of Canterbury], who will abuse the high charge confided to him, by giving mission and charge of souls within the limits of my diocese.'

'But the opinion of the Queen's Privy Council was not long in being given, and it was to the effect that each individual had a right to hold the opinion which seemed to him best as to the nature and effects of baptism. The Anglican Church humbly submitted to this sentence, and the terrible Bishop of Exeter, not to lose the favour he enjoyed, judged it expedient to grant investiture to Gorham; and thus finished the noisy disputes which this affair had stirred up. Gorham had not, in the main, done anything more than conform to Article 15, by maintaining that the doctrine of baptismal regeneration is not founded *on the written Word of God*, interpreted in his manner, and no one had a right to condemn him.'[33]

These facts, and thousands of others we could relate, give convincing proof that a fallible Church cannot lay down a rule of faith, since she has not the authority necessary for producing unity, and can give no certainty.

[33] Perrone, *Regola di Fede*, vol. i. p. 545.

CHAPTER III.

The contradictions existing between the Protestant rule of faith and those who profess it—Bible colportage—Results obtained.

1. *The Bible, all the Bible, and nothing but the Bible; the Bible interpreted according to each person's reason and feeling; no doctrine can be received as an article of faith if it is not contained in the Bible.* This is the fundamental principle of all the Protestant sects, whatever name they take and whatever may be their origin. Now this principle is by no means contained in the Bible, as we have already shown. These sects, therefore, cannot admit their own fundamental principle without believing something which is not in the Bible. This is a *first contradiction.*

2. Not only is this principle not contained in the Bible, but it is altogether in opposition with the testimony of Holy Scripture. The truth is, Jesus Christ Himself wrote nothing; then, when He chose His Apostles, He did not say to them, 'Go and write Bibles, which you shall distribute all over the world;' neither did He say to the faithful, 'Take a Bible, read it, understand it as well as you can, and make of it a rule of your faith and of your conduct.' But He said to His Apostles, 'Go, teach all nations, baptising them in the name of the Father, the Son, and the Holy Ghost, teaching them to observe what I have commanded you;

and behold I am with you even to the end of time.' He says again to them, 'Go to the whole world; preach the Gospel to every living creature: he who believes and is baptised shall be saved; he who believes not shall be condemned.' He adds elsewhere, 'He who hears you hears Me; he who despises you despises Me;' 'He who hears not the Church, let him be to you as a publican and a heathen.' Then might be seen the Apostles preaching, and preaching incessantly; some of them writing Epistles and Gospels, but only to meet the necessities of certain persons or certain particular churches, the greater number of them writing nothing. Their successors preach equally, and do not busy themselves much with propagating that Bible, which, if we believe the Protestants, is nevertheless so necessary, so indispensable. Everywhere and at all times they teach with authority; the faithful are submissive to them on all points; there is no trace of this individual liberty in the interpretation of doctrine laid claim to by Protestantism. Can there possibly be found a more striking opposition than that which exists between the fundamental principle of our adversaries and the word of Jesus Christ, and also with the constant and universal practice of the Church? If this is not a contradiction of their own principle, it is at least an evident contradiction of the words of our Saviour as contained in the Bible, for which they profess such profound respect. *Contradiction the second.*

3. Protestants admit the inspiration, the authority, the integrity of the sacred books contained in their Bible; the greater number recognise the validity of infant baptism, or of baptism conferred even by heretics

and infidels; a great number among them distinguish between fundamental and non-fundamental articles, &c.

Now none of these points of doctrine, none of these articles are contained in the Bible; they have borrowed some from the Catholic Church, and have simply invented the others. Behold them guilty of *contradiction the third*.

4. Nearly all Protestants celebrate and sanctify the Sunday, and yet the Scripture speaks only of the Sabbath, or the Saturday. Whence do they take this general custom, in contradiction to their Bible? From the Catholic Church. Whence have the Anglicans taken the Liturgy to be found in their Book of Common Prayer, everything concerning the ordination of bishops, priests, and deacons? The greater part of these things are taken by them from the Church which they renounced in the sixteenth century, and are not to be found in the Bible. In this it is easy to see a *fourth contradiction*.

5. The Protestants will only have a Bible which is to be left to the free interpretation of each individual. But then why have pulpits in their churches? Why do their ministers and bishops make it their duty to preach? Why do they come with their sermons, extempore or written, to interpret the Bible to people deemed able and bound to interpret it themselves? Have we not a good right to reject their opinions, and to proclaim them false or stained with error? On the high-roads, and even in the most retired parts of the country, may be found thousands of Protestant books, pamphlets, tracts; are all these nothing but the pure

Bible, or a means of upholding liberty of interpretation of the Scriptures? Would the authors of these writings, would all these preachers, approve the faithful who, reading the Bible, should interpret it in the Catholic sense, finding there, for example, a divinely instituted Church for teaching the nations, seven sacraments destined to sanctify man in the different conditions of his life? No, certainly; and every one knows what abuse has been heaped on Catholics and their doctrines by certain writers. It is, then, easy to discover a *fifth contradiction* between the fundamental principle of Protestants and their manner of acting.

Might not the disciples of the Reformation well retort on these numerous Protestant preachers in the words which M. Merle d'Aubigné[1] directed against the Catholics: 'We admit without restriction the need of a supreme, absolute, and sole authority to conduct men in the way of salvation, but this authority we do not place in the hands of the sinner, in those of man; it is not on the word of the creature that we believe in the word of the Creator; we do not wish for a revelation of revelation, a rule for rule; we wish for no reflection of light; we do not warm ourselves by the light of the moon.'

6. 'The Bible, all the Bible, and nothing but the Bible,' you say. But why, then, these synods got together with so much pains? Apparently some questions have to be elucidated, some points about which to arrive at an understanding, otherwise there would be no sense in them. Why these confessions of faith, elastic enough, if you will, and most

[1] *Appel à la Conscience des Catholiques Romains*, ap. Maguin, p. 306.

vague, if not for the sake of giving some uniformity to their belief, and of binding the faithful to conform to them up to a certain point? Why this Evangelical Alliance, which the Rev. Mr. Wells asserts to have been more œcumenical[2] than the Council of the Vatican? *Risum teneatis, amici.* It is manifest that all these little means of cohesion indicate something more than the free interpretation of the pure Word of God and the clear shining light of the Bible. *Sixth contradiction.*

If Protestants were logical, if they were persuaded of the truth of their fundamental principle, all their religious propaganda would be reduced to an immense *colportage* of the Bible; preachers would completely disappear to make way for colporters.

It is true that these latter might be puzzled if, while distributing their Bibles as divine and inspired books, they were asked: 'But who has told you that these books contain the Word of God? Did this Bible fall from heaven into your hands? The originals of it are said to be in Hebrew, Greek, Syro-Chaldæan; are you very certain that the volume you offer me contains all the inspired books, and is a faithful version of them? May it not, perhaps, be a purely profane book instead of a divine one? Why should not the Book of Common Prayer or the *Imitation of Jesus Christ* not be inspired? Why do you reject the Deuterocanonical books of the Old Testament, the gospel of St. Nicodemus, the apocalypse of St. Peter, the epistles of St. Clement and St. Barnabas? There must be some reason for including some and excluding others.'

[2] Quebec *Morning Chronicle*, February 26, 1874.

It does not moreover require a great mental effort to discover that the colportage of Bibles is not the method of apostolate chosen by Jesus Christ, by the Apostles and their successors. Before Luther's time the thing was morally impossible; since that time it has become easier, but evidently it cannot have changed the divine institution of the Apostolic ministry.

The Bible Societies established in England and Germany at the commencement of the present century have caused an enormous quantity of Bibles in all languages to be distributed on all the shores of the known world. They count the number of conversions by the number of Bibles distributed. We cannot help seeing that this way of reckoning is more visionary than real, more founded on the earnest desire than on facts. In the last meeting but one of the Bible Society, held at Quebec (1872), a reverend orator thought it incumbent on him to pronounce a special eulogium on an individual who as colporter had disposed of thirty thousand Bibles;[3] but I much doubt whether, with that prodigious number of Bibles, he has obtained thirty sincere conversions to Protestantism; whilst St. Francis Xavier, with only one Bible and his really Catholic ministry, converted millions of barbarians to the Catholic faith.

It is now well proved that at least ninety-nine out of a hundred of those who receive these Bibles either cannot read them, or understand nothing about them, or else do not take the trouble to read them, or only do so out of pure curiosity, or even throw them into

[3] Quebec *Morning Chronicle*, February 15th, 1872: Rev. Mr. Bancroft's speech.

the fire like damaged goods. Let there be an end, then, to this boasting about the good done by this Bible Society, and the conversions it has effected. No one who is in earnest can be taken in by these sonorous phrases for which there is no foundation.

CHAPTER IV.

What Catholics think about reading the Bible—Their respect for this divine book is greater and more sincere than that of Protestants—There is no precept about reading the Bible—The Church and reading the Bible in the vulgar tongue—Necessity of an infallible interpreter of the Bible—Wiseman—What the Catholic Church has done to preserve the Bible intact.

1. CATHOLICS believe that the Bible contains the Word of God. This is why they have such profound respect for that Divine Word. When the holy Gospel is read in the church, all the people stand, and make the sign of the cross on their forehead, lips, and heart, to show they do not wish to be ashamed of it, that they wish to profess it openly and to love it; then the priest kisses the text itself.

The Church imposes as a duty on all those who are in sacred Orders daily to recite the Breviary, which is principally composed of Holy Scripture. It is this extreme veneration in which she has always held the Sacred Books which has caused her to keep them so carefully, preserving them from any alteration or erroneous interpretation. The Protestants' mode of proceeding is quite contrary; they have rejected a part, mutilated the other, and most terribly distorted the evident and natural sense of the whole. How many strange variations have there been, what arbitrary opinions with regard to the Holy Scriptures, from Luther who called St. James's Epistle an *epistle of straw*, to our modern rationalists who deny the divinity, authenticity, and veracity of all the Holy Books! Let the reader judge which has shown, and still shows, the most respect for the Bible— the Protestants or the Catholics; those who possess only scattered fragments of it, or those who have preserved it intact.

2. The Bible has divine authority among Catholics. No Catholic has yet dreamt of denying that the Holy Scriptures were the Word of God; with us, no one has a right to reject certain books or certain texts of the Bible which either do not please him or do not suit his views. No; the most constant and universal uniformity is to be found on this as on all other points. Whoever would dare lay a sacrilegious hand on the smallest portion of this heavenly Book would be looked on as guilty of profanation and impiety. Protestants cannot say as much; the first comer, armed with the scissors of criticism, or guided by passion, caprice, or reason, lost to all sense of shame, cuts right and left, makes his own comments, and in many places retrenches. One would think it was a professor of literature employed in removing from his young pupils' compositions all useless digressions, long periphrases, high-flown and inappropriate expressions. This is how the Word of God is treated. One day Luther was found translating these words of Scripture, 'Justificari hominem per fidem,' by 'Man is justified by faith *alone*.' As a justification of his audacious temerity, he made the following presumptuous answer: ' Your Papist makes a good deal of fuss about this addition of the word *sola;* tell him Dr. Martin Luther wills it should be so, and he says that a

Papist and an ass are one and the same thing: *sic volo, sic jubeo, sit pro ratione voluntas.* We do not wish to be the disciples of Papists, who look on altering the Scriptures as a sin, but of their Master,' &c.[1] Catholics make use of the Scriptures every moment. Our preachers in their instructions invariably comment on some texts of Scripture, and deduce therefrom enlightening and salutary thoughts for the people whom they guide. All the theses of dogmatic and moral theology, although founded on the constant teaching of the Church, generally repose also on passages of the Bible. Let us, then, be no longer accused of depreciating the authority of the Scriptures, or of looking on them as useless.

3. We believe and teach that the reading of the Bible is by no means necessary to all the faithful for obtaining salvation.[2] Here the question is only about the faithful simply, and not about the pastors of the Church, who ought to be the guardians of sacred science; for them reading and meditating the Scriptures is frequently ordered. But for the faithful, whence arises this necessity of reading the Bible? Can it be from the very nature of the Sacred Books? Evidently not; for at all periods of the world's history, even during the ages preceding the existence of Genesis, men could be saved without reading the Bible. Can any one venture to say, even since the Canon of Scripture has been completed, there have not been a great number of ignorant persons who have sanctified themselves without, however, having seen a single copy of the Sacred Book?

[1] Döllinger, *La Réforme*, vol. iii. p. 148.
[2] Perrone, *Prælect. Theolog.* vol. ii. part ii. pp. 217-228.

It would be ridiculous to assert such a thing, since, according to the testimony of St. Irenæus, many barbarian and ignorant Christians, without the help of the Scriptures, professed the true faith and conformed their lives to it. Can it be said that piety, faith, sanctity can neither be maintained nor increased without the help of the Bible? But faith comes by *hearing* (*fides ex auditu*); and how many means have not the faithful of knowing their faith—instructions, exhortations, sermons, ascetic books, &c.!

Is there not, at any rate, some divine or ecclesiastical precept compelling the faithful to read the sacred text? None; and of this I wish no farther proof than the impossibility in which our adversaries find themselves of producing any single one, although they have been often challenged to do so. We see certain of the Fathers *counselling* sometimes the reading of the Bible, but nowhere do they suggest any precept whatever; often they even manifestly exclude the Scriptures. Councils are still more explicit on this point; indeed, it may be seen that under certain circumstances they have forbidden reading them in the vulgar tongue, amongst others the Councils of Narbonne, Toulouse, Cambrai, Mechlin, &c.

4. The Church and the Sovereign Pontiffs have never in a general manner prohibited reading the Bible in the vulgar tongue, but they have sometimes disapproved, sometimes approved it, according to the circumstances of time, places, or persons, and for the greater benefit of Christian people. This is a question of discipline, and consequently it is variable. Until the Middle Ages, the

Holy Scriptures, translated into the vulgar tongue, were left in the hands of persons capable of reading them. But as at that period (thirteenth century), and more particularly at the commencement of Protestantism, heresy was commencing to corrupt the Word of God, to pervert its text and sense according to the caprice of the moment, and to proclaim the absolute necessity of reading it, Pope Pius IV., wishing to remedy so sad a state of things, gave the fourth rule of the Index, by which he forbade reading the Bible in the vulgar tongue under severe penalties. This prohibition, however, never extended to all the faithful without distinction, since the Pope left it to the bishop or inquisitor to judge in different cases of the utility or the inappropriateness of so reading it. As there was some abuse in the concession of this privilege, Clement VIII. limited the power of granting it to the Sacred Congregation of the Index.

But whenever the reading of the Bible in the vulgar tongue has appeared to be of use, the Sovereign Pontiffs, so far from condemning, have strongly encouraged it. Naturally they always took care to assure themselves of the correctness of the versions, and the addition of suitable notes in the parts more difficult to understand. They have given their approbation or encouragement to the different translations of Holy Scripture which have been made in German by D'Allioli, in Italian by Martini, in Spanish by Father Scio, in French by Glaire, in Polish by Wich, &c. It is in the letter which he wrote concerning the translation by Martini, Archbishop of Florence, that Pope Pius VI., in speaking of the Holy Scriptures, said: 'These are the abundant sources which *ought to be open to every one*, that from them may be imbibed holiness of morals and of doctrine,' &c. Before even the name of Protestant was known in Europe, several hundred editions of the Bible had been published; in all parts of Catholic Europe they circulated freely; indeed about two hundred translations into the vulgar tongues were already existing. From all this it is easy to draw the conclusion that the Church and the Popes have never forbidden the reading of the Bible in a general and absolute manner, but only under particular circumstances, when prudence and the spiritual good of the faithful seemed to demand such restrictions.[3]

5. Jesus Christ, by permitting a part of His doctrine to be placed in a book, did not deliver it over to the disputes, passions, prejudices, and ignorance of men, without establishing a supreme tribunal, competent to decide on the controversies which are inevitable in such a matter, and bound to do so; this tribunal is the teaching Church, which He Himself founded, and intrusted with teaching, keeping, and propagating the whole of His doctrine, written or unwritten, without any distinction. Each time, therefore, when doctrine is attacked, and error menaces to make any alteration in the deposit of faith confided to her, the Church speaks, repels the error with divine energy, and affirms the pure and simple truth; she throws light on biblical difficulties, she defines the precise sense of certain texts, and always lays violent hands on false interpretations. Decisions pronounced by the Church should

---

[3] See Perrone, *Prælectiones Theologicæ*, vol. ii. part ii. p. 229, &c. Rome, 1842.

be received with submission and respect, as being the manifestation of the Infallible Truth, which has said: 'He that receiveth you, receiveth Me; and he that despiseth you, despiseth Me.' 'If any one listens not to the Church, let him be unto you as a heathen and a publican.' Besides, it must necessarily be thus, if the Divine Legislator wished to preserve to His work that character of unity and immutability which is so essential to it. In the same way as a code of human laws, however clear they may be, is never submitted to the free interpretation of each individual, but delivered over to magistrates and tribunals, who are intrusted with deciding disputes arising about the meaning of these laws, so also the Supreme Legislator could not fail to place some curb on the license of the human understanding, which is always inclined to adapt everything, even the divine laws, to the caprices, passions, and needs of the moment.

Let it not be said, however, that we thereby place the authority of the Church above that of the Scripture or Word of God. By no means; in so acting we only prefer *the interpretation which the Church* gives us of the written Word of God, to *the interpretation we would give of it ourselves.* We show herein less presumption than Protestants, who prefer their private interpretation to that of the Church, as well as of all Catholics together, and even to that of all those Reformers who do not think as they do. For us, the Church is a *divine* and ever-living authority, which decides on the meaning of the written Word of God; we do not, then, place the authority of man above that of God. When a judge gives an explanation of a somewhat obscure law, nobody is foolish enough to believe that the judge thereby assumes an authority superior to that of the Queen, or the parliament which enacted that law.

6. This extreme solicitude which the Church manifests for the Scriptures is easily explained. As she is intimately convinced that the Sacred Books contain God's word to man, that these same books are confided to her care, and that human perversity could easily corrupt both the letter and the spirit of them, she watches over them with all the solicitude shown by a mother by the side of her child's cradle; she keeps at a distance such over-bold persons as would lay a sacrilegious hand on the precious deposit which she has received from God; she prevents the pure gold of the divine Word being changed into vile metal; in a word, she makes use of her incontestable right, at the same time as she performs the most imperious of all duties towards humanity. Before leaving this important subject, I wish to quote those beautiful words of Cardinal Wiseman, that eminent man whose loss the Catholics of England and of the whole world will long deplore. This quotation is somewhat long, but it is so thoroughly convincing as regards the question I am now treating, that I feel sure the passage in its complete form will not be displeasing to my readers:

'We are told that the Catholic loves not the Scriptures; that his Church esteems not the Word of God; that it wishes to suppress it, to put the light of God under a bushel, and so extinguish it. The Catholic Church not love and esteem the Word of God! Is there any other Church that places a heavier stake on the authority of the Scriptures than the Catholic? Is there any other Church that pretends to base so much of rule over men on the words of that book? Is there any one, consequently, that has a greater interest in maintaining, preserving, and exhibiting that Word? For those who have been educated in that religion know, that when the Church claims authority, it is on the Holy Scriptures that she grounds it; and is not this giving it a weighty importance beyond what any other Church will attempt? And not only has she ever loved and cherished it, but she has been jealous of its honour and preservation, so as no other religion can pretend to boast. . . .

'For, first, she caught up its different fragments and portions, as they proceeded from the inspired writers, and united them together. To those who pretend that the Catholic Church extended not so far back, I will say, that it was the Catholic principle of unity which alone could have enabled Churches to communicate to one another the respective books and letters addressed to them by the Apostles; and it was only on the communication of the authority which their testimony gave that the canon of Scripture was framed. Did she not afterwards keep men by hundreds and thousands employed in nothing else than in transcribing the Holy Word of God; ay, in letters of gold, and upon parchment of purple, to show her respect and veneration for it? Has she not commanded it to be studied in every religious house, in every university, in every ecclesiastical college, and expounded to the faithful in every place and at all times? Has she not produced in every age learned and holy men, who have dedicated themselves to its illustration by erudite commentaries and popular expositions? Were there not, in what are called the darkest ages, men like Alcuin and Lanfranc, who devoted much of their lives to the detection of such errors as had crept into it by accident? And is it not to all this fostering care that we are indebted that the Word of God now exists? Long before any Protestant version existed in any language in Europe there were not one, or two, or five, or ten, but almost innumerable translations, not only in manuscript, but in print, for the use of the faithful, in the short interval between the invention of printing and the rise of Protestantism. And as I know that a different opinion prevails, even among some Catholics, on this point, I will give a few particulars, that so you may be on your guard against similar misconceptions. Let us take Germany as an instance. A clergyman who was among the most active promoters of the late tercentenary festival speaks of Luther's version as the first published in Germany. He simply says, that "so early as the year 1466 a German translation from the Latin Vulgate was printed, the author of which is unknown. Scarcely, however, had the Reformation commenced, when Luther meditated a new version."[4] And a little later he observes, " that besides the versions made by Protestants, there are also translations made by Romish divines, some of which appeared *almost* as early as that of Luther." Now how accurate all this is you shall see, from the enumeration which I will give you of the Catholic translations and their editions made before that of Luther, which was

[4] Horne, vol. ii. Appendix, p. 88.

begun in 1523, but not completed until eleven years afterwards. In the first place, there is a copy yet extant of a printed version so old as to have no date; for the first printed books had neither a date nor name of place. In the second place, a Catholic version was printed by Fust in 1472, nearly sixty years before the completion of Luther's version; another had appeared as early as 1467; a fourth was published in 1472, and a fifth in 1473. At Nuremberg there was a version published in 1477, and republished *three times more*, before Luther's appeared. There appeared at Augsburg another in the same year, which went through eight editions before that of Luther. At Nuremberg one was published by Koburg in 1483 and in 1488; and at Augsburg one appeared in 1518, which was republished in 1524, about the same time that Luther was going on with his; and down to the present time the editions of this version have been almost countless.

' In Spain a version appeared in 1478, before Luther was thought of, and almost before he was born. In Italy, the country most peculiarly under the sway of Papal dominion, the Scriptures were translated into Italian by Malerini at Venice in 1471; and this version was republished seventeen times before the conclusion of that century, and twenty-three years before that of Luther appeared. A second version of parts of Scripture was published in 1472; a third at Rome in 1471; a fourth, by Bruccioli, at Venice in 1532; and a corrected edition, by Marmochini, in 1538, two years after Luther had completed his. And every one of these came out, not only with the approbation of the ordinary authorities, but with that of the Inquisition, which approved of their being published, distributed, and promulgated.

'In France a translation was published in 1478; another by Menaud in 1484; another by Guiars de Moulins in 1487, which may rather be called a history of the Bible; and, finally, another by Jacques le Feare in 1512, often reprinted. In the Belgian language a version was published at Cologne in 1475, which before 1488 had been republished three times. A second appeared in 1518. There was also a Bohemian translation, published in 1488, thrice reprinted before Luther's; not to speak of the Polish and Oriental versions. In our own country it is well known that there were versions long before that of Tyndal or of Wickliffe. Sir Thomas More has observed, that "the holy Byble was, long before his [Wickliffe's] days, by vertuous and wel-lerned men, translated into the English tong, and by good and godly people, with devotion and soberness, wel and reverently red." And if it be said that the Scriptures were not disseminated, it was because the want of printing and of a general literary education prevented this.

'I have mentioned these facts to show how unjust is the assertion that the spread of the Reformation gave rise to Scriptural translations, how unjust it is to say that the Church has withheld the Bible from the people. But mark the change. The Scriptures had been diffused among the faithful, and would have so continued, had not dangerous doctrines sprung up, which taught that men should throw aside all authority and each one judge for himself in religion; a system which we have seen fraught with such dreadful difficulties, that it is no wonder that it should have been made matter of discipline to check for a time its perilous diffusion. Sir Thomas More truly observes, that if we look at the act of parliament on this subject, we shall find that it was not any Church authority, but the civil government, which first interfered; because it was when the Scriptures had begun more to be read, from the times of the Waldenses and Wickliffe, that the doctrine was broached that the civil magistrate lost all his authority when he committed crime, and that no man had a right to possess jurisdiction, civil or ecclesiastical, if he was in a state of sin. When these doctrines had raised the arm of fanatics against social order, the civil authority called in the aid of the Church; although, in the first instance, the Church did not prohibit the diffusion of the Scriptures.'[5]

These observations are more than sufficient to show how unfounded was Dr. Cook's somewhat poetical tirade: 'All are not apostles; *all are not Luthers, to bring a hidden Gospel to light;* all are not Knoxes, to convert a nation.'[6]

[5] Cardinal Wiseman's Lectures.
[6] Quebec *Morning Chronicle*, February 15th, 1872.

CHAPTER V.

Unity of faith is radically impossible in Protestantism—Unity the peculiar characteristic of truth—Jesus Christ and the Apostles recommend unity—It is impossible without an infallible authority—Unity of faith and of communion between individual Churches among Catholics, under the supreme and infallible authority of the Popes—Protestantism perceives its own disorganisation and divisions—The Protestant rainbow.

THE peculiar and essential characteristic of truth is its being one and indivisible. It does not vary with countries, with times, with individuals or circumstances; it is not of one kind *beyond the mountains*, and of another kind *on this side of the mountains*; it is immovable, permanent, indivisible, like God Himself. Then if God, who is the essence of truth, has revealed a religion to the world, that religion must necessarily be true, and likewise identical at all times and in all places. To be indifferent to such or such a form of religion, to like to find there the *colours of the rainbow*, is to proclaim that God, the infinite Truth, is indifferent as to truth and as to falsehood; it is to declare that the one and the other are equally agreeable to Him; or else to recognise the impossibility of arriving at a certain knowledge of revealed truth; it is establishing the principle of religious scepticism; it is giving over souls to despair.

There is perhaps no doctrine on which Jesus Christ and His Apostles have so much insisted as on the unity of faith and communion necessary amongst Christians.

Jesus represents Himself under the figure of a good and vigilant Shepherd, who takes care of His beloved flock. 'I am the good shepherd; and I know Mine, and Mine know Me.... And other sheep I have, that are not of this fold: them also I must bring; and they shall hear My voice: and there shall be one fold and one shepherd.'[1] This God, who is so infinitely good, does not teach doctrines which contradict one another; He does not teach truth and falsehood, yea and nay. If then the sheep listen to His voice, they will be united in the profession of the same belief, the same faith. If they form but one flock under one pastor, then must they all be in one communion, and be subject to but one and the same authority. Now this one flock, which is no other than the Universal Church, was confided by Jesus Christ to one single supreme and visible pastor, when He thrice said to the Apostle St. Peter: 'Feed My lambs; feed My sheep.'[2]

This unity is no less strongly inculcated and recommended by the Apostle St. Paul, when he calls the Church the *body of Christ*,[3] and when he would that we should all remain in perfect union, in just subordination, as the members of the body are towards one another. 'You are,' writes he to the Corinthians,[4] 'the body of Christ, and members one of another;' that is to say, that each one among them is a member of that body. He had before developed the same thought in these terms: 'For as the body is one, and hath many members; and all the members of the body, whereas they are many,

---

[1] St. John x. 14, 16.   [2] Ibid. xxi. 16, 17.
[3] Ephesians iv. 12.   [4] 1 Corinthians xii. 27.

yet are one body; so also is Christ. For in one spirit were we all baptised into one body, whether Jews or gentiles, whether bond or free. . . . For the body also is not one member, but many. If the foot should say : Because I am not the hand, I am not of the body: is it therefore not of the body? God hath set the members, every one of them, in the body as it hath pleased Him. And if they were all one member, where would be the body? But now there are many members indeed, yet one body. And the eye cannot say to the hand: I need not thy help: nor again the head to the feet: I have no need of thee,' &c. It is, then, very evident that all the members of the Church—the mystical body of Jesus Christ—ought to have that perfect union with one another which we admire between the members of the human body, which members all participate in the same corporal nourishment, are all animated by one and the same soul, and are all subordinate or coördinate the one with the other. 'Be ye all,' writes the great Apostle,[5] *one body and one spirit;* as you are called in one hope of your calling. One Lord, *one faith,* one baptism. One God and Father of all, who is above all, and through all, and in us all.' Farther on,[6] 'Until we all meet into the unity of faith, and of the knowledge of the Son of God; that we be no more tossed to and fro, and carried about with every wind of doctrine by the wickedness of men, by cunning craftiness by which they lie in wait to deceive.' Elsewhere it is Jesus Christ Himself who compares His Church to *a kingdom, a city, a house, a family, a fold,* &c. It is by means of these figures that He

[5] Ephesians iv. 4, 5.   [6] Ibid. 13, 14.

shows us the necessity of unity and subordination in His Church.⁷

But how will Jesus Christ unite and contain these people all in one same faith, in one single communion? How will He succeed in forming a perfect body out of all these members? Superior to all times and places, on earth He substitutes for Himself an infallible authority—Apostles to teach everywhere the same doctrine, the same dogmas, all that He had prescribed to them Himself, and to administer the same sacraments, particularly Baptism, by which each individual could become a member of His mystic body; then He sends on them the Holy Ghost to teach them all truth The Apostles, faithful to the order of their Divine Master, preach everywhere the same doctrine. They found several Churches, but the faith they impart is identically the same in all places. In ordinary language we often say, the Churches of France, Spain, Italy, England, Canada; and in a similar way the Apostle St. Paul also mentions several Churches in his divers Epistles.

But this by no means signifies, as certain Protestants would make us believe, that these Churches held different creeds. No; what St. Paul preached at Ephesus, at Athens, at Corinth, at Philippi, St. Peter was preaching at Rome, St. James at Jerusalem, and the others in the different countries of the earth. This is what we also find at every period of the existence of the Catholic Church. Traverse the whole earth; go to Japan, to India, to China, into Africa, into Europe, into

⁷ St. Matthew v. 15; St. John x., xvii. 11; 1 Corinthians xii. 13; St. Matthew vii. 24, &c.

America, into Oceanica; penetrate into the churches; interrogate the clergy and the faithful: always and everywhere you will meet with the same profession of faith, you will see the same sacraments administered; you will find all submissive to their bishops, and hence to the Head of the Universal Church, to the Sovereign Pontiff, the successor of the Apostle St. Peter. The Creed sung by the Pope beneath the dome of the Vatican is the same as is sung with all their hearts by all the Catholics in the universe.

As we see, unity is inherent in the constitution, in the rule of faith, of the Catholic Church; whoever refuses to her infallible authority the obedience due to her, finds himself by so doing excluded from her bosom, and ceasing to be one of her members. Thus, then, a person can well separate himself *from* the Catholic Church, but he cannot separate himself *in* the Catholic Church. Such an anomaly could not exist. Whether it be emperor, prince, bishop, or one of the faithful, he no longer forms a part of the Catholic Church from the moment that he knowingly repudiates a doctrine which she has defined. But it is very different with the partisans of the Reformation; there is no limit to their negations; they may deny everything, and yet remain Protestant, provided, however, they do not dare to affirm that the Bible contains the divine institution of an infallible Church.

Many sincere Protestants have not hesitated to acknowledge that Jesus Christ wishes for unity in His Church. The first Reformers in particular strongly insisted on this point, declaring that separating from the

Church was denying Jesus Christ, was committing a terrible outrage.[8] Their books concerning their belief contain a profession of faith in *one Church, in which reigns unity*. 'I defy you,' says Samuel Parker,[9] 'to show me an article more imperiously prescribed, as frequently recommended to notice, as the maintenance of unity amongst Christians.' 'As to the sin of making divisions in the Church, we grant without difficulty that it is one of the gravest and most enormous crimes, as well as one of the most odious.'[10]

The efforts which Protestants of all denominations have made at different times to draw up creeds, common professions of faith, will always remain as an eternal monument of their adhesion to the Christian doctrine of unity of the Church, and at the same time an authentic testimony of their powerlessness to put it in practice. According to the expression of a celebrated Reformer, Protestant uniformity *is cut up into a thousand little pieces.*

How could it be otherwise? How without a living and infallible authority can doctrinal unity be arrived at? So long as Protestantism shall have no other rule of faith than the dead letter of the Scripture, each one will be free to believe what he wishes and as he wishes. An understanding more or less enlightened, more or less under the empire of preconceived opinions, may always think and judge differently from what it would think and judge under other circumstances; it

---

[8] Calvin, *Institut.* l. iv.   [9] *Religion and Loyalty*, 1684.
[10] *Serious Inquiry into the Causes of the Neglect of the Protestant Religion.*

might deny on the morrow what it had affirmed the evening before. If even a code of laws, the clearest that can be imagined, admits of many different interpretations, and raises such conflicts of opinion as only the authority of a judge can remove, what must it be with the Bible, which is far from being either clear or intelligible to all?

But to preserve intact the unity of the Church, it is not sufficient to have a living authority: this authority must also be infallible; for an authority that could make a mistake could never govern understandings and wills so as to command their absolute assent to its decisions; it would always be permissible to examine them, to reject them as stained with error, and from that moment unity becomes radically impossible. Let there be no illusion; whilst proclaiming that Jesus Christ certainly wished for unity in the belief of His Church, let it be admitted that this unity can never be anything more than a pure chimera for all those societies whose leading principle is not that of unity, of the living and infallible authority of the Church of Christ.

It is indubitable that Protestantism, with its free examination, and even with a fallible authority, has not in itself the power of bringing the multitude to a state of religious unity. Resting on so shifting a basis, it can only be swayed by every breath of doctrine, cast from shoal to shoal, without having any certainty of arriving in the port of Truth. Of how many souls might there not be written the exciting but dangerous *Odyssey* through the labyrinth of the Reformation!

Not only does the fundamental principle of free examination contain in itself the possibility of error, of disunion, of infinite subdivision, but it has already *in fact* produced these fatal results. This is what all Protestants cannot help acknowledging and deploring, without, however, finding a remedy in the bosom of their Church. They must go and ask it of Catholicism, of that divine authority which they repudiated in the sixteenth century. Let us hear the language used by some of their leaders: 'Three centuries of *exterior life*,' says Vinet, pastor of Geneva,[11] 'must not deceive us with regard to Protestantism. It still lives from the first and vigorous impulse which it received in the sixteenth century; it lives through its political antecedents, it lives through its element of nationality. But this impulse is becoming exhausted; the beams of the edifice are falling asunder; the edifice itself is cracking in every part. Accessory and auxiliary strength is failing it. Protestantism remains alone and disorganised. There are Protestants; there is no longer Protestantism. It is not only in principle but in fact, in a flagrant manner, that this kingdom is divided against itself.'

Elsewhere he says, 'that Protestantism is only the place of a religion; that at first it was not a principle but a fact; it was not Protestantism, it was protestation. Separation was only a *remedy*, which many mistook for an *aliment*. Strange state of things, it must be acknowledged.'[12]

'The Lutheran Church,' says Fröseisen, 'with regard to its various subdivisions, resembles a worm cut

---

[11] *Essai sur la Manifestation des Convictions Religieuses*, p. 495.
[12] Ibid. p. 180.

into a thousand pieces, each one of which writhes so long as the least life remains in it, but ends by dying.'[13]

'If Luther were to rise out of his tomb,' says Reinhard, 'it would be impossible for him to recognise as members of his Church the doctors who call themselves his successors.'[14]

'The difference,' adds Augusti, 'between the old and the new Protestants is so great, that if Luther returned he would solemnly protest against the new Protestantism; just the same as, more than once, the new Protestant theologians have announced their resolution of delivering Protestantism from the tyranny of Luther.'[15]

'It is not *a* Church,' says Planck, 'it is *some* Churches that we have got.'[16]

'Protestantism may be seen and conceived,' says Lehman; 'but nowhere can *a Protestant Church* be seen.'[17]

'Let us frankly confess,' says a Protestant review, 'that our Church is torn from within as much as from without; she is divided in principles and opinions within herself as without herself; she is divided into numberless sects infinitely divided and subdivided.'[18]

It would be easy to multiply indefinitely similar quotations. The most zealous partisans of the Reformation acknowledge with grief that their Church is a worm-

---

[13] *Discours de Réception au Doctorat:* Strasbourg, 1713.
[14] *Homélie pour l'Anniversaire de la Réforme*, 1810.
[15] *Souvenirs de l'Histoire de la Reforme Allemande*, 1814, c. ii. p. 727.
[16] *Situation du Parti Catholique et Protestant*, 1816.
[17] *Aspect et Danger du Protestantisme*, 1810.
[18] *L'Idée, Revue Trimestrielle*, 1835.

eaten edifice, threatening ruin. At times it seems to them, and rightly so, that they are as if abandoned to the fury of the waves, separated from the abyss only by the remains of a shipwrecked vessel; a terrible situation, which draws from them bitter tears, and sometimes cries of terror and despair. Certain Protestants, however, put a good face on the matter; they frankly acknowledge that doctrinal unity is impossible with them; but they undertake to justify the existence of the thousands of sects which swarm on the surface of the globe by affirming that Jesus Christ did not exact this unity. They even go so far as to compare the diversity of their doctrines to the thousand shades of colour which form the radiant beauty of the rainbow. They pretend to ignore, or not to understand, that Jesus Christ, true God and truth itself, cannot cherish error, can neither tolerate it, nor sympathise with it, under whatever colour, whatever form it may present itself. There is an invincible and essential opposition between the true and the false, between God, the absolute Truth, and error; how could He take pleasure in that which is the negation of His divine essence? Besides, a comparison is not a proof; and the rainbow, so beautiful in the physical order on account of the harmony of its colours, may, in the intellectual order, be a hideous monster. Above all, it must be clearly demonstrated that Jesus Christ could will, and did really will, this astonishing diversity of doctrines. This is what can never be done, since it would be denying the divine character of Christ, annihilating the object of His mission into the world, and giving a formal contradiction to the doctrine of unity contained in many parts of the Scriptures.

The Rev. Messrs. Doudiet[19] and Burns[20] have the delicacy to tell us that they prefer these varied shades of doctrine to a uniformity of ignorance and obscurity. Leaving aside the entirely gratuitous insult they offer us, and to which it would be very easy to retort, I will content myself with asking them for proofs of this ignorant and obscure uniformity in Catholicism. Perhaps they may one day perceive that what they now call *darkness* is no other than the pure light of the sun of infinite Truth, which never ceases enlightening us, giving us warmth, movement, and life; whilst their rainbow only owes its apparent beauty to certain rays of the sun, and any way has but an ephemeral existence.

[19] Quebec *Morning Chronicle*, Feb. 15th, 1872.
[20] Ibid. Feb. 27th, 1874.

CHAPTER VI.

The results of Protestantism—The civil authority substituted for the religious authority of the Holy See, or subjection of the Church to the State—Religious scepticism—Rationalism.

THE truth or falsehood of a doctrine may be deduced in several ways, according to the point of view from which we study it. The reader has already been able to become convinced of the falsity of the fundamental principle which rules Protestantism by our having proved that this principle is in evident opposition to the will of Jesus Christ; that it cannot of itself give any certainty in matters of faith, that it necessarily destroys doctrinal unity, and ultimately results in individualism. We are now going to consider it in some of its principal and fatal results, in order still farther to expose its mortal venom to all sincere Protestants. Protestantism has loudly proclaimed religious liberty, individual liberty, the exclusion of all spiritual authority, and particularly of that of the Pope; and yet, perhaps, there is not one single heresy which has worked harder to enthrall consciences, to tread liberty under foot. The religious power which was wielded by the Vicar of Jesus Christ has been transferred to the heads of civil society; all these big words of *liberty of worship, freedom of conscience,* were only destined to veil the chains of slavery. What power has been employed to retard the over-rapid action of this destructive principle of free examination? How has heresy been implanted in Europe? By what have they replaced the Pope's authority, which they wished to eliminate on any terms? By the civil authority in general; in Germany, by the princes of the empire; in Switzerland, by the councils of the cantons and the Grand Council of Berne; in England, in Denmark, and Sweden, by kings and parliaments; in Russia, by the czar; in Turkey, by the sultan. Heresy would have none of the beneficent guardianship of the Church; it looked on the Sovereign Pontiff as a stranger sovereign, usurping the domain of souls; but by withdrawing itself from legitimate authority it had necessarily to seek elsewhere for support to protect itself from approaching and inevitable ruin; it made itself a servant of kings, it sought to profit by political revolutions, it lavished caresses on the great; it cringed, and still cringes, to all powers, who are in reality the masters of its existence. From the beginning it had for high priest a debased debauched king, and for popess a queen 'who had all the faults without any of the virtues of her sex,' and who condemned even the Protestants who protested differently to herself.

From that time forward how many councils of ministers without faith, of atheistical parliaments, have named bishops, resolved questions of dogma and discipline, prescribed fasts, reformed the ritual! Is it not humiliating to have to submit to the orders of a usurped authority, of a power which, without any mission, obtrudes itself on consciences, at its own will forms the doctrine of Christ, and invades the sacred threshold of souls, over which it has not the smallest domain? See what is passing in our day, particularly in Prussia, in Switzerland, and in Russia; was there ever a Pope who behaved in such an odiously arbitrary manner? Was there ever more insupportable tyranny weighing on the conscience of a man, of a Christian? And yet after that Protestantism is represented to us as the father and natural protector of all liberty—liberty of conscience, of worship, of thought. Is not this bitter irony? The present bishops are banished, condemned to heavy penalties, thrown into prison, as in the glorious days of Elizabeth; and why? Because they will not be faithless to God, to their duty, to their conscience; and this is what is called *liberty!* They demand their religious rights; and in defiance of this much-boasted *liberty* they are given exile or the dungeon! The new era of liberty is proclaimed by sound of trumpet; there is a boast made of the full liberty enjoyed of spreading abroad falsified Bibles in Austria, Italy, even in Rome itself.[1] But at the same time impious revolutionary journals are multiplied, filled with insults to the Pope, the cardinals, the Catholic clergy; monks and nuns are hunted from their convents, their goods seized, they are forbidden to teach, Catholic children are compelled to frequent government schools, and there to imbibe Protestant or atheistical doctrines. In good truth, never in ancient times would the beautiful name of *liberty* have been thus profaned by leaguing it to a state of things which, in reality, are nothing but frightful tyranny on the one side and humiliating servitude on the other.

---

[1] Quebec *Morning Chronicle*, February 15, 1872, and February 27, 1874: speeches of the Rev. Messrs. Elliott, Bancroft, and Wells.

They would no longer have a Pope; his authority gave umbrage; it troubled the repose of kings. In one of those moments of delirium which occur sometimes to nations as to individuals the downfall of the Roman Pontiffs was decreed, or rather their spiritual supremacy was no longer recognised. Shortly afterwards, one is astonished to find pontifical authority attributed to Queen Elizabeth's distaff, and skilfully pilfered by several sovereigns, ministers, and petty princes of Europe. Instead of submitting themselves to the Pope's spiritual and legitimate power, they bowed down to the representative of material force, who arbitrarily and illegitimately ruled over consciences. Such was the result necessarily arrived at, if a semblance of unity was to be preserved to the Reformation, and if too rapid crumbling away of this ruinous edifice was to be prevented; the tiara then had to be placed on other heads, and the bondage of souls had to be determined on, to the destruction of all true religious liberty. Let it not be thought that these words contain any exaggeration; the logic of facts, which have for three centuries been occurring, and are still daily recurring, brings us rigorously to this conclusion. The minister Vinet of Geneva vehemently expressed as much when addressing his Protestant brethren: 'Was the Church oppressed when you could not exercise any discipline with regard to your flocks except at the risk of seeing yourselves disciplined and censured by the civil power? When you were not permitted to defend your altars against the intrusion of shameless scandal? When you were forced to admit catechumens to the Lord's table, not by right of their knowledge or faith, but by right of their age? When, in your differences with your flocks, you had as judge not the ecclesiastical authority but the civil one, which made itself directly a judge of your preaching and doctrines? When you might be suspended or broken without any previous warning from your peers? When, outside of your immediate functions, you could undertake nothing for the immense needs of souls and the service of your Divine Master without giving umbrage to a jealous authority, and risking its interdictions and menaces? When this authority could force you to keep in your midst and admit to your deliberations certain debauched and scandalous members whom it was of consequence to you to exclude? When all discussion of spiritual matters was, in real fact, almost impossible in your assemblies? When, in a word, to sum up all, you were nothing more than a body of civil functionaries, teaching and dogmatising in a circle which the government, a new Holy See, might extend or curtail at its pleasure? This is the state of things under which *you* have lived."[2]

In a remarkable discourse pronounced in November 1837 before the Legislative Council, the Syndic Girod of Geneva did not hesitate to affirm 'that *one of the principal objects* of the Reformation was to annihilate the Papal authority, *substituting for it that of the civil government*.' Then, by means of numerous and incontestable facts, he clearly showed that the Council of State has constantly, since the Reformation, given and enjoined dogma, moral and other discipline, &c., on the ministers of the Gospel.. 'What oppresses our Church' (the Pro-

[2] *Quelques Idées sur la Liberté Religieuse*, Lausanne, 1831, p. 13.

testant one of Saxony) 'is the domination of civil functionaries, the secularisation of the Church in all its institutions, to such a point that everything is ruled bureaucratically, and that spiritual matters themselves are transacted like business.'[3]

'Take away from the (Protestant) Church the support and force of cohesion which the political sovereign, as its head and guardian, has imparted to it to enable it to resist the commencements of division, which since 1848 have become more energetic, and you will at once see it break into a thousand pieces, which no one afterwards will be capable of putting together again.'[4]

Abbé Döllinger, who, unfortunately for himself, has separated from the Roman Catholic Church since the Council of the Vatican, well described the state of the Church in England when he wrote the following lines: 'The laws of the kingdom, which under the three Tudors, Henry, Edward, and Elizabeth, proclaimed the royal supremacy over the Anglican Church as an imprescriptible right, still subsist in all their vigour. The king, or the reigning queen, is in possession of the supreme ecclesiastical power. The authority of the bishops only flows from the royal authority. It is true that the crowned head is, in one sense, the least free person in the kingdom, for if the king were to enter into communion with the Holy See, if he became Catholic, or only married a Catholic, he would be deposed, and would lose the throne. In such a case, according to the statute of 1689, the nation would be absolved from its oath of

---

[3] Hengstenberg's *Kirchenzeitung*, 1851, p. 99.
[4] Messner's *Kirchenzeitung*, 1860, p. 84.

allegiance. As religious head of two Churches, the king must by turns admit two mutually opposed religions, for in Scotland it is Presbyterian and Calvinistic Protestantism which is the State Church.

'Outside the ministers and Parliament, it is the Privy Council which, since 1833, exercises supremacy over religion and the Church. Parliament has named it as the supreme court of appeal in all ecclesiastical discussions, whether concerning doctrine or discipline. Laymen form the majority of it, even when it is not entirely composed of them, and many of its members do not even belong to the Episcopal Church.'[5]

Let us now hear the remarkable testimony of M. Druey, member of the Council of State of the Canton de Vaud: 'The State and the Church form but one mass, one unity, one person morally. If we examine the ecclesiastical ordinances of 1758, which are a collection of all the decisions given by the Berne government since 1536 on points relative to religion, we see that everything with regard to religion has been enacted, ordered, and laid down by government. The smallest details of ecclesiastical economy are entered into. Doctrine, discipline, preaching, management of ministers and parishioners, nothing escapes. It is *religious despotism* carried to the extremest verge.'[6]

These results are found wherever Protestantism has flourished. Lord Molesworth, an Englishman who well knew the Protestants of the north of Europe, and particularly of the Scandinavian States, wrote in 1692: 'In

[5] *L'Eglise et les Eglises.* Translated from the German, 1862.
[6] *Compte-rendu des Debats du Grand Conseil en 1839.*

K

the Roman Catholic religion, with its supreme head of the Church, who is in Rome, there is a principle of opposition to an unlimited political power. But in the north, the Lutheran Church is completely subject to the civil power, and reduced to servitude. All Protestant countries have lost their liberty whilst changing their religion for a better.' Here is the reason he assigns for the abnormal fact of the entire dependence of the Protestant clergy on the sovereigns: 'The Lutheran body of clergy,' he says, 'preserved its political power as an individual chamber or state of the Diet, but it depended on the crown as being its spiritual and temporal superior.'[7]

In England, have we not seen Elizabeth and her Parliament ratifying the principle that the unlimited power of royalty extended for ever, in this country, over everything concerning the Church, and this all jurisdiction, all power with regard to doctrine, discipline, reform, ought to be attached to the crown? Have we not seen the following clause added to the statute concerning the ecclesiastical supremacy of the king: 'No act or decree of the present Parliament, in matters of religion, may be considered as erroneous'? Here, certainly, is a well-placed infallibility! Is it not this which made James I. exclaim, at the moment of his ascending the throne, and when contemplating the greatness of his royal prerogatives: 'Is it not I who appoint the judges? is it not I who create bishops? Yes, thanks be to God! I can make what I please: the law and the Gospel.'[8]

[7] *Geschichte von Rugen und Pommern*, vol. iv. pp. 2, 294.
[8] John Forster, *Historical Essays*, London, 1858, vol. i. p. 227.

Also 'the supremacy of the legislature is, according to Hallam's expression, like a watchdog's collar, which the State has placed around the neck of a Church it has endowed, and raised to the rank of a national institution. The State thus repays itself for the lodging and maintenance it gives to its Church.'[9]

Let us also hear the celebrated Dr. Newman, who ought thoroughly to know the English Church, since he had been one of its brightest lights:

'We see in the English Church,' says he, 'I will not merely say no descent from the first ages, and no relationship to the Church in other lands, but we see no body politic of any kind; we see nothing more or less than an establishment, a department of government, or a function or operation of the State, without a substance —a mere collection of officials, depending on and living in the supreme civil power. . . . It is responsible for nothing; it can appropriate neither praise nor blame; but whatever feeling it raises is to be referred on, by the nature of the case, to the supreme power whom it represents, and whose will is its breath. . . . As a thing without a soul, it does not contemplate itself, define its intrinsic constitution, or ascertain its position. It has no traditions; it cannot be said to think; it does not know what it holds, and what it does not; it is not even conscious of its own existence. . . . Bishop is not like bishop, more than king is like king, or ministry like ministry; its Prayer-book is an Act of Parliament of two centuries ago, and its cathedrals and its chapter-houses are the spoils of Catholicism. . . . It is as little bound by what it

---

[9] *Constitutional History of England*, vol. iii. p. 444.

said or did formerly as this morning's newspaper by its former numbers. . . . Its life is an Act of Parliament. . . . It will be able to resist (its enemies) while the State gives the word; it would be unable when the State forbids it. Elizabeth boasted that she "tuned her pulpits;" Charles forbade discussions on predestination; George on the Holy Trinity; Victoria allows differences on holy baptism. . . . As the nation changes its political, so may it change its religious, views; the causes which carried the Reform Bill and Free Trade may make short work with orthodoxy.'[10]

I might multiply *ad infinitum* quotations from Protestant writings, where the fact of the supremacy of the State over the Reformed Church is recorded. All honest or moderately well-informed minds deplore this sad state of things; but what is to be done? The remedy would be worse than the disease itself; in fact, it is not difficult to see that without the principle of unity found in the civil authority, and which establishes certain natural relations between individuals, the Reformed Church, by whatever name it may be known, would disappear as a society; it would instantly crumble away; there would be as many religious systems, as many churches as individuals. The first effect, the first result of Protestantism is, then, to lessen, or rather to destroy, the authority of the Church in favour of the civil authority; it is to transfer the spiritual power, which was divinely conferred only on the Pope and on the bishops, to secular princes, to the different sovereigns who govern the earth. The falsely-called Reformation of the six-

---

[10] *Difficulties felt by Anglicans in Catholic Teaching*, 4th ed. pp. 5-8.

teenth century has not only given rise to the bondage of the Church to the State, but it has also produced *indifferentism* and religious scepticism. Question the first comer among Protestant ministers; ask him what ought to be believed. He will invariably reply: *The Word of God contained in the Bible.* 'But,' you will say to him, 'are you quite sure that it is the Word of God which is to be found in this Bible? Who told you so? From whom have you received this Bible?' 'From our fathers, who always have given it us as a divine book.' 'I readily grant that; but who gave it to your fathers?' 'Luther, Calvin, and all those who reformed the Roman Church in the sixteenth century.' 'That again is true; but you evade the question. The Bible did not fall from heaven into the hands of Luther and Calvin; where did they get it?' 'In the Catholic Church, from which they then separated themselves.' No other answer can possibly be given. The Catholic Church, which they have vilified so much, which they have loaded with abuse, which they have accused of so many misdeeds, so many corruptions, and even of idolatry, must, then, have been the only guardian of the Bible from the days of Jesus Christ. 'But has she not falsified it, interpolated passages, altered it in some manner, in order to justify her own doctrines?' 'A Church liable to error and subject to corruption may well have made no scruple of modifying the Sacred Text.' Here is a *first doubt*, inevitable for every reflecting Protestant who does not wilfully close his eyes: it is only the Catholic Church which can tell whether the Bible be an inspired book, whether the text has been faithfully preserved. Now, as he repudiates the testimony of the Church, it follows that he has but the quicksand of doubt on which to build the edifice of his faith. We will go farther; let us again question a Protestant pastor; let us ask him to explain to us certain passages of that Bible whose brilliant clearness he so praises. Let us see what sense he will give to the words of the Saviour during the Last Supper: *This is My Body, this is My Blood.* He will doubtless answer, like the greater number of modern Protestants, that the bread and wine which Jesus Christ gives us are not changed into His Body and His Blood, but are only a sign, a figure, a remembrance. On the one side, then, we have Jesus Christ, who says as explicitly as possible that this is His Body and His Blood, and on the other Protestantism, which dares sustain that it is not His Body nor His Blood: on the one side, the Apostles, the Fathers of the Church, the Councils, all the Christian people, the greatest geniuses of all centuries, who rise to affirm that the Real Presence is expressed in these words; on the other side, Protestantism, a Church which but yesterday was in the cradle, a Church whose birth and decay were pretty nearly simultaneous, a Church without any traditional basis except rash censure, and which finds in the Eucharist nothing more than a remembrance of Jesus Christ. And again, how many Protestants have there not been, from Henry VIII.'s time and the first Lutherans down to the Puseyites of our day, who, like us, have believed in the Real Presence, and have interpreted our Saviour's words in the same sense as the Catholic Church! It is very evident that, even only considering things from a purely human and rational point of view, the Catholic interpretation of these words is infinitely safer, since in its favour it has the lights of natural sense joined to the unanimous testimony of all Christian ages.

The same reasoning may be applied without distinction to any text of the Sacred Scripture. A Protestant can never say, '*I am very certain,*' &c. At the most he can but say, '*I think* this text ought to be understood in such or such a sense; *that is my opinion;* but I may very well be mistaken, seeing that millions of persons give it another sense.' The comforting light of certainty can never shine on these unfortunate people; they must perpetually live in the anguish of religious doubt, always uncertain as to the truth of their faith, the purity of their belief; always buffeted by the capricious winds of contrary opinions, always uneasy as to the road they are in, and as to the future reserved for them. Doubt is a bottomless abyss; never can the anchor of hope be thrown there. Who can describe this state of continual suffering? What feverish anxiety, what mental fatigue in this incessantly seeking for truth, each moment thinking to have found it, and always falling back into the same uncertainty! Involuntarily we recall the punishment of Tantalus, devoured by thirst, and never able to put his parched lips to the water which shrinks away from him; or again of the unhappy Sisyphus, condemned to roll an enormous stone to the top of a steep rock, whence it incessantly rolls down again. This state of uncertainty necessarily ends by engendering indifference with regard to no matter what communion, and produces complete scepticism.

Let us look at the portrait drawn by M. Scherir of the Reformed Church: 'The ruin of all truth, the weakness of subdivision, the dispersion of flocks, ecclesiastical anarchy, Socinianism shameful in itself, diluted rationalism, without doctrine, without consistence. . . . The name of this Church remains, but only designates a corpse, a phantom, or, if you will, a remembrance and a hope. . . For want of a dogmatic authority unbelief has invaded three-quarters of our pulpits.'[11]

Indifferentism goes side by side with *rationalism*. How many Protestants have commenced by piously examining the Scriptures, and have ended by religious scepticism and pure rationalism! Individual reason, obliged to form for itself a canon of Scripture, to penetrate its meaning, and thence extract a code of faith, exhausts itself in vain efforts; it is borne from one doctrine to another; its convictions disappear one after another, and leave a void from which it naturally recoils in horror. Fatigued with so much useless work, in despair of ever placing its foot on the solid ground of truth, it ends by no longer believing divine revelation, or else by only admitting what does not pass the narrow limits of its own domain. From the moment that it does not intrinsically understand any particular doctrine, even though it be taught by Jesus Christ Himself, it unscrupulously rejects it, or else gives it some milder sense which will not offend its own pride. Hence it ensues that all supernatural facts, the most evident miracles, the most sublime mysteries, the best accomplished and the most extraordinary prophecies, dis-

---

[11] *De l'Etat actuel de l'Eglise Réformée en France*, 1844.

appear before these short-sighted critics. It seems that for them revelation is like a tree encumbered with dead branches, with barren boughs, which must carefully be lopped off if we wish to gather any fruit; right and left they cut away everything that is beyond the reach of their weak reason, at the risk even of impairing the very substance of revealed doctrine.

Hence Germany and England, which broke off all relations with the Roman Church in order to embrace Protestantism, have already partly fallen into rationalism; many learned men, such as Niebuhr, Heyne, Wegscheider, &c., interpret the whole Bible in a manner to make away with the miracles, prophecies, mysteries, everything *supernatural;* everything is reduced to myths, to allegories which mask facts, which are purely natural. Thus the temptation and fall of our first parents in the terrestrial Paradise, the Tower of Babel, &c., are allegorical poems figuring the struggle of good and evil in the world. The apparition of the angels at the birth of the Saviour was but a burning meteor; His temptation in the desert, to the eyes of Eichorn and Augusti, is but the recital of the ambitious thoughts which arose in His mind whilst He was preparing for His public ministry; the voice from heaven which was heard at the moment of His baptism was but the noise of thunder; and that which was mistaken for a descent of the Holy Ghost was but the flight of a pigeon. His transfiguration is explained by a violent storm, His miraculous cures by His knowledge of medicine, His death by a swoon. His resurrection and ascension are allegories expressing the final victory of truth over error and spirit over matter.

White linen placed on His sepulchre by laundresses was taken for angels, &c.

Some have even gone so far as to reject all idea of the Incarnation of the Word, and of the redemption of man by the effusion of the blood of a God; they have tried to sap Christianity through its base. What do I say? With Strauss, they have tried to make a myth of the Person of Jesus Christ, or at the most to make of Him a humble personage, on whom have been centred all the prophecies of the old law concerning the Messiah.[12]

Each day the abyss of rationalism yawns wider, swallowing up numerous victims. Others—those who wish to cling to a revealed and supernatural religion, or who seriously study Christian antiquity—return to the Catholic Church, to ask of her that light of truth of which they feel such deep need.

[12] See Audin, *Vie de Luther*, t. ii. p. 376.

Part the Third.

THE CATHOLIC RULE OF FAITH.

THE refutation of the Protestant rule of faith has already led us to give the broad outlines of the majestic edifice of Catholicism, and to show the basis on which it rests. It will not, however, be useless to proceed farther, so that each and every one may easily discover this ark of salvation, and there find a refuge from storms. How many in the bosom of the Reformation do nothing but travel from one sect to another, without finding that repose they so ardently long for! They are driven from one shoal to another, like miserable shipwrecked mariners, who, meeting with nothing but barren and uninhabited islands, end by sinking with fatigue, exhaustion, despair.

What a happy chance for these poor victims of doubt if, before the momentous hour of death, they perceive the divine bark of the Church of Christ sailing on the sea of this world, and having been charitably welcomed into it, there have their wounds dressed and their exhausted strength renewed by the life-giving nourishment of grace! There, there is no more danger; Jesus, in His omnipotence, calms the troubled waves when it pleases Him. The very source of grace and truth, He gives to souls that supernatural food of which they stand in need; by means of His Vicar He commands, and all obey; hosts of ministers and faithful servants execute the most difficult tasks, and the vessel advances full sail towards the port of a happy eternity.

This bark, which thus braves the fury of the waves, is *the Church of Jesus Christ, the Catholic Apostolic Roman Church,* the visible society which the Divine Saviour Himself founded to preserve revealed truth in the world, and to save men. It is to her that He made His infallible promises; it is she who has received the precious deposit of the holy truths which He came to bring down to earth, and which are contained in the *Holy Scriptures* and in *tradition;* it is she who is charged with propagating this revelation, with preserving it intact, with interpreting it in its true sense, with putting an end to any controversies which may arise with regard to it. Scripture and tradition, then, constitute for Catholics the *remote rule of faith,* whilst the infallible *magisterium* of the Church is their *proximate rule of faith.* I will treat each of these subjects as briefly as possible.

CHAPTER I.

THE REMOTE RULE OF FAITH—HOLY SCRIPTURE AND TRADITION.

FIRST ARTICLE.

Of the Holy Scriptures—The collection of the books of the Old Testament looked on as divine by the Saviour and the Apostles—The canon of the Council of Trent is conformable to Christian antiquity—Authenticity and origin of the Vulgate—Protestantism recognises its exactness.

IT is beyond all doubt that, at the time of our Saviour and the Apostles, the synagogue was in possession of a collection of books which, in the opinion of the Jewish people, were all divine, and had been transmitted to them by their ancestors. Several books of the Old Testament infer the well-known existence of this collection, since they form, so to speak, a homogeneous body, a collection of doctrines destined for public use in the religious and civil life of the Hebrew people.

The *Law* (or five books composing the Pentateuch of Moses), the *Prophets*, and the *Hymns* or *Psalms*. Such are the three great divisions generally found among the Jewish writers who have spoken of this collection. Scrupulous care was taken not to alter the slightest thing in these books; they would have suffered death rather than have added or retrenched, no matter what, because they were convinced that they contained the pure Word of God; they therefore enjoyed divine authority. But, as I have already pointed out, besides the books which the whole nation looked on as certainly inspired, there were others held in great veneration, although a certain amount of doubt existed as to their divine origin, on account of the obscurity which existed about the succession of the Prophets. These are the Deuterocanonical books of the Old Testament, which the Catholic Church has admitted into her canon of Scripture, whilst Protestantism has rejected them. It would take too long to discuss this question from an historical point of view; it will be sufficient here to state the existence of a collection of Sacred Books, without examining its component parts.

It is this collection which our Lord Jesus Christ and His Apostles designate under the generic name of *Scripture*, of *Holy Scripture*, or *Holy Letters*. They quote a great many texts from it, taken from the different books of which it is composed. They look on it as of incontestable authority; they make use of it as bringing forward peremptory proof. Jesus Christ Himself affirms that He has not come on earth to destroy, but to fulfil the Law and the Prophets. He adds elsewhere, that everything written concerning Him in the Law, in the Prophets, and in the Psalms, must necessarily be realised. Never does He pronounce a single word of blame, never does He give the smallest indication of disapprobation with regard to the belief of the Jews in the inspiration of the Old Testament; on the contrary, He confirms it by making use of their books to prove the divinity of His mission, calling them *divine oracles, inspired writings*, proclaiming that even the least *iota* of the Law will receive its full accomplishment, and manifesting the most profound veneration for them.

Now, our Saviour's way of acting could not be understood if the faith of the Jewish people was erroneous in this matter; doubtless it was befitting that a God, come down to earth to restore truth, should have corrected this error, if error there were. It is, then, very evident from these remarks that, following the example of Jesus Christ and the Apostles, we ought to consider this collection of books as having a divine origin. Anyhow, this testimony of our Saviour's does not point out to us which are all the books and the only books, all the texts and the only texts, that are inspired.

As for the entire collection of the New Testament, and each one of the books composing it, we can only prove their divine inspiration by the writings of the Apostles or Fathers of the first ages. If we put aside the authority of Catholic tradition, as Protestants do, it is perfectly certain that we could never decide the canon of the New Testament in an incontestable manner. In fact, as we have remarked above, the testimony of St. Peter[1] and St. Paul[2] may well have some value in proving the divinity of what had been previously written, but not of what might be written later. As to the Deuterocanonical books of the Old Testament, it is the Catholic Church alone which can decide whether or no they are inspired.

Besides, without here entering into details, we willingly admit and firmly believe that the Holy Scriptures have God for their Author, that they contain the Word of God, a part of Revelation; that it is God Himself who has enlightened the understandings and prompted

[1] 2 Peter iii. 16.   [2] 2 Timothy iii. 16.

the will of the sacred writers, so as to make them write all that He wished, and only what He wished, to be contained in the Sacred Books. It is sufficient to read the decree of the Council of Trent on the canonical Scriptures (sess. iv.) to be convinced that such is the faith of the Roman Church. The Reverend Messrs. Wells and Burns, speakers at the meeting of the Bible Society, may be very certain that our respect for the Holy Scripture is not inferior to theirs; we may even fearlessly affirm that we profess a more profound veneration for this Divine Book than the Protestants, since we do not, like them, allow it to be mutilated, retrenching sometimes a book, sometimes a somewhat troublesome text, which perhaps does not quite suit preconceived ideas.

Neither can any one reasonably contest the legitimacy of the canon by which the same Council determines which are the inspired books. Besides the fundamental argument of the infallibility of the teaching Church, which is unassailable to every Catholic, there is also the scientific or historical proof, which ought even for Protestants to have at least a human authority. Now it is very certain that the canon of the Scriptures, as settled by the Council of Trent, is founded on the testimony of Christian antiquity, and can resist the attacks of criticism. In fact, we find the whole of it admitted by the Churches of Africa and Rome in the fourth century, recorded in the oldest versions of the Scripture; all the books contained in it are named by the different Fathers of the Church as divine and inspired, although each of these Fathers does not name them all in order, sometimes for one reason, sometimes for another; the Oriental

Churches even separated from the Roman Church since the first ages of Christianity, such as the Nestorians, the Jacobites, the Eutychæans, equally look on all the books enumerated by the Council of Trent as divine. Then, even considering the canon of Scripture only from a scientific and human point of view, it is far more reasonable to admit it such as we find it among Catholics.

There is no need to insist farther on the fact that Holy Scripture contains the Word of God, since Protestantism agrees with us on this subject. But there is one point which is often disputed, and which it will not be useless to elucidate. This is the authenticity of our Latin version of the Vulgate.

For greater clearness let us here recall to mind that the Old Testament was originally written in the Hebrew language, with the exception of the book of Wisdom and the second book of Machabees, of which the original text was Greek, with the exception also of the books of Tobias and Judith, and some fragments of the first book of Esdras, of Daniel, and of Jeremiah, which were written in Chaldaic. The New Testament was written in Greek by the sacred writers, if we except the Gospel according to St. Matthew and the Epistle to the Hebrews, of which the original text was probably in Hebrew.

The divine instructions contained in the Old Testament had been revealed to the Jews in their own language. This little nation, confined within the narrow limits of Palestine, had gained the favour of God; it was to this people that God had confided His heavenly doctrine. But other people were soon to be called to receive the light of revelation and the benefits of

Christianity; therefore the benign providence of God permitted that the Sacred Books should be translated into the languages of several nations. It was thus that in the third century before Jesus Christ there appeared that famous Greek version of the Old Testament, generally known under the name of the Alexandrine version or Septuagint, and destined for the use of the hundred thousand Hellenist Jews whom the king Ptolemy Lagus had transported from Palestine to Egypt. Everywhere this version was received with respect and veneration; the historian Josephus made use of it the same as of the original text. Jesus Christ and the Apostles accorded it a like authority, and transmitted it to the rising communities; all the Greek Churches received it favourably, so much so that St. Augustine wrote that in his time the Greek nations converted to Christianity seemed to think it was the only version, and appeared to be unaware that there were others.[3]

In the second century of the Christian era were published the Greek versions of Aquila, Symmachus, Theodotion, and several anonymous authors, which the great Origen, the oracle of the schools of Alexandria, carefully collected in fifty volumes of his immortal works. It was from the Septuagint that towards the end of the fifth century were made the different translations into Ethiopian, Armenian, &c. The Syriac version, called *Peschito*, was made from the Hebrew text.

In the West the Latin versions became infinitely multiplied. As Hebrew was but little known, and on the other hand Greek was extensively known, the text

---

[3] *De Civit. Dei*, l. xviii.

of the Septuagint was most frequently used for the Latin translations. Among these latter there was one more widely spread than the others; this was the one that St. Augustine and others call the *Italic*, and to which St. Jerome gives the name of Vulgate or Common. It was of long standing, it perhaps even dated from the apostolic times; it had also the merit of being clear and accurate. The author, whose name is unknown to us, translated the Old Testament from the Alexandrine version of the Septuagint, and the New from the common Greek edition.

In time different readings crept into the Latin text of this version, owing to the ignorance or negligence of the numerous transcribers. It is this version that St. Jerome undertook to correct at the request of the Pope St. Damasus. This great man, who, by means of constant study, was familiar with Greek, Hebrew, and even Chaldaic, was far more capable than our modern linguists of giving to the world a really satisfactory translation of our Sacred Books. After persevering labour, which lasted nearly twenty years, the chief work of his life was accomplished (405). First he had corrected the Italic version of the Old Testament from the Hexapla of Origen; but afterwards convinced, and rightly so, that the original is always better than a translation, he translated from the Hebrew itself all the books of the Old Testament except Wisdom, Ecclesiasticus, the two books of Machabees, Baruch, the letter of Jeremiah, the additions to the book of Esther, the two last chapters of Daniel, the Song of the Three Children in the furnace. Our present Vulgate comprises the Italic version of these last-named books as well as of the Psalms (corrected, however, from the Septuagint by St. Jerome), joined to that of the other books of the Old and New Testament taken from the Hebrew, the Chaldaic, and the Greek by the same illustrious doctor.

Notwithstanding the numerous criticisms that this version gave rise to, it was almost immediately adopted in several Churches of Spain, of the Gauls, and in Africa, and shortly afterwards in the other Western Churches. On account of its clearness and accuracy, it has been the only one used in the Latin Church since the eighth or ninth century.

It is this Vulgate that the Council of Trent declared *authentic in every part*. That certainly does not mean to say that this version should be preferred to the original texts from which it sprang, and which serve to throw light on the most faithful translations; but only that *among the Latin versions in use* at the period of that Council, the Vulgate ought to have the preëminence; it is that of which we ought habitually to make use. This decree does not mean that the Vulgate is perfect in every respect, that it contains no expression which might not advantageously be replaced by some other; but it simply means that it contains no fault from which an erroneous dogmatic or moral doctrine could be deduced, and that in all the texts which concern the faith and the moral precepts it gives us the veritable Word of God in all its integrity, so that in such matters we can draw valid proofs from it which no one can reject under any pretext whatever.[4] Protestants pretend sometimes to be

---

[4] Franzelin, *De Divinâ Traditione et Scripturâ*, p. 465.

scandalised at the revisions which the Popes have made or caused to be made in the Vulgate, even after the Council of Trent; but if they had understood the true sense of the decree of the Council, they would not have indulged in these puerile recriminations; the corrections made in the text were generally but of little importance, and in no way affected the doctrine, nor consequently the authenticity, which was established by the Council.

All ages are agreed in recognising the excellence of the Vulgate; Protestantism itself, by the voice of its principal men, cannot do otherwise than proclaim its superiority. Listen to Hugo Grotius, who declares that he 'always has a great esteem for the Vulgate, not only because it contains no unsound doctrine, but because it contains much erudition.'[5] See Michaelis, who affirms that 'this version is the most perfect of all;' and he calls on all his hearers, Protestant and Catholic, to bear witness to the authority he has always granted it.[6] In the judgment of Gerard the best and most ancient manuscripts decide in favour of the Vulgate; it is generally well done, faithful, and often renders the sense of Scripture better than the greater number of the modern versions.[7] Albert Schultens says similarly that he 'does not hesitate in general to award the palm to the Vulgate over the other versions, even the modern ones, to which it is often superior.'[8] Let us now hear what Dr. George Campbell writes on this subject: 'It must

---

[5] *Præf. Annot. in V. Test.* Amst. 1679, t. i.
[6] *Supplem. ad Lex. Hebraic.* pt. iii. p. 992; and *Biblioth. Orient.* vol. xxi. no. 311.
[7] *Institutes of Biblical Criticism*, § iv. nn. 269, 270.
[8] *Præf. in Job.*

be taken into consideration,' he says, 'that even the last part of this translation [the Vulgate] has been finished for about fourteen centuries.' . . . 'There are in this circumstance two things which should recommend the work in question to the serious examination of the critic. The first is, that this version having been made from manuscripts more ancient than the greater part, or even than the whole, of those which remain to us, it occupies to a certain extent the place of these manuscripts, and furnishes us with a probable means for discovering what were the lessons which Jerome found in the copies which he had collected with so much care. The second is, that having been completed long before the rise of those controversies which are the foundation of most of the sects at present existing, it is, we may rest assured, exempt from all party influence.'[9] I might also quote the testimony of Horne, Mill, L. Cappel, and a number of others who cannot help acknowledging the merit of the Vulgate. Before these straightforward attestations of Protestant science, what becomes of the insolent attacks of the coxcombs of modern criticism, who set themselves up as severe censors, and would substitute their own personal infallibility for that of the Church of all ages; who think themselves superior to St. Jerome, and who affect the greatest contempt for the Vulgate? On studying a little the grounds of these pretensions to biblical science, it will generally be discovered that they may be reduced to one or two years' study of Hebrew and Chaldaic in some academy or other; what I say is founded on fact. With this small stock of knowledge

[9] Dissert. x. p. 394.

people think themselves capable of demolishing at one blow that which centuries have built up and respected. Real science has none of this effrontery, and knows better how to render justice to truth.

Let it once more, then, be well established—1. that Catholics admit the Holy Bible to be the Word of God to men, and profess the greatest respect for it. 2. That they, by their preaching, do much more for its propagation and for making it known, than Protestantism does by means of its Bible Societies. 3. That the Bible has been left to the care of the teaching Church, which is bound to preserve it intact and give it an authentic interpretation, but that it is not left at the mercy of the first comer, who, at his own fancy, might retrench sometimes a verse, sometimes a whole book. 4. That the Vulgate is still the most faithful of the Latin versions of the Bible, and contains nothing that can substantially affect the heavenly doctrine which God came down from heaven to bring to man.

SECOND ARTICLE.

Of tradition: its nature—*Objective* tradition—Protestants must necessarily admit tradition, under pain of losing all foundation for their rule of faith and several of their articles of belief—The Scripture and the Fathers of the Church admit *objective* tradition as a part of Revelation—St. Vincent de Lérins—Testimony favourable to tradition of several Protestant writers—Jesus Christ only rejects vain and false traditions—Revealed truth is written everywhere in ineffaceable characters—Christian monuments—*Active* tradition—Transformations undergone by Catholic churches that have been taken possession of by Protestantism—The Anglican Liturgy has only preserved the accessories of worship.

Whilst refuting the Protestant rule of faith, I have demonstrated that if Catholic tradition is rejected, the Bible itself falls from our hands; Christianity is no longer anything but a vain shadow, a theory without a foundation; for the Christian religion is, properly speaking, nothing but a tradition, and rests entirely on tradition, so that to suppress the one is to annihilate the other.

Nothing frightens Protestants so much as *tradition;* this word rouses a multitude of prejudices. An idea is formed of human teaching added to the Word of God, a confused mixture of superstitions that have accumulated in the course of centuries, a collection of formulas transmitted to us by word of mouth, and consequently inevitably altered and distorted. We have only to read the works of the leaders of the Oxford school to become convinced that they have formed ideas altogether false about Catholic tradition, and that they are attacking nothing but chimeras.

What, then, is tradition? 'It is,' answers Father Perrone,[10] 'the whole of the oral teaching which the Apostles received from the very lips of the Divine Saviour, and that other interior teaching which was suggested and inspired by the Holy Ghost. A teaching which does not consist in mere formulas, in words alone, but in truth and in things themselves. A teaching which, so to speak, incorporated itself with the budding Church, at once penetrated and entirely filled it, and from that time forward has never ceased to live in her, to preserve itself in her, and to propagate itself in her, as it will preserve and propagate itself in her to the end of time. A teaching which had even attained its ple-

[10] *La Regola di Fede,* vol. ii. p. 43.

nitude and perfection before the books of the New Alliance were written, and which, consequently, already contained all those truths which have since been in a great measure consigned to those Sacred Books, but truths which, far from being only a dead letter printed on mute paper, have always been truths living or verified by faith, by instruction, by the practical life and interior spirit of the entire body of the Church. A teaching which lost none of its divine authority nor of its efficacy, as regards its quality and dignity as a rule, when a part of it was drawn up in writing, so as to form by degrees the canon of the New Testament, the books of which, incontestably of later date than this traditional teaching, have never offered, whatever may be said to the contrary, more than a part of the Word of God. I say *a part of that Word*, for no one can assert that all oral teaching is to be found in the Gospel composed by St. Matthew, since in St. Mark we find many things omitted by the former. We might say the same thing about the Gospel of St. Luke with regard to the two preceding Gospels, and in an inverse sense of the different Epistles of the Apostles, the Apocalypse included, with reference to the Gospel by St. John, the latest in date of all the books of the New Testament, and where are to be found many things omitted in all the others. And let it not be said that all which remained of oral teaching was contained in this last Gospel; for not only no document proves it, but, what is more, we find in that very book a protestation to the contrary, since the Evangelist there declares in express terms that Jesus Christ has done many other things which are not written in this book;[11] and that which was said about what Jesus Christ did, may, for the same reason, be affirmed about what He thought.'

As may easily be remarked, we are here considering Christian tradition *objectively* and in its broadest sense; it comprises, therefore, all the Word of God, written or unwritten, promulgated by God Himself or by those sent by Him. But this expression is more generally employed to designate a mode of transmission different from writing; it is thus that the Fathers of the Church term *tradition* whatever teaching comes to us from our ancestors, and cannot be proved by Scripture;[12] it is thus that they present to us tradition and Scripture as a double source of Christian doctrine,[13] as having an equal authority,[14] &c.

Now, it is this tradition *distinct* from the written Word of God which Protestantism openly repudiates, to which it denies all authority when it is isolated from the Scriptures, and which it even looks on as the principal and most fertile source of the corruption which in its eyes sullies the Roman Catholic Church.

Judging from the vehemence to which some of our adversaries give way, one would be led to believe that they had never allowed the smallest particle of divine and dogmatic tradition to filter into their belief, but that the Bible alone was the rule of their faith and their conduct. Still, as I have already abundantly proved,

---

[11] St. John xx. 30; xxi. 35.
[12] Tert. *De Corona*, c. iv.; Cypr. Ep. lxiii. ad Cœcil.; August. *De Bapt.* l. ii. c. vii.; l. v. c. xxiii.
[13] Iren. l. iii. c. v, n. 1; Tert. *Præscript.* c. xix.
[14] Basil. *De Spiritu Sancto*, 27; Chrysost. in 2 Thess. Hom. iv. n. 2.

it is radically impossible for them for an instant to maintain their rule of faith without the help of tradition; impossible for them to determine which books compose their Bible; impossible to prove the inspiration of those books; impossible to fix the dogmatic and legitimate sense of them.

Doubtless on some of these questions help may be borrowed from the Holy Scripture; but then a thing is proved by itself, and the vicious circle becomes inevitable; or history must be interrogated for the necessary proofs, and by so doing we are in the full tide of tradition. Supposing it be human, it cannot give the authority of divine faith to the bases of your faith; if you proclaim it divine, then you are agreed with us, and you become Catholics.

Is it not from tradition that Protestantism has taken its belief in the validity of Baptism conferred by heretics or infidels? Is it not from the same source that it takes its dogmas of the validity of infant baptism and the form of administering that sacrament? Is it not thence, again, that it has learnt to keep holy the Sunday instead of the Saturday; not considering obligatory the prohibition to eat blood and animals that have been strangled, as decided by the Council of Jerusalem;[15] not considering the reception of the Eucharist absolutely necessary for the salvation of children, notwithstanding these words of our Saviour: 'Except you eat the Flesh of the Son of Man, and drink His Blood, you shall not have life in you;'[16] not strictly keeping to the formal precept: 'You also ought to wash one another's feet'?[17]

[15] Acts xv. 29.   [16] St. John vi. 4.   [17] Ibid. xiii. 14.

I know that some have an easy manner of getting out of all these difficulties; they boldly affirm that they are not fundamental articles. It seems to me, however, that it ought to be a fundamental article to know which are the books and the only books containing the Word of God; nothing appears to me more fundamental than the knowing whether one has received Baptism validly or invalidly; whether one is Christian or infidel; whether one has a right to the kingdom of heaven, or ought to be excluded from it for ever. If these are not fundamental questions, I acknowledge that we may well renounce finding any in the Christian religion. But who cannot see that this distinction has been invented to avoid an inconvenient enemy? Who is the man shortsighted enough not to perceive in this a subterfuge imagined to support an imperilled cause?

These traditional truths which Protestants are necessarily obliged to admit enable us to mention a fact which has existed at all periods of history: it is that tradition, when it does not exist alone, goes hand in hand with Scripture. Open the annals of the people of God from the commencement of the world until the Reformation in the sixteenth century, you will always find in its profession of faith dogmas which it considered as divine, and which are not contained in the Scriptures.[18]

The Holy Scripture itself, of which Protestantism so loudly proclaims the authority, gives testimony against it by admitting the existence of divine traditions. In his second Epistle to the Thessalonians (ii. 14) St. Paul says to them: 'Brethren, stand fast, and *hold the tradi-*

---

[18] Franzelin, *De Divinâ Traditione et Scripturâ,* p. 209, &c.

tions which you have learned, *whether by word* or by our epistle.'

The great Apostle seems to wish to prevent the term *tradition* being confined later on to instruction given in writing only; this is why he takes cares to add 'which you have learned *whether by word*, or by our epistle,' in order to show us that his word, written or unwritten, has always the same authority. The Catholic Church, faithful to St. Paul's doctrine, has constantly manifested the same respect for the truths which have reached us by the channel of tradition as for those contained in the Scriptures.

St. John Chrysostom,[19] commenting on these words of the Apostle, reasons in the following manner: 'It is clear that the Apostles have not written all that they have taught, but they have left many truths without committing them to writing, and these truths are no less worthy of faith; this is why we believe tradition to be worthy of faith; it is tradition. Ask no more.'

Writing for the first time to the Corinthians, St. Paul says to them: 'I rejoice in you, my brethren, because in all things you think of me and keep my precepts, such as I have given them unto you,—*sicut tradidi vobis*.' The Apostle had already evangelised the Corinthians, and it was this oral teaching which he recommended them to preserve carefully; whence St. Chrysostom draws the following conclusion: 'St. Paul, then, has given several lessons, without committing them to writing, which he points out in several other texts.'[20]

---

[19] Hom. v. in cap. ii. Ep. ad Thessal.
[20] Hom. xxvi. in cap. ii. Ep. i. ad Corinth.

It is thus St. Epiphanius expresses himself as to this passage: 'Recourse must be had also to tradition, because we do not find all in the Holy Scriptures; the Apostles have transmitted us certain things by the Scriptures, and others by tradition, as the Apostle teaches us.'[21]

Do you wish for other testimony of St. Paul's on this matter? In the second Epistle to Timothy he says expressly: 'And the things which thou hast heard of me by many witnesses, the same commend to faithful men, who shall be fit to teach others also.'[22] St. John, at the end of his second epistle, says: 'Having more things to write unto you, I would not by paper and ink: for I hope that I shall be with you, and speak face to face.'

The existence of divine and unwritten traditions is confirmed by the testimony of a number of the Fathers of the Church; I quote some taken at hazard. 'What then!' exclaims St. Irenæus; 'if the Apostles had not even left us the Scriptures, ought we not to have followed the order of the tradition which they have deposited in the hands of those to whose care they have confided the Churches? Many nations who have received the faith in Jesus Christ have followed this order, preserving without letters or ink the truths of salvation written in their hearts by the Holy Ghost, and carefully keeping the ancient tradition. These men, who have embraced this belief without any Scripture, are ignorant as regards our language; but as for doctrine, the customs and manners prescribed by the faith, they

---

[21] *Hæres.* lxi. ed. Petav. [22] 2 Tim. ii. 2.

are well instructed and agreeable to God. If any one proposed to them dogmas invented by heretics, they would at once stop their ears and flee away, so as not to listen to such blasphemies. Thus, being constantly attached to the venerable tradition of the Apostles, they would not even admit into their thoughts the least image of these prodigies of error.'[23]

'There is nothing true,' says Origen, 'except that which is in all points conformed to ecclesiastical and apostolical tradition.'[24] And elsewhere: 'It is the tradition of the Apostles which teaches the Church the necessity of Baptism conferred on infants.'[25] 'Tradition, like Scripture, forms a part of the whole of Christian doctrine,' says Tertullian. And elsewhere: 'If you are a Christian, believe tradition,—*Si Christianus es, crede quod traditum est.*'[26] 'If you ask,' he adds, 'that these and similar usages should be confirmed by the authority of the Scriptures, it cannot be done; they have no other source than tradition confirmed by practice and sanctioned by obedience; this is why the Scriptures should not be appealed to.' Often even he appeals to tradition against his adversaries, against the heretics of his day, because the greater number of them, like the Catholics, admitted the force of an argument founded on tradition.

St. Basil, in his book on the Holy Ghost, demonstrates the necessity of admitting tradition, and makes use of it to establish the divinity of the Holy Ghost, saying that there are written dogmas, but that there are

---

[23] *Adv. Hær.* l. iii. c. iv.   [24] *De Principiis*, l. i.
[25] In Epist. ad Rom.
[26] *Præscript.* xix.; *De Cor. Militis*, c. iv.; *De Carne Christi*, c. ii.

also others which we have received from the tradition of the Apostles; then he adds, 'that the latter have as much authority as the former—a fact which no one disputes, however small a smattering he may have of the ecclesiastical laws. . . . For my part,' he says, 'I hold for Apostolic whoever remains attached to unwritten traditions.' Then he establishes his proposition by means of those texts of St. Paul which I have cited above, and at the same time by a natural comparison taken from the secular tribunals, where written proofs and proofs given by eye-witnesses are alike received; which answers to the two proofs in use among Catholics to establish the truth concerning faith and morals, that is to say, Scripture and tradition.

It is to tradition that St. Augustine principally and often has recourse to prove that Baptism conferred by heretics ought not to be reiterated. 'The Apostles,' he says, 'have ordained nothing on this subject in writing; but we should look upon this custom [of not rebaptising], although contrary to St. Cyprian's sentiments, as a tradition taking its origin from the Apostles themselves; in fact, there are several things which the Universal Church believes, and which, for that reason, are considered as having been commanded by the Apostles, although these things cannot be found written down.'[27]

I might cite twenty other analogous passages taken from the works of the great Bishop of Hippo; but I shall again have occasion, when speaking of the Church, to cite some texts which will confirm the same doctrine. However, I will not terminate this chapter without giving

[27] *Cont. Donatist.* l. v. c. xxiii.

the testimony of St. Jerome and that of St. Vincent de Lérins.

The former wishing to refute the Luciferians, who despised tradition, and only took the Bible as authority, addresses these energetic words: 'Let not the sectarians boast that they cite the *Holy Scripture* to prove their doctrines; the demon himself has quoted passages of it; Scripture does not consist in the letter, but in the sense. If we held to the letter only we should have to forge a new dogma, and to teach that we should not receive into the Church those who have shoes and two coats.'[28]

St. Vincent de Lérins is still more explicit on this subject when he gives us his famous rule of faith, that is to say, what must be looked on as revealed doctrine, *which has been believed in all places, at all times, and by all the faithful.* Here is that simple, precise, clear rule which overthrows all innovators, that immutable rule by which Catholic truth may be distinguished from all heresies, and all controversies may be decided. He shows that the Scripture cannot serve as the only rule, because all do not understand it in the same sense; he lets us see that the Church has the mission of preserving, developing traditional faith, and determining the sense of immutable faith by new and special means of expression. 'As for making use of the testimony of the Fathers, we must only cite,' he says, 'the words of those who have lived, taught, and persevered in the Catholic communion and faith, holily and faithfully, and who have been judged worthy of dying for Jesus Christ, or of consecrating their lives to Him. Any way, nothing must

[28] *Dialog. adv. Lucif.* in fine.

be received as entirely certain and indubitable except what has been believed by all or nearly all, and then the unanimity of their consent is equivalent to a General Council. If any one amongst them, however holy, however learned he may have been, be he bishop, confessor, or martyr, has taught a doctrine contrary to that of the greater number, this doctrine must be placed among the catalogue of private opinions, uncertain, obscure, destitute of all authority as well as of the sanction of a universal, public, and prevailing belief.'

Speaking of the heretics who, at that period as in our days, boasted of having the Bible with them: 'They affect,' he says, 'to cite Scripture continually; there is hardly a page of their writings where we do not find texts. But herein they resemble poisoners, who give imposing names to their murderous potions, and they imitate the father of lies, who, when tempting the Son of God, quoted Scripture.'

After having established the immutability of Catholic dogma, he asks himself, 'Will there then be no progress in the Church of Christ? There will be, and even much; for who will be so jealous of the welfare of men, so cursed of God, as to prevent this progress? But let it be progress and not change. With the progress of ages and centuries there must be an increase of intelligence, of wisdom and science for each man as for all the Church. But the religion of souls must imitate the progress of the human body, which, whilst developing and growing with years, is still the same in mature age as it was in the bloom of youth.' This doctrine, which St. Vincent de Lérins has recorded in his celebrated *Com-*

monitorium adversus Hæreses, is absolutely the doctrine of the Roman Church of our days.

The authority and necessity of tradition have often been recognised by Protestants themselves. 'Above all,' says Grotius, 'it must be supposed that everything which is generally adopted, without our being able to discover the origin, comes from the Apostles.'[29]

'Without tradition,' says Collier, 'we cannot prove that either the Old or the New Testament contains the Word of God.'[30]

Lessing[31] is no less explicit. 'It is tradition and not Scripture which is the rock on which the Church of Jesus Christ is built.' And elsewhere: 'All antiquity speaks in favour of tradition with a voice which our Reformers have too much slighted. They ought to have allowed to tradition, at least tradition such as St. Irenæus understands it, the same divine authority as they see fit to allow exclusively to Scripture.' Further on, wishing to anticipate a somewhat common objection, he adds: 'If tradition may have been falsified, may not the Sacred Books have been falsified also?'

From all which precedes it is easy to conclude— first, that the unwritten Word of God has an equal title to our faith and respect; secondly, that there really do exist veritable divine *traditions*, that is to say teachings, which the Word of God imparted orally to His Apostles, without these latter having committed them to writing,

---

[29] *Votum pro Pace*, p. 137.

[30] Hæninghaus, *La Réforme contre la Réforme*, c. v., quoted by Rev. Father Nampon, p. 121.

[31] Ibid.

and others which the Holy Ghost dictated to them, and which they were to transmit to the Universal Church; thirdly, that in the New as in the Old Testament the existence of these traditions is undeniable, since it is affirmed by the Scriptures themselves, by the Fathers of the Church, by Christian writers of all times and in all places; fourthly, that Protestantism itself is forced to admit these traditions, or submit to having nothing to rest on.

It is with reason, then, that the Council of Trent, in its fourth session, gave the following definition: 'There are truths and rules of conduct which, without being written, have been received from the very lips of Jesus Christ, or which, dictated by the Holy Ghost, have been handed down from one to another; these are the divine revelations that form the traditions which the Council receives with the same piety and veneration as it receives the Scriptures.'

The majority of the objections offered to us on this subject by Protestants rest on texts of Scripture which are badly interpreted. There is no doubt that Jesus Christ, like the prophet Isaias, rejects *human doctrines, vain and false traditions, the traditions of the Scribes and Pharisees*, precepts contrary to the law of God; but this is not the case in point, for the question here is only concerning divine traditions, which can have for their authors neither the Pope, nor the holy Fathers, nor Councils, but only God, speaking in the ancient law by the mouth of Moses and the prophets, and in the new by that of Jesus Christ or the Apostles. It is against all evidence that God can consider as false or as opposed to

His law doctrines which He Himself has taught to men either directly or by those He has sent.

When we speak of unwritten divine revelations or traditions, we do not by this mean to say that these revealed truths have never been written anywhere; but only that they are not contained in the inspired writ of the Old and New Testaments. In fact we may find them everywhere else. Whether we study, however slightly, the monuments of Christian antiquity, the works of the Fathers of the Church, the guardians and witnesses of Catholic truth; whether we read the creeds and professions of faith, the acts of the martyrs, the lives of the saints, the liturgical books; whether we look through the decrees concerning discipline, the collections of civil and ecclesiastical law, the history of the Church and even of heresies; whether we carefully scrutinise more particularly the definitions of the Councils, the pontifical acts, we shall easily be convinced that our dogmas are everywhere written in ineffaceable characters. Doubtless the Apostles were not sent by Jesus Christ to write books, but to promulgate the Gospel by the authority of preaching, to found Churches, to preserve the faithful in the faith by a living and authentic *magisterium*. Still, some of them were inspired by the Holy Ghost to write a part of the revealed doctrine. In the same way, although the mission of the apostolic succession or teaching Church may not be to write, its essential function being that of the Apostles, there ensues from this, however, by a consequence which is, so to say, natural and consonant to the gracious providence of God—particularly if we remark that the Holy Ghost does not *inspire* the Church, and makes her no new revelations; but only *assists* her, directing her and preserving her from error—that she ought to watch over the entire and perpetual preservation of the doctrine revealed by means of written documents, which will bear witness to future ages of the belief of the present age.[32]

I have said that revelation is written everywhere; I might have added that it is even incrusted in stone and marble, that it is cast in bronze, that it is graven in the very bowels of the earth. See the catacombs of Christian Rome; there are paintings representing Jesus crucified, Jesus risen, the Blessed Virgin, the Apostles; most of the biblical scenes there are life-like. You may see altars where the august sacrifice of the Eucharist was offered, and beneath the stone on which Jesus was constantly immolated for the salvation of the human race were then placed, as at present, the bones of some martyr or some other saint; the Real Presence was believed; the Blessed Virgin and saints were venerated, as well as the martyrs who had given their life for the Faith.[33]

Without undertaking the arduous task of ransacking the old manuscripts and folios in the large libraries, let

---

[32] See Franzelin, *De Divinâ Traditione et Scripturâ*, pp. 132-3; Perrone, *Prælect. Theol.* vol. ii. pp. ii., 300, &c. 'The name of *active* tradition is often given to the whole of the means and acts taken together by which doctrine, whether theoretical or practical, has been propagated and preserved until now. It is clear that *active* tradition contains the transmitted matter, since that can only have been preserved with it and by it. Sometimes also the name of *tradition* is applied to the truth transmitted and the mode of transmission, as, for example, was done by the Fathers of the Council of Trent in the fourth session.' Franzelin, op. citat. p. 12.

[33] De Rossi, *Roma Sotterranea Cristiana*, Roma, 1864.

us halt for a moment near the immense basilicas, whose origin dates from the early ages of Christianity. Everywhere will be found the cross, that emblem of our belief in the redemption of Jesus Christ; the altar, which reminds us of the Holy Eucharist, which is at the same time a sacrament and a sacrifice; the confessional, where the pardon of our sins is obtained; the baptistry, which shows us the Catholic faith in spiritual regeneration; the relics of the saints exposed to the veneration of the faithful, &c. In the cathedrals you will easily distinguish a particular seat higher than the others, destined for the bishop; this is the emblem of his superiority and of his authority over the clergy and the faithful. Elsewhere, as at St. Paul's without the Walls, you can admire those beautiful mosaics in the form of medallions which represent the whole series of Popes, from St. Peter to Pius IX.; and if you have seen the Vatican basilica, you have doubtless contemplated that gigantic cupola, which exalts to the sky in colossal letters the dogma of the infallible authority of the Vicars of Jesus Christ: 'Tu es Petrus, et super hanc petram ædificabo Ecclesiam meam, et portæ inferi non prævalebunt adversus eam.' This is how revealed truths, written or unwritten in the Holy Books, are not only impressed on souls, but are graven in Christian literature, in sculpture, in painting, in monuments, in the objects of art produced by Christianity. This is how we may confidently appeal to Christian antiquity to show to the dissentient communions that our dogmas are not inventions of the middle ages, or of a relatively modern epoch, but are the veritable teachings of the apostolical ages.

I understand how Protestantism cannot bear to hear the word 'tradition' pronounced. It can never itself mount higher than Luther; its genealogy commences with the apostate monk of Wittenberg, and not with Jesus Christ. Besides, tradition cannot easily be reconciled with incessant innovations; and what has Protestantism been from its very birth except a schism with previous centuries, a perpetual metamorphosis, an uninterrupted fluctuation between the most conflicting doctrines? I admire the deep meaning of the answer given by a French grenadier to his Protestant comrade, who wished to win him over to his own sect. 'Do not talk to me,' he said, 'of your religion; it is not as old as my regiment.'

One is indeed painfully affected when one visits those grand Gothic churches of Westminster, Bâle, Lausanne, and others, built for Catholic worship and usurped by one or another of the Protestant sects. The altar has been completely taken away, or sometimes replaced by a table made of ordinary marble; the choir is despoiled of everything which furnished it with a reason for existing; the niches, destined for statues of the Blessed Virgin and the saints, are empty; the bas-reliefs, too, suggestive of Catholicism, are mutilated. There is no longer any life in such a church; one feels that God no longer dwells there, since a strange religion, an enemy to ancient traditions, has come and pitilessly chased Him thence.

After having spoken of the Anglican Liturgy, of which they vaunt the incomparable beauty, without remembering that it is but borrowed from ours which they have abolished, Cardinal Wiseman very justly remarks that the essential part of Anglican worship (Collects, Epistles, Gospels) is, with us, but a secondary part, an introduction to a more solemn act—to the Eucharistic Sacrifice. 'Assuredly, when I see this Church thus treasuring up and preserving from destruction the accessories of our worship, so highly prizing the very frame in which *our* Liturgy is but enclosed, I cannot but look upon her as I would on one whom God's hand hath touched, in whom the light of reason is darkened, though the feelings of the heart have not been seared; who presses to her bosom, and cherishes there, the empty locket which once contained the image of all she loved on earth, and continues to rock the cradle of her departed child!'[34]

Let us not, then, be told that revelation not contained in the Scriptures must necessarily be changed in the course of time, and become mixed up with the impure dross of a thousand superstitions: this objection necessarily supposes the existence of erroneous ideas in the minds of those who make them. Jesus Christ having established, as we are about to see, a teaching Church, to be the depositary and infallible guardian of all revealed truth, written or unwritten, it follows that the true doctrine can never be corrupted while in the hands of that Church. If, with the Divine assistance, she has been able to preserve the Holy Scriptures intact, she has also been able to preserve the truths which are not to be found in the Scripture: the one is no more difficult than the other, to Divine Omnipotence.

[34] Wiseman's *Conferences.*

CHAPTER II.

THE PROXIMATE RULE OF FAITH, OR THE TEACHING CHURCH.

FIRST ARTICLE.

Necessity of a doctrinal authority proclaimed by reason—Jesus proves His divinity; He preaches, but does not write—He gives a mission to His Apostles to preach His doctrine, but none to write it—He constitutes St. Peter head of the Apostolical College and of His whole Church, and pastor of His whole flock—He gives supreme authority to the teaching body, and the obligation to believe and obey to the faithful — The inspired writings of some of the Apostles in nothing change the primitive constitution of the Church of Christ; error of Protestantism on this subject—The Church is invested with infallible authority by Jesus Christ Himself; proofs taken from Scripture; promises of the Saviour; assistance of the Holy Ghost—It is the Catholic Church alone which lays claim to this infallibility, and that until the end of time—The Church of England proclaims herself fallible.

AMONGST revealed truths there are some which are contained in the Holy Scriptures, and others which are only to be found in tradition. But as all are alike divine, and God is not compelled to speak to us in a book, it follows that we ought to believe all indifferently without distinction, and profess an equal respect for all.

But this revelation, written or unwritten, is of itself a dead letter: it comprises, as we have already seen, a number of obscurities. Serious doubts arise on this subject, and sharp controversies, which place it in peril. Who will make these uncertainties cease, who will put an end to these religious disputes? It may be cut to pieces by a rash criticism; who will preserve it in its primitive purity? It is destined for all men; who will propagate it, always the same, to the very extremities of the earth?

We have already proved that neither the authority of a fallible Church, nor the supposed inspiration of the Holy Ghost, nor individual reason applied to the Bible, can lead to these results; existing facts, and an attentive examination of these different systems, have furnished us with an eloquent and persuasive demonstration of such being the case. Even considering things by the light of reason alone, it is easy to be convinced that it is radically impossible for revelation to be preserved always and everywhere the same without a living authority, supreme, infallible, perpetual.

Now this authority in doctrinal matters, of which reason itself proclaims the rigorous necessity, Jesus Christ has established in the clearest and most solemn manner. Striking miracles,[1] prophecies confirmed by the result,[2] intimate knowledge of the most secret actions and even of the recesses of the heart,[3] the realisation in His own person of the figures of the old Law, His transfiguration, and the celestial testimony rendered to His divinity on that occasion;[4] His whole life, His admirable doctrine; His death, considered by the light of the prophecies which had announced it and the prodigies which followed it; His glorious resurrection,—

[1] St. Matthew xi. 5; St. John x. 37; xv. 24, &c.
[2] St. Matthew xxiv.; St. Luke xviii. 31; St. John ii. 19, &c.
[3] St. John i. 48; ii. 24, 25; xiii. 18, &c.
[4] St. Matthew iii. 16; xvii. 2; St. John xii. 28; 2 Peter i. 16, &c.

here are so many incontestable historical facts, which had shown to the world that Jesus was indeed the Messiah promised for four thousand years; that He was the Saviour of whose mysterious advent the inspired writers had so often sung; that He was sent from God and was God Himself, united to our human nature. These supernatural facts were as His credentials to the men whom He came to save; it was impossible to deny that He had received a divine mission: also He taught with an authority that could be laid claim to by a God alone. His doctrines, His precepts, won their way to souls more easily after His miracles had gained the multitude to believe in Him; He exacted an entire submission, an absolute obedience; the sentence decreed by His orders was either endless happiness or eternal reprobation; He dies without having written a single word of that doctrine which He destined to enlighten the whole world.

But His work was not to end with His terrestrial life; His teachings were to be kept up and propagated until the end of time. To attain this end, did He command that His doctrine should be codified, that a book should be made of it for the *colporteurs* to bear to all the shores of the known world, and from which each individual was to gather his faith and his religion? By no means. He commences by Himself teaching orally, and thus implanting the faith in souls. From among the multitude of those who believed in Him He chose seventy-two disciples, and from among these He chose twelve Apostles, to whom at different times He communicated the most ample powers, as well as His own authority. Behold, according to St. John Chrysostom, the *books* of Jesus Christ, the *living codes* containing His divine law, who move in every direction, and whom He intrusts, aided by the Holy Spirit, with instructing, governing, and sanctifying the rest of the faithful.[5] The first origin, the first step, so to speak, of Christian teaching, the supreme source of the apostolate, which was to be perpetuated for ever, is, then, to be found in the Son of God made man, in His *oral preaching*, in His *living and personal magisterium*. The Apostles, to whom He communicates all His doctrine, with the injunction of preaching it everywhere, constitute the second link of that mysterious chain which stretches across ages without break, and which binds, and will always bind, the teaching body of pastors, first to the preceding ages, then farther back; and lastly, to the Apostles and the Man-God. 'Go,' said our Lord to the twelve poor fishermen whom He had gathered around Him, 'go ye into the whole world, and preach the Gospel to every creature. He that believeth and is baptised shall be saved; but he that believeth not shall be condemned.'[6] 'All power is given to Me in heaven and in earth. Going, therefore, teach ye all nations, baptising them in the name of the Father, and of the Son, and of the Holy Ghost; teaching them to observe all things whatsoever I have commanded you; and behold, I am with you all days, even to the consummation of the world.'[7] 'As the Father hath sent Me, I also send you. When He had said this, He breathed on them: and He said to

---

[5] In Matth. Hom. i. n. 1. [6] St. Mark xvi. 15, 16.
[7] St. Matthew xxviii. 18-20.

them: Receive ye the Holy Ghost; whose sins you shall forgive, they are forgiven them; and whose sins you shall retain, they are retained.'[8]

If there is anything clear in the Gospel, it is these words which I have just cited. Now what is the sense of them? It is very evident that Jesus Christ established thereby a body of pastors, and that He communicated to them all authority for teaching the nations, for governing them, for administering the sacraments. It is no less evident that He who received all power in heaven and on earth sends them, even as He Himself has been sent by His Father, and promises them His special assistance until the end of the world. The mission of the Apostles has no other limits than those of the entire universe, no other object than all the commandments of Christ. But from among these twelve Apostles, henceforward to be called His ministers, the dispensers of the mysteries of God, His ambassadors, He chooses Simon, and confers on him a special prerogative, which is already explained by the symbolical surname of Peter (Petrus) which He gives him. Later on He explains the reason of this singular appellation, at the same time recompensing him for having confessed that Jesus is 'the Christ, the Son of the living God.' 'Thou art Peter, and upon this rock I will build My Church; and the gates of hell shall not prevail against it. And I will give to thee the keys of the kingdom of heaven, and whatsoever thou shalt bind on earth it shall be bound also in heaven, and whatsoever thou

[8] St. John xx. 21, 22.

The Catholic Rule of Faith.

shalt loose on earth it shall be loosed also in heaven.'[9] The eve of His death, Jesus said again to Peter: 'Simon, Simon, behold Satan hath desired to have you, that he may sift you as wheat; but I have prayed for thee that thy faith fail not; and thou, being once converted, confirm thy brethren.'[10] Lastly, after His resurrection, Jesus confers on Peter the primacy, or supreme authority over the whole flock—over the universal Church—by saying to him three times: 'Feed My lambs, feed My sheep.'[11]

Here, then, is the Church of Jesus Christ definitively constituted: at its head a supreme pastor, charged with feeding, governing the whole flock; with maintaining unity in this edifice, of which he is, so to speak, the basis; of keeping the keys of the kingdom of heaven, a symbol of the divine authority; of confirming his brethren in the faith, his own never wavering by virtue of the prayer offered by our Saviour for him. Peter is the supreme head of that teaching body which is to preach the Gospel, baptise, remit sins, and to rule the Church of God, which Jesus has acquired by His own blood.[12] Even considering the Gospels only as ordinary historical and uninspired books, it is indubitable that

---

[9] St. Matthew xvi. 16-19. 'The idea of the rock on which the Church is built being Peter, and no other, cannot be as forcibly expressed in the English language as in either Greek, Latin, or French. The identity of the words is striking in the original Greek; for in that language the two above-mentioned nouns are rendered by Πετρος and Πετρα. In Latin they are *Petrus* and *Petra*, and in the French the very same word is used for both, with only the variation of gender—"Tu es Pierre, et sur cette pierre," &c. This would have to be expressed in English by, "Thou art a rock, and on this rock I will build My Church."' (Note to English edition.)

[10] St. Luke xxii. 31, 32. [11] St. John xxi. 15-17. [12] Acts xx. 28.

Jesus Christ chose for Himself Apostles; that He gave them the mission of announcing the Gospel to all the nations of the universe; that in order to accomplish this difficult task He has endowed them with all the authority which His Father had given Him in heaven and on earth; and lastly, that He charged Simon Peter to confirm them in the faith. Up to that time there existed no injunction to write a book and spread it throughout the world.

This authority confided to a teaching body supposes the existence of a body taught, and the strict obligation of this latter to credit the doctrine transmitted to it. Thus Jesus Christ expressly says: 'Preach the Gospel; *he that believeth not shall be condemned.*'[13] This is why St. Paul, writing to the Thessalonians, expresses himself in these terms: 'Therefore we give thanks to God without ceasing, because that when you had received of us the word of the hearing of God, you received it not as the word of men, but (as it is indeed) the word of God, who worketh in you that have believed.'[14] The same Apostle also calls the resurrection of Jesus Christ, 'by whom we have received grace and apostleship for the obedience to the Faith in all nations for His name.'[15] Lastly, the Holy Scriptures show us the Apostles dispersing all over the world, not to distribute Bibles, written codes, but *orally* to announce to the nations the good news of the Gospel.

This simple historical account of the origin of Christianity evidently shows on the one part a teaching hierarchy, a living authority, a personal and genuine

---

[13] St. Mark xvi. 16.   [14] 1 Thess. ii. 13.   [15] Romans i. 5.

magisterium; and on the other a corresponding submission, obedience, and obligation of receiving the Faith, as also the explanation given of it. Here are elements which are not extrinsic to the Christian religion, nor superadded accidentally, nor variable according to circumstances, but which constitute an intrinsic essential property, the very basis of the system instituted by Jesus Christ. If then, later, some of the Apostles, without interrupting the course of their preachings, write to various particular Churches founded by their care, or to divers persons and under special circumstances, a part of the revealed doctrine, these writings may well, in the views of Divine Providence, be of great service to the teaching body of pastors and to the faithful depending on them, but they never were more than a secondary means of preserving the doctrine; they can never affect the existence of the teaching Church, since that which is essential to the apostolate is not writing—never did Jesus Christ give such an order to His Apostles—but preaching, teaching orally; and this is what the greater number of the Apostles contented themselves with doing, doubtless persuaded that their divine mission demanded nothing further.

Now will it dare be said that substituting a book, a dead letter, for a living and personal authority, is not a radical change? Will it be said that it is no innovation substituting for the submission of the faithful to the Apostles the complete independence of individuals in religious matters by means of private examination of the Scriptures? Will it be affirmed that it is one and the same thing for the faithful to receive religious instruction such as given by their legitimate pastors, and to take their doctrine from a book, with no guide but their feeble reason, and oftener than not, without any other aim than that of finding a justification for preconceived ideas? It would be the same as maintaining that a government does not change in form when it passes from pure democracy to the most absolute monarchy. There has been, then, in the bosom of Protestantism a radical innovation, a change which essentially affects the constitution of the Christian Church. Now cast your eyes on Catholicism, and you will see without difficulty that it rests on absolutely the same bases as Jesus Christ gave to it; the bishops and the Popes have succeeded to the Apostles and their visible Head; they still teach with authority, like those of whom they are the legitimate heirs; they say to the world, such and such a doctrine is revealed, and the world unhesitatingly believes them, convinced that it is God who is speaking by the mouth of His emissaries. What, then, is the secret of this infinite distance which separates the authority of the Catholic Church from that of the Anglican Church? Why is the one obeyed most thoroughly, whilst the other no longer dares to issue commands? Why does the one behold its unity gaining strength daily, whilst the other is becoming subdivided, is breaking up, like those modern edifices, badly built, which fall to pieces without waiting for the weight of years? The explanation is easy: it is because the former possesses and claims as her own those prerogatives conferred by Jesus Christ on Peter and the other Apostles, whilst the latter, born but yesterday, having no roots in the past nor promises for the future, has but an ephemeral existence, is aware of its own weakness, and has not even the courage to proclaim itself heir to the divine favours: the one is infallible, proclaims itself to be infallible, and has been recognised as such since the time of the Apostles; the other contents itself with being fallible, and its most devoted partisans discuss its decisions—which certainly are but rarely given—sometimes accuse it of doctrinal error, of mistaken interpretations of Scripture, offer it a most determined opposition, and end by submitting their points of difference to the civil government, which pretty often reverses the ecclesiastical decisions.

Let us now see whether there is a solid foundation in the Scriptures for the pretensions of the Catholic Church to possessing, not only a certain authority, but an infallible authority in all that concerns the teaching and preservation of revealed doctrine.[16]

Jesus Christ having given Simon the name of Peter, told him that on that stone He would build His Church,

---

[16] It is not my intention here to treat *ex professo* of the question of the *subject* of active infallibility; that would lead me too far. Any way, it would be easy to deduce from my words the following conclusions, which I extract from the Rev. Father Franzelin's *De Diviná Traditione et Scripturâ*, pp. 105-10:

'*Subjectum ergo hujus infallibilitatis in docendo* sunt illi omnes et soli, quibus jus est et officium divinitus commissum authentice docendi universam Ecclesiam.

'(*a*) Ita infallibilis est *Ecclesia docens*, h. e. corpus *Pastorum et Doctorum* in unione, consensione, et subordinatione ad visibile caput Ecclesiæ: idque tum in universali et consentiente prædicatione doctrinæ de fide vel moribus, tum in solemnibus judiciis seu definitionibus ejusdem doctrinæ. . . .

'(*b*) Ex opposita ratione verba Christi, quibus Petro primatus et in primatu comprehensa infallibilitas magisterii promittitur et confertur, ipsum solum designant non tantummodo diserte distinctum a ceteris, sed etiam in relatione ad ceteros ab ipso confirmandos et pascendos. . . .'

and that 'the gates of hell should not prevail against it;' that is to say, against the Church which has Peter for its basis. If these words do not signify that the Church, as built on the foundations given it by the Saviour, will always be infallible, it seems to me it would be impossible to find other words to express that idea more clearly. What other sense the very least natural can be given them? None. Do not these words, in fact, contain a promise? Evidently, yes. And is not this promise made to the Church built on Peter, or to Peter who bears up the Church (for the edifice cannot be separated from its foundation without its crumbling to pieces)? This is no less evident. But of what nature is this promise? What guarantees does it offer? Jesus commences by affirming that *He will build His Church* on a rock, *on this stone.*

Does that mean that the Church will soon crumble away and fall into error? Is it probable that our Lord, whose glance penetrated the future, descrying its most minute and hidden secrets, should have made use of similar words if He had clearly known the future fall of the Church? Would He ever have said that He would build it on a stone, if that stone were not to serve it as a solid and durable foundation?

But the Saviour replied beforehand to these questions when He compared whoever performs good works 'to a wise man that built his house upon a rock; and the rain fell, and the floods came, and the winds blew, and they beat upon that house, and it fell not, for it was founded on a rock.'[17] Whence it is clear that Jesus Christ, by promising also to build His Church on a stone, wished

---

[17] St. Matthew vii. 24, 25.

thereby to show us that its basis would be so solid, so immovable, that it would be capable of resisting the shock of storms, of persecutions, and of all the violent means employed to overturn it. He develops this thought still farther by adding that 'the gates of hell shall not prevail against it.' These words contain at the same time a general prediction and a promise. The *prediction* is that the powers of hell would be hostile to the Church, would seek to prevail against it, and would make use of all their energy and malice to destroy this kingdom of truth by trying to corrupt the revealed doctrine. This prediction has been fully accomplished, and it is easy to prove by considering all that the Church has constantly had to suffer from schismatics, apostates, pagan and even Christian princes, enemies of the Faith and jealous of its authority; and lastly, from thousands of different sects eager for its downfall. The *promise* is that, in spite of all these efforts, all these ever-recurring hostilities which our Saviour designates under the name of *the gates of hell*, the Church will remain immovable; it will stand against the blind fury of heresy, of incredulity, of schism, of persecution, and of apostasy, exactly like the edifice which, founded on the solid rock, resists the violence of the storm. But the Church of Christ can only be that one which absolutely believes all the doctrine taught to the world by Jesus Christ and His Apostles.

If, then, we can suppose for an instant that this Church is fallible, that she undermines the Faith, that she corrupts her moral teaching, that she teaches error, by these very facts she ceases to be the Church of Christ, and it would be true to say that she had apostatised, that she is no longer His chaste spouse; that she was not built upon the rock, but upon sand; that the gates of hell have prevailed against her, and that consequently the Saviour has not been faithful to His promise, or else had not foreseen her future ruin. This is the rigorous conclusion; but as this conclusion contains a blasphemy against God, it ensues that the premises are false, and that the Church of Christ is necessarily infallible.

The partisans of the Reformation do not fail to reply to us that God alone is infallible, and that all men are subject to error. This is true, if we lay down as a principle that God cannot communicate to man the privilege of not erring; but would it not be a manifest absurdity to maintain such a proposition? Can His power be limited? Is He not free to communicate to one or several the prerogative of preserving intact the deposit of revelation? Why could He not confer on the successors of the Apostles what He conferred on Peter and the other Apostles? No doubt that, without the special assistance of God, any man may make a mistake even in the most ordinary things, and still more probably in matters of faith, which often far surpass our weak intelligence; deep study, profound science, the lights of talent or even of genius are not sufficient to shelter us from error, and if Jesus Christ had not given a more solid foundation to His Church than these afford, He would have acted like that foolish man in the Gospel of whom He Himself speaks, and who built his house on the sand; the rain, the floods, the winds beat down upon that house, and it fell.[18] But the Saviour did not act

[18] St. Matthew vii. 26, 27.

thus; and if He has promised to His Church that the gates of hell shall not prevail against it, He has, at the same time, promised the necessary help for attaining that end; this help is that of an infallible guide, of infinite wisdom,—it is the assistance of the Holy Spirit. Let us for a moment open the Holy Scriptures, and let us meditate on those explicit words addressed by our Saviour to His Apostles.

'I will ask the Father, and He shall give you another Paraclete, that He may abide with you for ever, the Spirit of Truth, whom the world cannot receive, because it seeth Him not, nor knoweth Him; but you shall know Him, because He shall abide with you, and shall be in you. . . . But the Paraclete, the Holy Ghost, whom the Father will send in My name, He will teach you all things, and bring all things to your mind, whatsoever I shall have said to you.'[19]

Elsewhere He adds: 'I have yet many things to say to you, but you cannot hear them now. But when He, the Spirit of Truth, is come, He will teach you all truth.'[20]

Jesus Christ has, then, surrounded His Church as with a wall of brass, impervious to the waves of error, and strong enough to protect it against all the powers of hell. This protecting wall is the Holy Spirit, the *Spirit of truth,* which is to *abide eternally* with the Apostles, *bringing to their minds whatsoever He shall have said to them, teaching them all things, all truth.* The Apostles

---

[19] St. John xiv. 16, 17, 26.
[20] St. John xvi. 12, 13; see also St. Luke xxiv. 49; St. John xv. 16; Acts ii.; 1 Peter i. 12.

are, then, the depositaries of all revelation; for such is the precious treasure over which the Holy Ghost watches, so to speak, with particular care through the medium of the Apostles.

This solemn promise, as well as a number of other truths contained in this same discourse of our Saviour's, not only concerned those to whom He spoke at that moment, but also all their legitimate successors. In fact He promises to remain *eternally*, or *for ever*, with them. It is, however, very evident that the Apostles were not to live for ever, unless it was in their successors. Now the Holy Ghost continues teaching all truth to His Church. This conclusion is clearly confirmed by those other words which our Saviour addressed to these same Apostles after His resurrection: 'Go, teach ye all nations, baptising them . . . teaching them to observe all things whatsoever I have commanded you; and behold, I am with you all days, even to the consummation of the world.'[21]

How, indeed, could Jesus Christ promise to be always with His Apostles when He was evidently on the point of withdrawing His visible presence from them, and ascending to heaven? Doubtless He wished to speak to them of His invisible presence by means of the assistance and protection of the Holy Ghost, whom He was about to send them. But as this presence was to be perpetuated to the *consummation of the world*, it becomes manifest that this promise is not made to the Apostles alone, but to the teaching Church of all ages.[22] The

[21] St. Matthew xxviii. 19, 20.
[22] Cardinal Wiseman proves most clearly by all these texts, and by

Church of England itself, when claiming obedience to its bishops, founds its claims on no other words than those we have just quoted; the societies which occupy themselves with preaching the Gospel in foreign lands do the same.

It is then clear, according to the Scriptures considered only even as a simple historical document, uninspired and capable of being equally well understood by Catholics as by Protestants,—it is clear, I say, and altogether undeniable, 1. that Jesus Christ has instituted a teaching Church, intrusted with announcing the Gospel to all nations; 2. that He has given to that Church the mission of teaching with supreme authority; 3. that this authority is infallible in all things concerning the revealed doctrine by virtue of the assistance of the Holy Ghost; 4. that this privilege of infallible authority was not confined to Peter and the first Apostles, but was to be perpetuated to their successors until the end of the world.

Once this doctrine of infallibility is proved and admitted, it can easily be understood how Jesus Christ could say to His Apostles, 'He that heareth you heareth Me, and he that despiseth you despiseth Me. And he

---

biblical parallelism, that Jesus Christ promised the prerogative of infallibility to the Apostles and their successors. He enters into many details, and with profound erudition proves that the perpetuity of the divine mission in all the apostolical succession is recognised by all such Dissenting communions as lay claim to their churches or pastors being possessed of any jurisdiction whatever. *Conferences on the Doctrines*, &c. pp. 115-22. See also Father Murray, *Tractatus de Ecclesia*, disput. ii. t. iii. p. 169; Franzelin, *De Divinâ Traditione et Scripturâ*, p. 28, &c.; Rev. R. Manning, *The Shortest Way to end Disputes about Religion*, Boston, 1846.

that despiseth Me despiseth Him that sent Me.'[23] It can easily be understood how our Saviour declared that 'he who will not hear the Church let him be to thee as the heathen and the publican.'[24] Could there be any rational explanation of the obligation to obedience and the ignominy attached to disobedience, if there were question of a fallible Church—of a Church of which the faith, moral teaching, and all revealed doctrine could be corrupt? We do not wonder that St. Paul has said of an infallible Church that she is the 'pillar and ground of the truth;'[25] that she is 'without spot or wrinkle or any such thing, but holy and without blemish.'[26] We can understand Jesus Christ in this case having pronounced categorically, 'he that believeth shall be saved, and he that believeth not shall be condemned.'[27] But, tell me frankly, is it possible for a moment to suppose that a Church spotted with error or even simply fallible can receive the glorious name of 'pillar of truth,' and be declared 'without spot, without blemish'? Is it credible that the Saviour of men can have ordered us, under pain of eternal damnation, to submit ourselves to an authority which could pervert His holy doctrine, which could lead to the most monstrous errors? Such questions require no answering; they are determined as soon as proposed.

The Church of England has declared herself fallible; it is the only truth which she has raised to the dignity of a dogma. But this dogma is the ruin of all others; it saps the very foundation of the Thirty-nine

---

[23] St. Luke x. 16. [24] St. Matt. xviii. 17. [25] 1 Tim. iii. 15.
[26] Ephesians v. 27. [27] St. Mark xvi. 16.

Articles, all the creeds, and even the Scriptures. In fact, a defined dogma is a truth concerning which we are not permitted to doubt.

Now the Church of England, proclaimed by herself to be fallible and recognised as such by the whole world, cannot propose any doctrine as absolutely certain; the clouds of doubt inevitably hover over all her decisions. Let her proclaim from the housetops that the Thirty-nine Articles, that the creeds of the first ages, are contained in revelation. She may be mistaken, and may maintain that she is mistaken, in affirming such doctrine; any way she cannot force it on any one, and these Thirty-nine Articles will never be more than thirty-nine opinions. She may perhaps err in presenting the faithful with the Scriptures as inspired, and, in point of fact, every one curtails or rejects them according to his caprice; in a word, the whole system reduces itself to the Bible, accepted or not as one will, and interpreted by oneself. If she wishes to maintain the absolute necessity of Baptism for salvation, she will be told by her Majesty's Privy Council that she is in error, and that any one can be saved without Baptism, which is but a simple ceremony; for the words of Jesus Christ, 'If any among you be not born again of water and of the Spirit, he cannot enter into the kingdom of God,' mean 'he can enter into the kingdom of God and be saved.' If she dare affirm with Luther, with the Puseyites and Ritualists, that Jesus Christ is really present in the Eucharist with the substance of bread and wine, thousands of voices are raised against her, crying out about the encroachments of Popery, maintaining that the doctrine of the Real Presence is an intolerable superstition, seeing that the Saviour, by saying, 'This is My Body,' meant to say, 'This is not My Body;' that that of the Sacrifice of the Mass is a dangerous and criminal invention; that the teaching of the High Church on this point is a remnant of 'pure Popery,' whilst that of the Low Church is 'dirty Calvinism.' Others again, the enemies of extreme doctrines, will leave it an open question, and will pretend that the doctrine of the Real Presence must neither be rejected nor admitted, but that it is sufficient to teach that the Lord's Supper should be made use of as a monthly, tri-monthly, or annual devotion, by which one feeds on a little bread and wine in remembrance of the Saviour. This is the Broad Church. This is how, with a fallible authority, which is none at all in religious matters, all belief disappears and melts away like snow before the rays of the burning sun. This is how violent hands have been laid on those dogmas which have been the most universally admitted by all ages; this is how men are led to deny the eternity of punishment and reward, the immortality and spirituality of the soul, the existence of God even; this is how men become rationalists, then materialists and atheists.

ARTICLE SECOND.

Distinctive characteristics of the only Church of Christ: unity, sanctity, Catholicity, and apostolicity—Peter dies at Rome; his successors on the throne of that city claim and exercise the same authority as Peter over the Universal Church; testimony of the earliest centuries on this question—The Roman Church the guardian and propagator of the whole Word of God, written and unwritten—Protestantism, by rejecting the supremacy of Peter and his successors, by denying

The Catholic Rule of Faith.

the existence of an infallible authority, and by making the Bible its only rule of faith, has changed the constitution of the Church of Christ—Protestantism possesses neither unity (avowals of the Reformers on this subject, Synod of Lausanne), nor sanctity (the heads judged by themselves), nor Catholicity, nor apostolicity—The Catholic or Roman Church is no other than the Church of Christ; she is founded on Peter; she is infallible; she is one; answer to objections concerning the dogmas of the Immaculate Conception of Mary and Papal Infallibility; concerning the disputes between the Thomists and Scotists, between the Jesuits and Jansenists; she is Holy, Catholic, and Apostolic—Conclusion—Some remarks on the Real Presence, on Transubstantiation, on confession, on the worship of the Blessed Virgin and the Saints—Answer to an objection.

Jesus Christ founded but one Church, and it is upon Peter that He has built it up; it is to this only supreme pastor that He has confided the care of His whole flock: 'On this stone will I build My Church; and the gates of hell shall not prevail against *it*. *Feed* My lambs, *feed* My sheep; *confirm* thy brethren.' There are other pastors who take part in the government of the Church, in the direction of souls, but they are subordinate to Peter, the same as the faithful are subordinate to the Apostolic College and to Peter himself. This magnificent hierarchy, at the summit of which our Saviour has placed the prerogative of infallibility, necessarily produces that unity of faith which is a distinctive attribute of the true Church, as I have proved already.[28] Thus constituted, this Church of Christ, which is *one only*, and not *triple*, as the Anglicans would have, can really be compared to a kingdom, to a city, to a family, to a sheepfold, to a human body. Each one of these metaphorical appellations, which are applied to the Church in Scripture, gives the idea not of an assemblage of beings having an equal authority independent

[28] Pages 112-116.

of one another, as in Protestantism, but a body of members subordinate to a supreme head, as in Catholicism; every one sees that our Lord has established one only society, one only government, and in this society there must be perfect unity of belief.

Unity is not the only divine ray which shines on the forehead of the Church of Christ; sanctity also attests to the world the vigour and force of its constitution, the presence of a divine soul in that human organism. Indeed, 'Jesus Christ has loved the Church, and delivered Himself up for it, that He might sanctify it... that He might present it to Himself a glorious Church, without spot, without wrinkle, holy and without blemish.'[29]

If He has established Apostles, pastors, doctors, it is that they may work for the sanctification of His mystic body, which is the Church.[30] He Himself is come into the world to shed abroad abundantly the light of grace;[31] He would that the virtues of the faithful should shine as a light before men, so that they may see their good works, and glorify their Father who is in heaven.[32] It is even conformable to reason that there are found in this Church of Christ many members who not only practise the precepts, but also the evangelical counsels—perfect charity devoting itself even to martyrdom, voluntary poverty, virginity, and obedience.[33] These virtues, practised to a heroic degree, are not absolutely necessary to the existence of the true Church, still they naturally flow from it.

[29] Ephesians v. 27.
[30] Ibid. iv. 11-13.
[31] St. John x. 10.
[32] St. Matthew v. 16.
[33] 1 John iii. 16; St. John xv. 20; St. Matt. x. 19; xix. 12-21; St. Luke ix. 23; St. John xiii. 15.

The tree may exist without flowers or fruit; flowers and fruit may certainly fall without the robust trunk losing life; but so long as the tree shall survive, never will it cease giving proofs of its vigour and its beauty, offering to the sight the charm of its flowers, to the palate the delight of its fruits.[34] So it is with the Church; Jesus Christ founded it to sanctify men; He has left it the necessary means of attaining that end; it must therefore produce works of holiness, which reveal themselves in an external manner.

Catholicity, or the moral diffusion of the Church throughout the earth, constitutes another mark, another characteristic of the society founded by our Saviour; it is, as it were, the geographical proof of it, the same as we might say that unity is its organic proof, and sanctity its moral proof.

The prophets represent to us the Church under the figure of a mountain which filled the universe;[35] they assign it all nations and the ends of the earth as its heritage.[36] Our Lord Himself destines His religion for all men, because He wishes for the salvation of all.[37] We should therefore expect to find it again in all ages and throughout the universe. It should be always identical, constantly the same in all places; for Jesus Christ did not come to bring *religions*, Christianities, societies to men, but one *only* religion, one *only* Christianity, one *only* society, to last to the end of time. Catho-

---

[34] Balmès, *Protestantism compared with Catholicism*, vol. ii. c. xxxviii.
[35] Daniel ii. [36] Psalm lxxi.; Mal. i.
[37] St. Luke xiii. 19; Romans xi. 15; St. Matt. xxviii.; Acts i.; St. Mark xvi.

licity infers, then, a Church possessing unity in universality.

The fourth distinctive note of true Christianity, and consequently of the true Church, is apostolicity; it is, as it were, the chronological proof. Indeed every Church which has not the apostolical sap in its veins, every Church which cannot prove its antiquity by showing the uninterrupted course of its pastoral lineage from Jesus Christ Himself, is evidently human and false; the true Church of the nineteenth century must be able to exhibit the long and glorious genealogy which connects it with its Divine Founder. The legitimate pastors must have succeeded each other uninterruptedly since the Apostles, forming, as it were, the different links of a living tradition.[38] Already the mark of apostolicity has been well compared to the different telegraphic wires which, starting from the centre of a vast empire, bear the sovereign's wishes to the most distant villages; here, Jesus Christ is the centre of that kingdom which is the Church, and the legitimate pastors who have succeeded one another since the Apostles on all the shores of the world are like the conducting wires of the divine wishes, bearing the teachings of the Saviour through the course of ages and to all the countries of the universe. The Fathers of the Church frequently bring forward this living and tangible proof of real Christianity against heretics, because by virtue of the assistance of the Holy Ghost promised by Jesus Christ to His Apostles and their successors, Christian revelation must necessarily have been kept intact in the teach-

---

[38] Ephesians ii. 19; Apocalypse xxi.

ing body which He Himself constituted. They never fail, therefore, to unroll before the eyes of innovators the series of legitimate bishops, particularly in the Roman Church, the Mother and Mistress of all Churches, because in her dwell all the prerogatives of the blessed Apostle Peter; with one word they confound all rising heretics. 'You are but of yesterday,' they say to them; 'your commencement dates from a certain epoch posterior to Christ; such or such an innovator is your head, consequently you are not of divine origin, but of purely human; therefore you are in error.'[39]

Here, then, is the Church, such as it appears to us in the Bible, considered simply as an historical document. She proves her divine mission, she acts constantly as mistress and infallible guardian of the truth; in the views of her Divine Founder she will always be One, Holy, Catholic, and Apostolic, and by so being will prove to the whole world her Divine origin. It is on these bases that she develops without changing, absolutely like the human body, which increases in size and yet never forms other than the individual who first existed; humble in her commencement, like a grain of mustard-seed, she becomes a great tree whose powerful branches shelter the whole universe.

After the ascension of the Saviour and the great feast of Pentecost, Peter, having become the essential basis of the Church of Christ, acted as chief of the Apostolic College and of the whole of the new society. After having been the first to preach the resurrection and divinity of the Saviour, to work miracles, to give a

[39] Tert. *De Præscript.* c. xxxii.; Iren. l. iii. *Adv. Hæreses*, &c.

successor to the traitor Judas, to receive gentiles into the Church, to preside at the Council of Jerusalem, he fixes his seat at Rome; and from the period of the sanguinary death of the Prince of the Apostles in that city, the Bishop of Rome possesses and claims as a heritage all the privileges divinely conferred on St. Peter; that is to say, universal supremacy and infallibility. From the time of that glorious martyrdom of the Head of the Church, Rome has never ceased to be called by the fathers, the doctors, and the saints, 'The Seat of Peter'—and the Bishop of Rome, the *successor* of Peter; the authority of the Pope, the authority of Peter; and the communion with Rome, communion with Peter.[40] Then the Apostles preach, baptise, found Churches, solve difficulties, excommunicate the guilty, choose themselves successors whom they place at the head of particular Churches; they confer the sacrament of Order on these successors; they charge them with watching over the deposit of the Faith; they exhort them to fulfil their duties faithfully; they trace them a line of conduct with regard to the different classes of the faithful; they lean upon Peter as on an immovable foundation, and it is with Peter and by Peter that they have this stable and uniform faith which they propagate throughout all the world. Such is the part which has always been played by the Catholic Episcopate with regard to the Popes and in their relations with the faithful.

Follow the Church in her course through centuries,

---

[40] Orig. *in Exod.* Hom. v.; Epiph. *in Anchora;* Tert. *de Præscript.* c. xxii.; Cyp. Epist. lv. and lix.; Hieron. Epist. xiv. *ad Damasum et Dialog. adv. Lucif.;* Athan. Epist. *ad Felicem Papam.;* Leo M. Serm. i. and ii.; Euseb. *H. E.* l. ii. and iii.; Chrysost. Hom. lv. *in Matth.*, &c.

you will always find her united in the same faith, always submissive to her supreme and infallible head, whether he is deciding controversies of himself, or whether he is submitting them to the examination of a General Council presided over and confirmed by himself; or, again, whether fixing certain points concerning discipline, always you will see her watching with scrupulous care over the preservation of orthodox doctrine; always she is commanding with sovereign authority; always she is advancing with a brilliant train of the Thaumaturgi—martyrs, confessors, virgins, saints of all conditions—which she has given birth to; always she is known and venerated by the whole earth as the true Church of Christ, as the legitimate heir of the divine promises.

These are not gratuitous assertions, which every one is free to deny; they are founded on the testimony of all the writers of different ages. Protestantism does not choose to see in the unanimous consent of all the Fathers of the Church a criterion of the revealed truth; but at least it ought to consider these illustrious personages as historians or witnesses to the belief of the Church. Let us now look at what is said of the constitution of this society; we shall thus ascertain whether they have given the Catholic or Protestant sense to our Saviour's words. I will only select a few passages among thousands which it would be easy for me to reproduce here.

St. Irenæus in the second century teaches us the necessity there is for the faithful and for particular Churches to seek conformity with the Roman Church. 'It is with this Church [Roman], on account of its superior dignity, that all the Churches should necessarily be in accordance, that is to say all the faithful, wherever they may be found. It is in her that the tradition of the Apostles has been preserved by the faithful from all parts of the world.' Then, after having cited the names of the first twelve bishops who occupied the See of Rome, starting from St. Peter, he adds the following remarkable words: 'It is in this order and by this succession that the tradition of the Apostles in the Church and the preaching of truth has come down to us. By which we prove fully that the faith preserved down to our days, and transmitted in all truth, is the one and vivifying faith confided to the Church by the Apostles.'[41] This text has no need of comment; it clearly contains the belief in the primacy of the Roman Church, and in its infallibility, since she preserves the doctrine of the Apostles, since she preaches the truth, and that all the Churches should necessarily be in accordance with her; it is thus that everywhere is preserved the one and vivifying faith confided to the Church by the Apostles.

'Let us again hear this great Bishop of Lyons. 'The Church,' he says, 'spread over the whole world, carefully keeps the faith which she has received from the Apostles and their disciples, as if she dwelt in but one house... She imparts it, teaches it, proclaims it with such conformity, that she seems to have but one mouth. No matter that the people speak different tongues; the tradition which is current among them preserves everywhere one and the same force. Neither the Churches founded

[41] *Adv. Har.* l. iii. c. iii.

in Germany, nor those established among the Iberians, the Celts, in the East, in Egypt, in Libya, or in the centre of the earth, have any different belief or tradition; but even as God created but one sun to illumine the universe, there is also but one only preaching of the faith, whose light shines everywhere, and enlightens all those who wish to know it.' Elsewhere, after having spoken of the dissensions of the heretics, he adds: 'It is quite different with those who follow the way traced by the Church; they faithfully observe the tradition of the Apostles in all parts of the world. Their faith is the same everywhere. They keep the same commandments, retain the same forms in the constitution of the Church. .... The teaching of the Church is uniform and constant over all the surface of the globe; everywhere she shows to men the same way of salvation. It is to her that has been confided the light of divine faith, that wisdom from on high by which men are saved, which speaks without, which makes itself heard in public places, for the Church preaches the truth everywhere. .... There is no need to seek the truth elsewhere than in the Church, where it is easy to learn it. The Apostles have placed in her bosom the rich deposit of the truth; they have communicated the exact knowledge of it to the succession of bishops, to whom they have confided the charge of governing the Church spread everywhere. There, by means of faithful transmission, the deposit of Scripture has been preserved until our time, without additions or retrenchments; there it may be read without any intermixture of error; there care is taken to explain doctrine according to the Scripture by means of a legitimate interpretation, which averts all danger and avoids all blasphemy.'[42]

Here, then, is the doctrine of the second century. There is but one true Church, which adheres to the Apostolical tradition; her faith is one; everywhere may be heard the same doctrine, as if there were but one mouthpiece; this Church is spread everywhere; it is she who possesses the truth; it is she who holds the deposit of Scripture and keeps it intact. There is no question of the *colportage* of Bibles, nor of reading the Holy Books in the vulgar tongue, nor of private interpretation of the written Word of God; the only question is of preaching, of oral teaching, of unity of faith. At that time it was only the Gnostic sects, swarming with compounds of absurdities, which took upon themselves to deface the Scriptures and make rainbows out of them.

Origen, in the third century, commenting on the words of Jesus Christ to St. Peter: *Thou art Peter, and on this rock I will build My Church*, &c., gives them the following sense: 'If then the gates of hell prevail against any one, it will neither be against Peter, upon whom Christ built His Church, nor yet against the Church, which Christ built upon Peter. They have only power against whoever finds himself without Peter, without the Church, with regard to whom they are powerless.'[43] It is impossible to express more precisely the infallibility of Peter, and of the Church which reposes in surety on Peter; but can Protestantism, that will have neither Peter nor his successors, nor the Church founded on

---

[42] *Adv. Hær.* l. i. c. x.; l. v. 20; l. iii. c. iv.; l. iv. c. xxxiii.
[43] *In Matthæum*, t. xxii. n. 11; Opp. t. iii. Migne, p. 1003.

Peter, but who take refuge in the Bible alone, or in a fallible Church,—can Protestantism believe itself secure against the powers of hell? Does it understand the words of the Saviour in the sense given to them in the third century? St. Cyprian, writing about the same period against the Novatians, is no less explicit as to the prerogative which Jesus Christ conferred on Peter of being the foundation of unity; his words merit serious consideration: 'He who does not keep the unity of the Church, does he think that he keeps the faith? He who goes against the Church, who abandons the chair of Peter on which the Church is founded, can he flatter himself that he is still in the Church?'

Speaking elsewhere of the unity of the Church, he attributes it to the source whence it emanates, the chair of Peter: 'The rays of the sun are numerous,' he says, 'but the light is one. The branches of the tree are numerous, but the trunk is one, and springs from an immovable root. Many streams flow from one only source. .... Try to detach a ray of the sun from its centre; the unity will not allow of this division of its light. Take away a branch of a tree by breaking it off; broken, it loses all vegetation. Isolate the stream from its source; in its isolation it will dry up. Thus the Church, enlightened by the light of the Saviour, darts its rays all over the universe; there is, however, but one light spreading everywhere, and the unity of the body is not broken. The Church extends its vigorous branches over all the earth; she diffuses her abundant streams afar; but there is one only source, one only origin, one only mother, whose abundant fruitfulness is ever increasing. We are born of her, nourished by her milk, animated by her spirit.'[41] As we see, the Church of the third century professed perfect unity, such as still exists in Catholicism; but she could never have accommodated herself to those thousand and one dissentient and dissimilar communions, which must inevitably exist wherever there is no infallible authority to produce unity.

In a letter to Pope Cornelius, he complains of the heretics who went to Rome with the design of deceiving the Holy See. 'They dare,' says he, 'sail towards the chair of St. Peter and accost the *principal* Church, which is the source of sacerdotal unity.'[45] Are not these titles which we still give to the See of Rome? Elsewhere he calls the Church of Rome 'the mother and root of the Catholic Church,' the same as he gives the Pope the name of 'chief and root of the Church which is one.' 'There is,' says he, 'but one God and one Christ, one Church and one chair, founded on Peter by the Word of the Lord.'[46]

In his book against Jovinian, St. Jerome writes: 'Although the Church is equally founded upon the twelve Apostles, Jesus Christ has, however, chosen one of them to be chief, in order to prevent the dangers of schism.' In the midst of the dissensions which laid waste the Church of Antioch he writes to Pope Damasus: 'I ally myself by communion with your Holiness, that is to say, the chair of Peter; I know that the Church is built on this stone: whoever will have eaten the lamb outside of this Church is a profaner; whoever dwells not

[41] *De Unitate Ecclesiæ*, c. iv. and v.　　[45] Ep. iii. l. i. edit. Casil.
[46] Epist. ad Corn. ad Jubaia, &c.

in the ark of Noe shall perish in the waters of the deluge.' It appears that in the fourth century people were not yet of the same opinion as Luther, Calvin, and the numberless heads of sects which have sprung up since the sixteenth century; they admitted the necessity of unity of faith and communion, and they placed the source of this unity in the Popes, the successors of Peter, whom the Saviour had constituted supreme pastor of His flock.

St. Augustine professed the same doctrine when, in the First Book *ad Bonifacium* (c. i.), he addresses these words to the Pope : 'We all who are called to fill with you the functions of the episcopate, we also share with you pastoral vigilance, although your preëminence places you much higher.' Every one knows the celebrated words which fell from the lips of the great doctor with regard to the Pelagian error: 'The acts of the two Councils [Carthage and Mileve] relative to this affair have already been sent to the Apostolic seat; the decisions have arrived from Rome; the cause is ended; God grant that the error may be also!'

St. Leo the Great, addressing Rome herself, 'You are become,' he says to her, 'by being the sacred seat of the blessed Peter, the head of the Christian world; your power extends further by the religion of Heaven than it was extended by human force.'[47] Did not St. Ambrose say excellently well, 'It is Peter to whom the Lord said: *Thou art Peter, and on this rock will I build My Church?* Where Peter is, there the Church is. Where the Church is, there death is not, but life eternal.'[48] It is

[47] Serm. *de Nativ. Apost.* ed. Quesnel, p. 161.   [48] Enarratio in Ps. xl.

easy to see that the great Bishop of Milan did not share the ideas of Protestants, but that he was a sincere Catholic.

Would you hear on the same subject the great voice of the Councils, and consequently the heads of all the individual Churches in the universe? They declare at Nice, 'That the Roman Church has always had the preëminence;' at Sardica, that 'if a deposed bishop appeals to Rome, no one can be appointed in his place until the Bishop of Rome has pronounced:' at Ephesus, that 'Peter lives and will always live in his successors, and that he judges by them;' at Chalcedon, that 'Peter has always preserved the truth without any admixture of error;' at Constantinople, that 'Peter has spoken by the mouth of Agathon,' &c. It is useless further to insist on the value of these testimonies, which show us with all the clearness of which evidence is capable the universal belief of the Church of the first ages in the primacy and infallibility of the Bishops of Rome, successors of St. Peter.

In those days no one ever thought of converting nations by putting a Bible in their hands, and leaving to them the onerous task of extracting a creed from it, at the risk of breaking that unity of faith and communion desired by the Saviour. Far from it; every one recognised a supreme head in the Bishop of Rome, the confirmer of his brethren in the faith; every one submitted to his decisions as well as those of the General Councils presided over and confirmed by him; every one admitted the absolute necessity of preserving the most perfect unity. The Bible, as well as the unwritten Word of God, was confided to the keeping of the Church; it was from her that the faithful received the different books, both text and interpretation. Hear St. Augustine saying to the Manichæans: 'As for me, I would not believe the Gospel, did not the authority of the Church determine me to do so. Those whom I obeyed when they said to me: Believe the Gospel, why should I not obey when they say to me: Do not believe in the Manichæans?' Addressing the heretic Faustus, he challenged him in these terms: 'Either you wish I should believe in the Catholic Church, or you do not wish it; make your decision. If you think it well that I should listen to the Catholic Church, retire; for this Catholic Church has condemned you, and she orders me to look on you as innovators. If you forbid me to listen to her, again I say retire, and bring forward no more texts of the Gospel against me, since the tribunal of the Catholic Church being overthrown, for me there is no longer any Gospel.' 'You would,' continues this great doctor, 'that I should obey this Church when she tells me to receive the Gospel as the Word of God; but you would not that I should obey her when she tells me to explain this same Gospel otherwise than you explain it! Is not that unreasonable, wishing that I should believe what pleases you, that I should not believe what does not please you, and wishing to treat me as a simpleton, who would sacrifice all his lights and his most sacred interests to purely arbitrary decisions?'[49] Here certainly are words very little in harmony with Protestantism, but which at the same time are so true, so striking, that they forced from Luther the

[49] *De Doct. Christ.* l. ii. c. xxxvi.

following avowal: 'We are forced to concede to the Papists that the Word of God is with them, that we have received it from them, and that without them we should have had no knowledge of it.'[50]

By looking into the Bible as we might look into a simply historical book, we have, then, proved that Jesus Christ has instituted *one only Church*, composed of pastors and faithful, of a teaching hierarchy, of a body taught; the one endowed with *supreme authority* and the prerogative of infallibility by virtue of the assistance of the Holy Spirit; the other obliged to receive the teachings given to them, and to *submit* to such heartily, as if submitting themselves to God Himself. This Church, which the Redeemer has acquired at the price of His blood, and to which He confided the care of His doctrine, ought to show exteriorly her titles of nobility, her heavenly origin; she ought to reveal herself at all times and in all places as the true Church of Christ; she ought to bear on her forehead a particular mark by which to be recognised, and signs so manifest, so characteristic, that she might be distinguished from all false Churches, since God wills the salvation of all men, and the means of salvation are only to be found in the Church of Jesus Christ. These distinctive marks are perfect *unity, sanctity, catholicity*, and *apostolicity*. This is how all Christian ages have interpreted the words of the Saviour concerning the constitution of the Church and her particular characteristics.

Let us now examine to what actually existing Christian society this divine plan can be applied; let us see

[50] Luther's Commentary on St. John's Gospel, c. xvi.

which is the one that evidently realises all the conditions desired by the Saviour; in other terms, where real Christianity is to be found, that revealed religion which our Lord brought to man. Is it in any one of the Protestant communions? Is it in the Catholic Church? Whoever will take the trouble of looking ever so little into the actual state of Protestantism, will easily be convinced that the society founded by Jesus Christ is not to be found there. In fact, the Christian Church has received Peter and his successors for its basis, and to them the Saviour has conferred supreme authority over all His flock. Now Protestantism, under whatever form it presents itself to our view, only sees in Peter an ordinary Apostle, having perhaps more talent than the others and an honorary title; nothing more. As for his successors, it recognises no greater authority in them than in any other bishop whatever. Now I will ask of the different Protestant sects, how can you flatter yourselves that you are in the true Church, when you proclaim by sound of trumpet that the Church to which you belong adheres neither to Peter nor to his successors? You are, then, beyond the boundaries of the basis which the Saviour laid down for His Church, and, consequently, you are not in the true Church of Christ, or, as St. Jerome expresses it, you are outside the ark of Noe; you will perish in the waters of the deluge. Peter has been constituted universal pastor of the flock of Jesus Christ; but by refusing this title to Peter and his successors you no longer belong to the flock of Jesus Christ; in other terms, you cease to be members of His Church.

I know that our adversaries are accustomed to limit

our Lord's words to Peter; they will not hear heirs or successors spoken of.

To this objection I will reply, with Abbé Magnin: 'Was not the Church to live except during the lifetime of Peter? Was the foundation, laid by the hand of its Divine Author, to end with that Apostle, after barely a quarter of a century's existence? Should time, which affects human institutions, triumph over its divine constitution, and that so soon? And if the nature and the government of the Church are to be to-day what they were in the time of Peter, how could that Apostle be the foundation-stone of the Church, if it was not in the person of his successors? The foundations are not laid for a day, when the duration of the edifice ought to be (as is the case with the Church) for centuries; they should support it to its very last day, for if ever the foundation fails the edifice falls in; and it is this which proves that Peter must have successors, who, together with him, would make but one moral being.' A little farther on he adds: 'What Church is it against which the gates of hell are not to prevail? It is the Church built upon Peter, the Church of which Peter has the keys, in which he has the power to bind and to loose. Now how can it be otherwise than that the individual Church of Rome should belong to that Church?—Rome, the special Church of St. Peter, the Church founded not only on him, but by him, governed by his successors. Without considering anything even in Rome but the individual Church, it is historically, and will be eternally, true that it is specially built on the stone upon which that Church shall be raised against which the gates of hell shall not prevail; and no interpretation of the text before us can destroy an historical fact, proclaimed by the whole Christian universe.'[51]

I sum up, then, by saying: Jesus Christ founds a Church, which is to last to the end of time, and He establishes it on Peter, who will always be its basis, either in himself or in his successors. Now the successors of Peter are, and can only be, the Bishops of Rome, as is attested by the whole history of the Church. Then Protestantism, which does not admit the authority of the Bishops of Rome or Sovereign Pontiffs, does not rest on the foundations which the Saviour gave to His Church, and, consequently, is outside the true Church of Christ.

I have already said that Jesus Christ had instituted in His Church an infallible authority, living and personal, to which every Christian ought to submit as to Jesus Christ Himself. Now Protestantism—that which admits a living authority—does not possess this infallibility; not only does not possess it, but takes care to proclaim itself fallible, subject to error, and consequently capable of leading into error those who would have the simplicity to adopt its decisions blindly. Protestantism, then, cannot be the true Church of Jesus Christ.

In place of the infallible authority instituted by the Saviour there have been substituted sovereigns, male and female, as if Jesus had placed the Cæsars at the head of His Church; as if the history of the Christian ages did not give the lie most solemnly to this sacri-

[51] *La Papauté aux Prises avec le Protestantisme*, p. 265, &c.

legious innovation; as if these popes and popesses of modern manufacture had received a mission to govern the Church and serve as its basis. Certainly it is not of a similar authority that our Lord said, and could have meant to say: 'He who hears you hears Me, and he who despises you despises Me. If any one will not hear the Church, let him be unto you as a heathen and a publican.' Rather would contradictory propositions to these be true, particularly when we see this Reformation proclaim that Baptism is not absolutely necessary to salvation, that faith *alone* justifies, without works, &c.

There are some who boast of having their infallible authority in the Word of God contained in the Bible. But, as I have already shown, Jesus Christ has not given us a book, so that each individual may go to it and extract his belief, but He has given us a teaching body, a living personal authority, to which He has intrusted the keeping His heavenly doctrine intact. I do not deny that the written Word of God is necessarily true; but what I deny is, that He has left to each one the task of interpreting it in his own manner, and making it say the most contradictory things. It must be acknowledged, too, that this infallible authority, which rests on a dead letter, does not inconvenience the religious liberty of individuals, since it suffers, without saying a word, the most absurd as well as the most impious doctrines; and I can understand that some persons find it suits themselves admirably. Any one can interpret at his will this divine text, without fear of being the least in the world inconvenienced. Human pride there finds its own advantage, but do not the interests of revealed truths suffer? Are they not even completely sacrificed to the caprices, passion, or ignorance of each one?

Not only does Protestantism lay no claim to the infallible authority which the Saviour had communicated to the teaching body—an authority so clearly expressed in the Bible—but it possesses none of the marks which ought to characterise the true Church of Christ, and manifest it to the eyes of the nations as such. Is it possible to find unity in Protestantism, that characteristic which is so essential to the true Church of the Saviour? By no means. It is not to be found there, and never will be. That unity does not exist in the various Dissenting communions is a fact which is as clear as the sun at noon. This fact has already been abundantly demonstrated when I proved that the fundamental principle of Protestantism is irreconcilable with unity; also we may draw attention to the jeremiads uttered by the heads of the false Reformation and their partisans up to the present day, concerning the interminable dissensions which are constantly arising. They admit that Protestantism is going to ruin, is being divided into numberless sects, into fractions of fractions, *ad infinitum*, is giving birth to a number of incongruous and contradictory confessions of faith, and is producing *Churches* instead of the *one Church* which should exist. Melancthon, writing to Calvin, said: 'The whole stream of the Elbe would not furnish water enough to weep the misfortunes of the divided Reformation. The most important things are doubted; the evil is incurable.'[52] *La*

---

[52] Epist. c. l. iv.

Gazette Ecclésiastique wrote on this subject: 'It is easy to prove, as it has indeed been proved more than once, that among all our pastors there are not two who believe alike.' 'They are all laughed at as so many false prophets' (*Lüdke*). 'The people, seeing their inconsistencies, treat their guides as simpletons and impostors' (*Fischer*). 'It may be affirmed without hesitation that there is not a theologian amongst us who has not renounced some one important article of our belief, which was so judged by the first Reformers' (*Planck*). 'Satan himself has more faith than our commentators, and Mahomet was far better than they are' (*Ewald*). These are avowals made by Protestant writers as to the present state of the Reformation; it would be easy to bring forward a thousand other quotations analogous to those I have given.

Still Protestantism has often tried to save itself from the anarchy into which it must result. All has been useless. It has had to resign itself to contemplating with its own eyes the alarming spectacle of complete disorganisation and approaching death, like those unhappy creatures who, eaten alive by a cancer or consumed by a mortal gangrene, feel life abandoning them, and the tomb opening to them as their dwelling-place. Confessions of faith have been published, people have been sworn to defend them always, and in all their respective parts; but soon some error being discovered in them, each individual thinks himself obliged to bid adieu to the standard of deceit: hence arise doctrinal disputes, as well as divisions and subdivisions without end. In what have the Protestant synods, the Evangelical Alliance, resulted? In making every serious man laugh, and in pointing out to Protestants themselves their radical powerlessness to extract from their Bible one single truth of the faith which must be admitted by all.

I will content myself with giving one example.

In the month of March 1838, a Protestant synod was assembled at Lausanne. Convoked by a Council of State—of which the members might be Catholics, Jews, atheists—thirty-two pastors assembled daily in the hall of the Grand Council, who were to give decisions from which there was no appeal. The question was first asked, what was the Church—whether it was a school or a society, or at once school and society, or by turns society and school; which means that from the very beginning doubt was thrown on the existence even of a teaching ministry in the Church. Nothing was decided; nevertheless, they discussed the following grave question: Is Baptism necessary for belonging to the Church? Upon which a member made the observation that to preserve greater harmony with those who do not baptise their children—a practice which, *in a few years, may possibly become general with us*—it was only prudent not to exact this condition! Baptism provisionally provided for, they next occupied themselves about a confession of faith. And first, must there be one? The majority said 'Yes.' Should it be declared variable or invariable? 'Essentially variable,' answered twenty-one voices out of thirty-two. And must the ancient Helvetic confession be changed? Fifteen voices said 'Yes,' fifteen said 'No.' It was at length determined that the Helvetic confession should be retained, not as rule of faith, but as a rule of teaching—a distinction that appeared subtle to several. These men, calling themselves ministers of the Church and pastors of souls, asked of one another, in the nineteenth century of the Christian era : To whom does it belong to govern the Church? Is it to us or to laymen? Some capital things were said on this subject; amongst others the following most just observation was made, that for three centuries it had been the State—the State alone—which had governed Protestant Churches. Struck with this truth, 'I ask, then,' said a candid minister, 'that we propose to the Council of State that the Church may at last become something.' On this question : Are laymen competent to judge of doctrine? sixteen said 'Yes,' sixteen said 'No;' and ultimately the controversy was submitted to the decision of the Great Council! With regard to this, some said they had a mission, that they believed in their ordination; others that they had no authority but that which resulted from the force of their own reasoning, that their ordination conferred on them no distinctive character. In short, they were ignorant what the Church was, what they were themselves, what they had to teach on the most essential points, such as Baptism; they were only assured of one thing, which was, that with them the State ruled over the Church and governed it, if really there was a Church.[53]

By means of the Evangelical Alliance it was thought to imitate the Œcumenical Council of the Vatican, and show to the world that Protestantism also possessed unity. Such was the aim clearly expressed by the Rev.

[53] Nampon, *Etude de la Doctrine Catholique*, Paris, 1852.

Dr. Adams at New York, and by the Revs. Dr. Cook and James Davies at Quebec. Vain effort! They succeeded in getting laughed at, and that was all.

If, indeed, we examine each discourse pronounced on this occasion, it is easy to see that the orators are in the clouds, and fear going beyond generalities; their domain is the undefined and undefinable; they do not know where to set their foot; they fear seeing the ground open to swallow them up.

A good many people set out from Europe to go to New York, in order to manifest Protestant unity. But what unity? Is it unity of the faith? Certainly not. Amongst themselves they would have found ardent adversaries of baptismal regeneration, of the divinity of Jesus Christ, of the Holy Trinity, of the Incarnation of the Word, of sanctification by the sacraments; they could not even have come to an understanding as to the books of which the Bible is composed, still less as to the sense to be given to the clearest texts of Scripture. Indeed, Dr. Stoughton of London took care at the very beginning to declare, 'that they had not come together to decide any ecclesiastical question, nor to propose a dogma, but only to express their views on religious matters.' This declaration was superfluous, for no one is ignorant that Protestantism is incapable of imposing a dogma on the human conscience, since it has neither authority nor infallibility: any attempt of this sort would only result in making every one laugh. The rev. doctor did not tell us what were the *religious matters* in question. Once more it suited him to remain in generalities. This is the true style of modern Protestantism. Was it the unity of ecclesiastical government or of discipline that they came to exhibit in Quebec? But who is not aware that on these subjects, as on all the rest, there is a prodigious divergence of opinions, and that, from the Episcopalian to the Quaker and Socinian, every possible and impossible shade of difference may be met with? Did they wish to show union of hearts? Yes, if we believe the reverend speakers; but this union hardly exists, as every one knows, except in their profound aversion to Romanism—that is to say, to the Catholic religion. Apart from this unity in protestation and hatred there is no tie, no common principle, to serve as a basis of so-called evangelical alliance. Had it been their object to make a caricature of unity, they could not possibly have succeeded better than in these omni-coloured assemblies.[54]

Some very nice things could be related also with regard to the Protestant Synod held at Paris in 1848, and more particularly about the famous Pan-Anglican Synod assembled in London some years ago, and which was turned into ridicule so cleverly by a certain writer.[55] But this would lead me too far; and, besides, I think I have more than sufficiently proved that unity never has existed, and never will exist, in Protestantism.

Certain Protestants have from time to time pretended that the Church of Rome alone is responsible for the separation, since she was the cause of it by excommunicating the Reformed Churches. But it is easy to

---

[54] *Morning Chronicle* of the 6th, 29th, and 30th October 1873.
[55] *Comedy of Convocation in the English Church*, by Archdeacon Chasuble, D.D. New York, 1868.

understand that the sentence of excommunication pronounced by Rome did not precede the separation or the schism, and, consequently, was not the cause of it; but that it was pronounced after the schism, and was but a just punishment inflicted on rebel subjects. In the second place, it must not be forgotten that it was the Reformers who separated themselves from the Church by their innovations, and not the Church which separated from the Reformers. In fact, the Catholics took not a single step. They maintained the doctrine, such as it was at that period and had been during previous ages; their faith is absolutely that of the Middle Ages, and that of the first Fathers of the Church. 'You cannot, then, say,' I will add, with one of the Protestant writers (answer to Dr. Sharp, Bishop of York)—'you cannot maintain that the Catholics made a schism with you, unless you mean to say that when a vessel sails away from the shore where it was at anchor, it is the shore which goes away from the vessel, and not the vessel which goes away from the shore.'

It has been well said that the false Reformation 'protests, but does not unite;' that in its bosom are only to be found 'individualities which seek one another to agglomerate together, like the atoms of Epicurus, without being able to succeed in doing so; aggregations of scepticism, amalgamations of incredulity of every species—in fact, a regular pulverisation of evangelical doctrine.'[56]

Protestantism can hardly be said to possess the mark of sanctity any more than that of unity. I will not here

[56] Caussette, *Le bon Sens de la Foi*, t. i. p. 392.

descend to personal questions: polemics that give rise to irritated feelings rarely produce any good, and I am but too glad to recognise among Protestants *of good faith* many noble, great, sincere souls, to whom God will grant the happiness of the heavenly kingdom, as is acknowledged by the greatest theologians, such as De Lugo.[57] But here I wish to compare particularly societies as they stand revealed before the eyes of impartial men—in their *origin*, in the *means of sanctification* which they employ, and specially in the *results* they obtain.

As to the heads of the Reformation in the sixteenth century, I do not wish to judge them myself, for fear of being accused of partiality. I prefer only quoting some short passages of their writings, and repeating the polite speeches they make about one another; the reader can then pronounce for himself as to the sanctity of the origin of Protestantism. The sincerity of Luther is well described in this confidential letter to his friend Melancthon, August 30th, 1530: 'When once we have nothing more to fear, when we shall be left in peace, then will be the time to rectify our deceits, lies, and errors.' 'Peter,' he says elsewhere, 'the greatest of the Apostles, lived and taught contrarily to the Word of God.'[58] Moses, he says, had a tongue, but a hesitating tongue, which stammered—a tongue of death, of anger, and of sin. Collect all the words of wisdom of Moses, of the gentile philosophers, and you will find that they only express idolatry or hypocrisy.[59]

[57] *De Fide.* xii. 3, 30.
[58] *Comment. in Ep. ad Gal.* c. ii. edit. Wittemberg, Opp. t. v. p. 290.
[59] T. iii. in Ps. xlv. p. 425.

I will not quote anything from his 'Table Talk' (*Tischreden*), which forms a folio volume of 1350 pages. I would fear being found wanting in that respect which I owe to my courteous readers. It is of him that Zuinglius wrote: 'When I read that book [Luther's] I fancy I see an unclean pig smelling here and there among the flowers in a beautiful garden, in such indecent, untheological, and unsuitable terms does he speak of God and holy things.' 'This,' he exclaims elsewhere, 'is how Satan seeks to gain entire possession of this man.'[60] In his turn, Luther says of Zuinglius that he is *satanised, insatanised, supersatanised.*[61]

In a letter addressed to Bucer, January 9th, 1538, Calvin accuses Luther of pomp, backbiting, ignorance, of having fallen into gross mistakes, and of being guilty of insolent pride. Bucer, a disciple of Calvin's, called his master 'a writer possessed of a passion for backbiting —a mad dog.'[62] In his work entitled *De Vera et Falsa Religione*, p. 202, Zuinglius wrote: 'We return here to what we have said elsewhere, on condition, however, that what we write in the forty-second year of our age should be admitted in preference to what we wrote in the fortieth year only, at a time, as we have said, when we rather consulted the interest of the moment than the truth—*ne inter initia canes et porci nos rumpant.*' Too truly, then, can we say, with the Protestant W. Cobbett: 'Perhaps the world has never, in any age, seen a nest of such atrocious miscreants as Luther, Zuinglius,

---

[60] Zwingle, Opp. t. ii. *Resp. ad Conf. Lutheri*, pp. 474 and 478.
[61] Audin, *Vie de Luther*, t. ii. p. 376.
[62] Freudenfeld, *Origine de la Réformation de Calvin*.

Calvin, Beza, and the rest of the distinguished Reformers of the Catholic religion. Every one of them was notorious for the most scandalous vices, even according to the full confession of their own followers. They agreed in nothing but the doctrine that *good works were useless,* and their lives proved the sincerity of their teaching; for there was not a man of them whose acts did not merit a halter.'[63]

What might not be said of Carlostadt, Melancthon, Beza, Bucer, and others? But we can already judge by the above quotations that these brave *Reformers,* who well knew one another, were not more ready to canonise each other than we would be so disposed ourselves.

If such an origin is neither pure nor holy, it can be affirmed with no less truth that the doctrines and means of sanctification are not any more so. Let it suffice for me to bring forward the following principles, admitted by Luther, Calvin, and Zuinglius: first, the dogma of justification by *faith* alone, and the inutility of good works to salvation; secondly, the abominable doctrine that God is the author of sin, in that He urges man to sin by an irresistible necessity—'*Nam et mala opera in impiis Deus operatur,*' wrote Luther; thirdly, that original sin deprived Adam and his posterity of free-will; fourthly, it has become absolutely impossible to keep the commandments of God; fifthly, God only created the greater number of men in order to damn them eternally; sixthly, the elect alone are justified, and as soon as they are baptised they can no longer sin,

[63] *A History of the Protestant Reformation,* London, 1829, c. vii. n. 200.

or at least their sins are no more imputed to them; seventhly, the simple exterior imputation of the merits of Jesus Christ by means of faith alone is sufficient to confer holiness even equal to that of the angels or of the Blessed Virgin, were the conscience of the recipient even laden with all the crimes in the world. Such are the frightful doctrines which we find expressed in plain language in many parts of their writings. If they were rigorously applied in the ordinary concerns of life, they would ruin public morals and overturn society. Fortunately heretics and schismatics, as has already been said, are often better than their heresies and their schisms. By taking away the Sacraments of Penance and the Holy Eucharist, the two greatest sources of sanctification in the Christian religion have been taken away from man.

As to the results obtained by the pretended Reformation, volumes might be written on the subject, showing how low has sunk the Christian devotedness of their missionaries among the heathen and among the lower classes of society. It would be easy to show that the doctrine of the inutility of good works for salvation has produced the fruits that might be expected from it. Where are the saints produced by the Reformation? Where are the men she has formed to the practice of the evangelical counsels? Why this species of horror she shows with regard to the religious who unite themselves to the Lord for their whole lives by vows of poverty, virginity, and obedience? Why this persecution to the death directed against men who are guilty of no other crime than that of wishing to flee from the dangers of the world; who have no other social crime to expiate but that of spending their lives in study, in the practice of piety, in the exercise of the works of apostolic zeal? In what have resulted all the efforts that have been made, in one place or another, to found convents of religious men and women, as in Catholicism? In nothing—everything has ended in a general dispersion. What part has been played, and is still being played, by these propagators of the pure Bible among infidel nations? That of good citizens, carefully taken care of by a wife and children, travelling for the faith and not confessing it; or, again, as the Rev. Father Caussette expressed it, that of commercial travellers of the Gospel, leaving to others the glory of being its apostles.[64] Whoever thinks I am in the very least exaggerating has only to read the writings of the heads of Protestantism, or else Döllinger's work entitled *The Reformation*, in three volumes. They will easily be convinced that I have not said a thousandth part of the truth on this question.

From the very fact that unity does not exist in Protestantism, it is evident that the mark of Catholicism, or universality, cannot be found there either. In fact, when it is said that a religious society is Catholic, or universal, it ought to be understood of a society whose members profess, and are bound to profess, one and the same positive belief, under pain of no longer belonging to that society. But what is to be found in the Reformation? Is there any unity whatever in the faith? None. Is any one obliged to adhere to certain particular positive doctrines? By no means. There may

[61] *Le bon Sens de la Foi*, t. i. p. 428.

be as many Christianities as Christians, as many Protestantisms as Protestants? Without any doubt, since each one believes what best pleases himself, and nothing farther. But how form a society with such dissimilar elements—with men whose only principle of cohesion is the persevering negation of the Roman Church? The problem does not appear to me to be easy to solve, unless, with a certain clever writer, we place the sign of Catholicity on 'the harmony of universal divergences;' or else compare the Church 'to an artificial nosegay, composed of a rose, a cabbage, a tulip, and an onion, the whole carefully tied together by a shoe-string.'[65]

As for apostolicity, I know that many Dissenting communions lay not the slightest claim to it, and they are right. They have even divorced themselves from all kind of priesthood. Their religion is summed up in the infallibility of human reason, or of the sovereign's reason, when applied to the Bible. Going back to the Apostles in an unbroken line of succession of legitimate pastors is a glory to be found only in the Roman Catholic Church. Still, there are certain sects which wear themselves out in vain efforts to show to the world that they are not illegitimate; but how can they succeed? How find a connecting link beyond Luther, Calvin, Zuinglius, and Henry VIII. or Elizabeth? It is very evident that the Churches which they founded are not apostolical, since they only date back three centuries; nor are they grafted on the Apostolic Church, since, on the contrary, they have either been cut off or have separated themselves from it. Starting from the period when

[65] *Comedy of Convocation in the English Church*, pp. 62-3.

this criminal rupture took place, Protestant communions can no more boast of being the true Apostolic Church than can the Arians, the Nestorians, the Eutychians, and the Monophysites. They are branches lopped off from the tree and condemned to die; they no longer receive the life-giving sap of the doctrine of the Apostles. Of them might be said what the *British Review* said in 1838 of the Anglican Church: 'It is a mummy, a solemn corpse, which can neither walk nor breathe.' There is no doubt that the genealogical tree of Protestantism extends its branches no farther back than the sixteenth century, unless it be maintained that Henry VIII. was the legitimate successor of Pope Leo X., and Cranmer the representative of Catholic faith and virtue in the see of Canterbury, which is a manifest absurdity. There are Protestants who fabricate for themselves strange titles of nobility. They pretend that, from sect to sect, they go back to Jesus Christ! They are at perfect liberty to choose such ancestors; it is hardly to their honour. But it would be easy to prove (if it did not take too long) that these sects differed in belief from Protestants on a number of important points. Besides this genealogical tree, which at every branch shows different kinds of schismatics or rebels, conducts us at length to Simon the Magician, and to certain sects which had but one drawback—that of professing a doctrine diametrically opposed to that of Jesus Christ. Others take refuge in the apostolicity of the doctrine which they pretend to have retained. But they ought to bear in mind that this is precisely the difficulty which is to be solved, and that doctrine cannot be a note, a distinctive and visible characteristic of the true Church, although it must necessarily be a quality of the same. In fact, the apostolical succession may be clearly seen—it is a patent historical fact; but can doctrine be visible in the same manner?

Presbyterianism would hardly agree to the Real Presence, auricular confession, and a liturgy which is in a great measure Roman; but Ritualism pronounces differently on these subjects, and on many others, both, however, believing that they are in possession of apostolic doctrine. Who shall decide between them? I might reason in the same way about each article of the Apostles' Creed and about all the sects. The question would always remain insoluble for the same reason.

But let us take a particular example, in order to show that the first Reformers abandoned the faith of the Apostolic Church, and have never received any Divine mission. At the commencement of his career, did Luther believe in the pontifical supremacy, in the reality of the holy Sacrifice of the Mass, in the worship of saints, in the necessity for the confession of sins? Yes, without any doubt; his writings attest it. Did the Catholic Church, which was then spread over all the earth, teach the same doctrines; and had she taught them during the Middle Ages and during the first centuries? That is absolutely certain; Protestants themselves are sometimes pleased to acknowledge this, and it is for that reason that the greater number of them divorce themselves from tradition and take refuge in the pure Bible. There was then a sacrilegious innovation on the part of Luther and the other Reformers; they rose up, therefore, against the Church founded by Jesus Christ, and with which He had promised to be until the end of time; they put their individual reason above that of the whole Church; they rejected the religion of the Pope in order themselves to become popes of their religion; they accused the Church of idolatry, superstition, impiety, &c. When a man takes on himself so important a part as that of reformer of the Church, when he has the boldness to contradict what has been believed for sixteen centuries, when he even goes so far as to deny the accomplishment of the Saviour's promises, the plainest common sense tells us that such a hero ought to prove in an authentic manner that he has an apostolate—a divine mission—that of leading back Christian society to its earliest condition. But what, then, can these heads of the Reformation show to prove to the world that they have received the mission from heaven of reëstablishing the apostolic doctrine? Not a single miracle, not even the cure of a lame horse, says Erasmus; but a sensual and scandalous life, principles worthy of Paganism, cynical language, a frightful death. From whom did they receive their mission? From themselves. It is very rarely that God chooses similar instruments to accomplish His work, and it is incredible that He charged them with reforming the whole world and yet gave them no credentials. This would be attributing to God a wisdom inferior to human wisdom. It may, then, be concluded that in the Reformation there is neither apostolic succession nor apostolic doctrine, nor a divine mission to purify the belief of the Catholic Church; the spirit of revolt and error is alone to be found there.

Protestantism, then, possesses none of the characteristics of the true Church of Christ, such as she is represented in the Holy Scripture.

We have now arrived at the Catholic Church. Does this Church possess all the prerogatives, all the distinctive characteristics of the Church of Christ, such as the Holy Books (considered as historical documents) represent it as issuing from the hands of its Founder? Let us examine this question a little.

We have seen in the Bible that Jesus Christ founded one only Church, to which He gave, as an indestructible and permanent foundation, Peter, the Prince of the Apostles, and as a necessary consequence his successors, for His Church was to last as long as the world. Thus it is evident that no Church can be considered as built upon Peter and his successors except that one which has for its head Peter and his successors. Now no Church can lay claim to this glorious prerogative except the Roman Church, where Peter was Bishop, where he died, and where the succession has been uninterruptedly kept up down to our days. Then the Catholic Church, the seat of which is in Rome, is that one to which Jesus Christ promised that the gates of hell should not prevail against her. The Saviour constituted Peter the basis of His indefectible Church, the pastor of His flock, the confirmer of his brethren in the faith; He prayed in a special manner that his faith might not fail; in other words, He promised infallibility to the head of His Church. Now the Bishops of Rome, or the Popes, are the only ones who have constantly laid claim to this privilege—the only ones in whom it has been acknowledged and to whom it has been attributed; the only ones who can show in their teaching an invariable doctrine always in harmony with that of their predecessors and with that of their successors, always conformable to that of St. Peter and the Apostles. Then the Roman Church is the legitimate heiress of the divine promises contained in the Bible.

Jesus Christ promised to the Apostolic College, having Peter for its head, His special guardianship and the assistance of the Holy Ghost, not only for a time, but for ever—*in æternum*. Now apart from the teaching Catholic Church, united in council under the presidency of the Popes at the different periods of history, can any other be found which has even dared to call itself infallible, the pillar and foundation of the truth, or assisted by the Holy Spirit so as not to be able to err? None; all take care—which is, however, not necessary—to proclaim themselves fallible, subject to error, and consequently not assisted by the Spirit of Truth. These Churches are not, then, the society founded by Christ; they do not possess the infallible power of ruling which He established for the teaching of the nations until the end of time. Apart from the Church of Rome, is there a single one which dares to teach with the authority of a divine mission, and which seriously consents to having our Saviour's words to the Apostles applied to it: 'He that heareth you, heareth Me; he that despiseth you, despiseth Me. If any one hear not the Church, let him be to you as a heathen and a publican'? None.

Outside of the Roman Catholic Church will you find a single one which believes itself, as she does, strictly obliged to *preach the Gospel to all men*, to teach the nations *all that Jesus Christ had commanded them, keeping the deposit of the faith, avoiding profane innovations*, transmitting the revealed doctrine—even unwritten—to persons capable and legitimately charged with teaching it to the nations? Not one. On the contrary, each one of them has limited itself to a little corner of the earth, to a nationality, or to a part of the revelation; all have sacrificed the unwritten Word of God; all have let the Bible be torn to shreds in the hands of their adepts; all have abandoned the deposit of revelation to the caprices and passions of individuals. The Roman Church alone has accomplished the divine mission of preaching *all* the revealed truth and to *all* nations.

That the Roman Church is *one*, is a striking and incontestable fact. Traverse one after another the different regions of the globe, and you will everywhere hear the same *Credo* repeated and the same doctrine taught. It cannot be otherwise; for whoever would dare knowingly to reject the smallest portion of doctrine defined by the competent authority would be excluded from the Church; she has but to speak, but to give a definition of faith, every one submits to her decision heartily, and makes the sacrifice of any particular opinions he might before have held. We had a magnificent example of this in the Council of the Vatican; its decrees met with the most unanimous and complete adhesion on the part of the bishops and the faithful; all previous disagreements were effaced in the presence of the pontifical sanction attached to the decrees of the venerable assembly. Now put her faith to the test of ages; go back to the Catacombs, pass on to the Middle Ages or to the time of the Reformation, and compare the doctrine of the Roman Church at these periods with that which she now professes, and I defy you to discover the smallest change in it or the faintest divergence.

But, our adversaries say to us, did not the Roman Church change in her faith when, in 1854, she defined the dogma of the Immaculate Conception of the Blessed Virgin, and, in 1871, that of the Infallibility of the Pope? The Reverend Messrs. Bancroft[65] and Burns[66] are astonished that these dogmas were not discovered before if they existed; whereupon they gave utterance to something ineffable, not to say anything stronger; they even went so far as to assign this latter definition as the cause of the Franco-Prussian War; then Dr. Burns recalled to mind the great schism of the West, the disputes between the Thomists and Scotists, between the Jesuits and Jansenists, and drew from thence the conclusion that there is no more unity in the Roman Church than in Protestantism.

To this I reply, first in a general manner, that the Church never creates new dogmas; they are all contained in written or unwritten revelation, although all are not there contained in an equally clear and precise manner; it is this latter reason which establishes a *difference of date*, not between such and such a *belief* of the Church, since the Church has always implicitly or explicitly believed everything which she now believes; but between such and such a *definition* of the faith of

[65] Quebec *Morning Chronicle*, Feb. 15, 1872. [66] Ibid. Feb. 27, 1874.

the Church. A *new dogma*, as our adversaries express it, is not, then, a new doctrine taken outside of revelation, imagined by the caprice of the Pope or the bishops; no, it is only a *definition* or *new declaration which the Church* gives us of an old doctrine, revealed from the first, but which, on account of its *less explicit* revelation in Scripture and tradition, had up to then been only *implicitly* believed in the Church.[67] In other terms, the Church does not change the *object* of her faith, she does not fabricate beliefs at her own will; her part is confined to that of undeniably establishing, when circumstances require it, that a certain doctrine is really revealed, that is to say contained in Holy Scripture or in tradition; it is always the Word of God which is taught to us and propounded to us, not by individual reason, as in Protestantism, but by the infallible authority of the Church aided by the Holy Ghost. Is this clear enough?

Let us add another example, so that there may be no room for any obscurity on this point. I will suppose that our gracious sovereign Queen Victoria might publish a code of civil laws, and that she might, as was the case with our Saviour, confer on the Privy Council the prerogative of interpreting these laws with infallibility, that is to say in a manner so as never to give them a different sense from that which she herself attached to them. Some centuries later, the jurisconsults interpret a particular law of this code some in one sense, some in another; there are even some who go so far as to deny the existence of such a law. But the Privy Council

[67] Rua, *Cours de Conférences sur la Religion*, t. ii, p. 339; see also Franzelin, *De Divinâ Traditione et Scripturâ*, p. 238.

steps in, and, always infallible in this matter, solemnly declares that *this law exists, and that such and such was the sense attached to it by the Queen*. Would you, perchance, say that the Privy Council has made a new law, that it has introduced an innovation into the royal code? No; it would be clear that it had only proved the existence and the sense of a law already promulgated. So it is with the definitions given by the Church; she only proves the existence of revealed doctrines, or explains and develops what might before have been obscure.

I will allow myself to put a question to the above-named reverend orators: When the Council of Nice, in the fourth century, defined the divinity of the Son of God, did they invent that doctrine? *Was that doctrine unknown to anterior centuries?* Before the year 325 had no one believed that Jesus Christ was God? It would be absurd to assert this; the Council only defined a doctrine certainly revealed and already admitted in the Church. What else, then, was done concerning the dogmas of the Immaculate Conception and Pontifical Infallibility?

The greatest fault I find with these reverend ministers is speaking of things with which they are not sufficiently acquainted; at the same time they too easily disregard the most ordinary rules of logic. What indeed can be said of philosophers who attribute the Franco-Prussian War to the definition of Papal Infallibility, because the one came after the other—*post hoc ergo propter hoc?* If I wished to reason in the same manner as my adversaries, I would attribute the Crimean War to the doctrinal judgment pronounced by the Privy

Council in the Gorham case; or again, ascribe as the cause of the financial crisis in the United States and the troubles in Manitoba to the last assemblies of the *Evangelical Alliance*, held at New York and Quebec!

I do not wish here to correct the historical error into which Dr. Burns has fallen, when he confounds the sojourn of the Popes at Avignon for seventy years with the dissensions which followed this sojourn, and which led to there being as many as three claimants of the pontificate. Evidently he has as confused an idea of history as of the doctrine of the Catholic Church. I have already answered elsewhere the objection made against the unity of the Church founded on this fact.[63] Let it suffice for me here to recall to mind that during all that troubled period it never came into any one's head whatever that there could be two or three legitimate Popes at once. The error, then, under which some were lying was not an error of *doctrine* or of *right*, but simply an error of *fact* concerning the one legitimately elected. This case was absolutely analogous to that we often see occurring in electoral disputes: certain elections are contested; no one knows which candidate is legally elected; still all agree in saying that there can be but one member to represent the county.

The divergencies of opinion existing between the Scotists and Thomists with which the Roman Church is reproached turn entirely on points with regard to which authority has defined nothing, and which it abandons to the activity of the human mind; but in nothing do they

---

[63] *La Primauté et l'Infaillibilité des Souverains Pontifes*, pp. 393-406: Quebec, 1873.

affect the unity of faith and communion, since on all definite points there is perfect identity of faith amongst Catholics, and on undefined questions each one is ready to submit his own judgment directly the Church shall have spoken. As for the Jansenists, if we look on them as forming a *sect*, an individual *Church*, for example, at Utrecht, they have always been subjected to the anathemas of the Roman Pontiffs, and formally looked on as heretics; it is clear that in this case they no more destroy the unity of the Church than do the Lutherans or Calvinists, since they are completely separated from it. As to the *individuals*, they have not generally been excommunicated each one by name, and consequently they continue materially to form a part of the body of the Church. But this does not prevent their being immensely guilty before God, nor their harming themselves; still they do not harm the unity of the Church, which incessantly repudiates their errors.[69] The Jesuits have fought with the Church against the Jansenist error, absolutely the same as the Dominicans against the Albigenses, and St. Athanasius against the Arians; their strife was honourable, since they strove with men who altered the doctrines of the Church, and would no longer submit their judgment to competent authority.

Unity, then, has always subsisted in the Roman Catholic Church; it exists now and always will exist, because it must necessarily be the effect of an infallible authority intrusted with keeping divine revelation intact. It is useless, let us say so *en passant*, for the Anglican Church to pretend being, with the Russo-

[69] *Regola di Fede*, p. 242.

Greek and Roman Churches, a branch of the true Church of Christ, since the first condition of forming part of it is submission to legitimate and divinely constituted authority.

The mark of *sanctity* is no less evidently found in the Catholic Church. Without doubt all its members are not saints, since everywhere man remains free to do evil; also Jesus Christ predicted that there would be scandals, and that the Church would be like a field in which tares and wheat grew at the same time, like a sheepfold where there were both goats and sheep. Still is it no less true to say that Catholicism, holy in its origin, in its dogmas, in its moral teaching, in its worship, has never ceased producing saints. I wish for no other proof than those saints who have appeared in the course of the last three centuries. Can there be found in the bosom of Reform many Christians like St. Charles Borromeo, St. Theresa, St. Ignatius, St. Francis of Xavier, St. Aloysius, St. Francis Regis, St. Vincent de Paul, St. Francis de Sales, St. Jane Chantal, St. Alphonsus de Liguori, and a number of others? Do we find in Protestantism many young persons who consent to separate from their families, banishing themselves from the world, sometimes renouncing a brilliant fortune, to consecrate themselves exclusively to the service of God by the solemn vows of poverty, chastity, and obedience? Can many be found who have worn out their lives in begging for the poor and infirm, nursing the sick in the hospitals, dressing wounds on the battle-field, or bringing back into the paths of virtue the unhappy victims of vice? Very few; disdain and hatred is even affected for this evangelical perfection. Catholicism, on the contrary, can count by millions those holy and courageous souls who sacrifice everything for God, and who believe with the Holy Scripture that faith without works is dead faith. And has the Catholic missionary ever recoiled before epidemics, persecutions, the dungeon—death itself? Never; nor has he anything which attaches him to the earth; he leaves behind him neither widow nor orphans; he belongs to himself entirely, or rather he belongs to God alone, to whom he has consecrated his labours and his life; he is happy to give his blood for the faith or for the alleviation of human suffering. I need but recall here his heroism during the plague at Milan and at Marseilles; during wars; during the cholera which raged at different periods even in our Canada. I have but to pronounce the names of countries such as Japan, China, Tonkin, the Corea, &c., to see rise up before me a cloud of courageous martyrs, who have never wanted for successors in the continuation of their work. Let not my words be taken for enthusiasm, for superannuated exaggeration; I only appeal to facts which are within the domain of history.

One more remark before going farther. When any one decides on passing from Protestantism to Catholicism, is it in the hope of leading a more free or easy life, of finding a less-exacting religion—one less severe with regard to pride and the other bad passions of the human heart? Quite the contrary; and what often prevents certain returns to the Catholic religion is the necessity of submitting to the restraint of obedience in religious matters, to the confession of faults, to rigid morality, or to fasting, abstinence, &c. All these matters are much simplified in Protestantism, as every one knows; but is that indeed the religion of Christ? The following saying of Fitz-William is well known: 'The passage from the Church to a sect is too often along the road of vice; that from a sect to the Church is always by the road of virtue.'[70]

The Roman Church is not only holy, but also *Catholic* or universal. Contrary to paganism, which never dreamt of universality in religion, and which took care to circumscribe itself within the narrow circle of the family, the city, or the kingdom; contrary to Judaism, which has remained stationary for two thousand years; contrary to Mahometanism, that 'phantom of religion raised on a pedestal of mud,' which contains no principle of progressive diffusion, and which is limited to some barbarous provinces; contrary, lastly, to the Greek schism, which is pretty nearly unknown in the greater part of the provinces of Europe and Asia, and is not to be found either in America, Africa, or Oceanica;—the Roman Church, with the Pope for her head, the legitimate successor of the Prince of the Apostles, is spread in all parts of the world, and counts a considerable number of faithful even in those regions where other societies predominate. Add to this that she does not profess a different belief in different countries; she is absolutely one in her faith as in her government and her worship.

The Roman Church is also *Apostolic*, and the only

[70] *Letters of Atticus*, 1826, p. 112.

Apostolic Church. In fact she is the only Church which can show her descent—her genealogy—from Jesus Christ and the Apostles down to our days. She alone has pastors, bishops, and priests who are still divinely sent as the first Apostles were by our Saviour, and who can say to the nations: 'We teach, we baptise, we remit sins, we exercise the power of the keys to bind and loose, to make disciplinary laws; we administer the other sacraments; we establish bishops, priests, and we send them as we ourselves were sent; and we do all that because the Apostles did it, because the successors of the Apostles have done it, because the Catholic Church has had the liberty to do so for 1840 years, and that all this, by the commands of Jesus Christ, is to be practised until the end of time.'[71] Nothing is more evident than public facts. Now the divine mission of the present Pope, Pius IX., as well as that of his predecessors, is the greatest of public facts. History is there to show us not only their names, but also their acts—their zeal to defend the holy doctrine, their universal and supreme authority; it leads us by the hand, as it were, up to St. Peter and to Jesus Christ, who constituted him the immovable basis of His Church, the pastor of His flock, the confirmer in the real truth.

What we have just proved of the Sovereign Pontiffs is equally applicable to Catholic bishops and priests in no matter what part of the world, since all have been ordained and consecrated by bishops who were in communion with the then reigning Pontiff of Rome. We can

[71] *Le Protestantisme dévoilé*, p. 18; Paris, 1841.

thus mount, link by link, along an uninterrupted chain of bishops as far as the Apostles, who ordained and consecrated the first bishops and the first priests—Titus, Timothy, &c. Here are incontestable proofs of our divine mission. But I should be curious to know whence the reverend orators of the Bible Society and the Evangelical Alliance have taken the titles of their mission, from whom they received it, and from how far back in the course of centuries it dates. I will allow myself to make a remark on this subject which P. Caussette[72] has already made before me, that 'the sects behave towards the Church as false nobles do towards the old race; failing the blood, they take the name, reckoning on the careless and inattentive, confounding the identity of the name with that of the blood.' 'But it is in vain they seek to mislead us,' says Bossuet:[73] 'we lay down as a fact that none can be named which, if traced up to its commencement, has not the point of junction marked at which a particle began to fight against the whole and separate itself from the stalk.' But it is altogether otherwise with the apostolic dynasty; never has it become extinct, and it never will.[74]

---

[72] *Le bon Sens de la Foi*, t. i. p. 415.

[73] *Instr. sur les Promesses.*

[74] Those who would know all the glories of the Catholic Church, and what she has done for the good of society in general, have only to read the admirable Conferences given in the United States by the Rev. Father Burke, of the Order of the Friar Preachers. These discourses, in which learning is united to the most exalted eloquence, have been published in New York in the course of the year 1873.

CONCLUSION.

I HAVE now attained the object I had in view. I think I have established with sufficient clearness, 1st, the necessity for a rule of faith as a means of knowing the revealed truth, which rule should be suited to the capacity of every one, certain, capable of deciding all controversy, and perpetual. 2dly. The insufficiency, the uncertainty, and the instability of the Protestant rule of faith, or the Bible. This rule of faith gives no certain proof of the inspiration of the Holy Books, nor does it fix any canon of them, nor verify their authenticity, nor determine their true sense; it cannot exist without an evident contradiction, that is to say without resting on tradition; it is incapable of establishing that unity which it was the will of Jesus Christ should reign in His Church. Let the Bible be interpreted by individual reason, or by the pretended inspiration of the Holy Ghost, or by a fallible authority, any way it only leads to uncertainty and infinite subdivisions; it results in the annihilation of religious liberty beneath the despotism of the civil authority, and ultimately gives rise to religious indifferentism and rationalism. I have shown, 3dly, the perfect harmony which exists on this question between the exigencies of human reason and the Bible on the one hand, and the rule of faith in the Catholic Church on the other. Divine revelation is contained entire in the Holy Scripture and in tradition; this precious deposit was confided by the Saviour to the care of a teaching Church, visible, permanent, and infallible; and this Church, which ought manifestly to be one, holy, Catholic, and Apostolic, is not Protestantism with its thousand sects, born yesterday, but the holy Roman Church; she alone still commands as the Apostles formerly commanded, and she is obeyed with the most perfect submission, because each one of her children is perfectly convinced that she is the legitimate heir of the divine promises—the true Church founded by Jesus Christ, and to which He said: 'He who heareth you, heareth Me; and he who despiseth you, despiseth Me. Whosoever believeth not shall be condemned.'

It is, then, absolutely indubitable that the Saviour has established one only Church; that He put her *in possession* of all revealed truth, so that she might be its *infallible guardian*. Hence it is absolutely necessary for those who are outside this only ark of salvation to hasten to enter it, if they do not wish to be condemned to perish. It is precisely to spare man so frightful a misfortune that He has rendered His Church visible, like a town set on the summit of a mountain; visible in her sacramental rites, visible in her supreme head, in her pastors, her members, her government, her worship, her judgments, her admirable hierarchy; above all, visible in the marks or distinctive characteristics which apply to her alone, to the exclusion of all the other so-called Churches. The fundamental question is, then, decided: Jesus Christ has founded an infallible Church.

Now this Church is the Roman Catholic Church, and can be no other. Then the Roman Church is absolutely the infallible and only Church of Christ. Now whoever listens not to this Church, whoever despiseth her, whoever does not believe in her teachings shall be condemned. Then from the moment she is recognised as being alone true, it is of rigorous necessity to become a member of this Church if we wish to escape from the terrible judgments of God.

'This conclusion is a true one,' I may be told; 'but how admit all the articles of belief of the Catholic Church? There are some of them which appear so little conformable to Scripture—so new, so arbitrary, so superstitious.'

They only appear so to those who do not sufficiently understand them, who from their childhood upwards have been imbued with a prejudice against everything Catholic, and have constantly heard reiterated the most absurd tales concerning our faith without having ever been able or willing to investigate their truth. A more attentive study, however, will amply prove this belief to be reasonable and founded on divine revelation. Doubtless there are mysteries which man can never thoroughly and completely comprehend, for they are beyond the power of reason. But even in the kingdom of nature are there not many things whose existence is well proved, and yet which we cannot understand? How much more, then, may not such be the case in the supernatural order? There are certain doctrines which we do not understand, but we believe them on the infallible authority of that Church which our reason has previously received, and which teaches us that they have certainly been revealed.

'But,' it is added, 'how believe in the Real Presence, in Transubstantiation, in the worship of the Blessed Virgin and the saints, in the confession of sins, &c.? All that is so evidently a mixture of superstition, idolatry, and fanciful errors.'

I do not here mean to treat at large each of these questions; that would carry me too far, and lead me beyond the limits I have imposed on myself in this work. Perhaps later I may develop these important questions; for the moment I will but say a word.

The Real Presence of Jesus Christ in the Eucharist appears to you to be a fiction. But what is there more incomprehensible in that than in seeing God, who is infinite in all His perfections, stooping so low as to take on Himself our poor nature, to be born in a manger, to suffer and die on a cross? The mystery of the Incarnation is as hard for human reason to compass as that of the Real Presence. What the love of God could do for humanity in one case, it might well do in another. Besides, when an infinitely powerful God tells us, 'This is My Body, this is My Blood,' reason itself shows us that we ought not to give the lie to God in a manifest manner by saying, 'That is not possible; this is neither the Body, nor the Blood, but only a figure—a remembrance of the Saviour.' This latter is what really might be called a fiction and a blasphemy; Protestantism will never be able to make it appear otherwise.

'Transubstantiation, or the changing of the substance of bread and wine into the Body and Blood of

Jesus Christ, is impossible.' And why? You admit that the Saviour changed water into wine at the marriage feast in Cana; that He multiplied the bread and fish; that He resuscitated Lazarus; that He Himself rose from the dead; that He created the heavens and the earth out of nothing; that the food which you take changes into your substance, &c. What reason have you, then, for making this choice, and believing the latter prodigies more than the former? This is simple arbitrariness. The Creation, which you admit, is it not even a still greater miracle than Transubstantiation? 'Confession of sins is a human invention.' But tell me in what century, in what country, by what mortal was it invented? Make every necessary research; fix whatever epochs you please to assign to this embarrassing institution; by means of historical tradition I will make you go back from century to century until that of Jesus Christ Himself, who addressed to His Apostles these memorable words: 'As My Father hath sent Me, so send I you. Receive the Holy Ghost; the sins ye remit shall be remitted unto men, and the sins ye retain shall be retained unto them.' I now ask whether an Anglican clergyman, pronouncing a form of absolution over persons who have just confessed to God in the secret of their heart, makes use often of the power expressed by the words: 'The sins ye retain shall be retained unto them?' How retain sins without knowing them? Impossible, except by acting arbitrarily. Jesus Christ, King of Heaven, judges like the kings of the earth, not in His own person, but by His plenipotentiaries, by His tribunals. He might without doubt have disposed of things in a different manner, but He has not done so; every objection disappears before His holy will.

'The worship of the Holy Virgin and the saints is pure and simple idolatry.' Yes, if we adored them, if we rendered them a worship which is due to God alone; but we venerate them only as the friends of God, as privileged souls who have made themselves agreeable to the Lord by their perfect charity, and who have faithfully corresponded to divine grace. We believe that their prayers, being more perfect than ours, may obtain from God that which we could not obtain for ourselves; consequently we invoke them, we honour them, we beg them to *intercede* for us. Is not such *cultus* conformable to reason, and, I might add, conformable to revelation? Do we not honour the mother of a king more than an ordinary mother, and the familiar friends of the sovereign more than ordinary citizens? Do we not have recourse to their mediation, to their intercession, to obtain royal favours? This is what we see every day; but is not the worship of Mary and the saints more rational even, since in them we honour the Mother and friends not of a man, but of God Himself? Let us, then, be no longer looked on as senseless idolaters, for that is an old tale which is perfectly ridiculous, and which should no longer be repeated in this nineteenth century.

You will often hear it said that we ought to die in the religion of our fathers; this is a pretext of which the faint-hearted make a convenience. I reply thereto, first: Yes, if the religion of those fathers was true and good; No, if it was false, for truth has imprescriptible rights over our intelligence. Acting on so erroneous a principle, the world would soon be plunged again into paganism. Besides, with regard to Protestants, it is easy to make them the same reply as was made by Count de Stolberg to a prince who was making this objection to him: 'Pardon, prince,' said he, 'it is still better to die in the religion of one's grandfathers.' This is the same idea as was expressed on his deathbed by a French ambassador in England: a friend asked him whether he were not grieved at seeing himself reduced to being buried amongst heretics. 'No,' answered the dying man; 'I will ask to have my grave dug very deep, and then I shall find myself in the midst of my own people.' And, in fact, abandoning the Reformation to become Catholic is returning to the religion of one's grandfathers, of one's ancestors, since up to the sixteenth century there was not a single Protestant on the face of the earth.

To those who render interior homage to the truth of Catholicism without choosing to profess it openly, under the pretext that God is satisfied with the good dispositions of the heart, and that a change of religion would involve too many sacrifices, too many disagreeables, and would grieve relations, friends, benefactors, I might bring forward our Saviour's most formal words: 'Every one therefore that shall confess Me before men I will also confess him before My Father who is in heaven; but he that shall deny Me before men, I will also deny him before My Father who is in heaven. He that loveth father or mother more than Me is not worthy of Me;' 'for what doth it profit a man if he gain the whole world, and suffer the loss of his own soul?' 'Seek ye therefore first the kingdom of God and His justice, and all these things (worldly goods) shall be added unto you.' 'Blessed are ye when they shall revile you, and persecute you, and speak all that is evil against you untruly, for My sake; be glad and rejoice, for your reward is very great in heaven.'[75] I might place before their eyes the noble examples of princes and learned men converted to the Catholic religion in our century: the Duke of Saxe-Gotha, allied to the Royal Family of England; Prince Henry Edward de Schönburg; Count d'Ingenheim, brother of the last deceased King of Prussia; the Duke A. F. of Mecklenburg-Schwerin, and his sister, the Duchess Charlotte Frederica; Prince F. A. C. of Hesse Darmstadt; the Duke and Duchess of Anhalt-Coethen; the Countess of Sohns-Bareuth; the learned Count Frederick Leopold de Stolberg; Frederick Schlegel, son of a Lutheran pastor; the celebrated Goerres; the Aulic Counsellor, Adam Muller; Count Charles Louis de Haller; Esslinger; the illustrious Frederick Hurter; Newman, Ward, Oakeley, Faber, Morris, Brown, Manning, Brownson, Forbes, Ives, Baker, and a number of others[76] who have had the courage to profess the truth

---

[75] Matthew x. 32-7, xiii. 26, vi. 33, v. 11, 12.

[76] I do not know whether the Rev. Dr. Cook meant to speak of these illustrious converts, when he recalls to mind the struggle to be maintained against 'the continual encroachments of Rationalism and Romanism led by renegade churchmen and advanced scientists' (*Morning Chronicle*, Oct. 29th, 1873). If it was his intention to award the title of *renegades* to these chosen intellects, the glories of Protestantism, what names should we not give to the chiefs of the Reformation, who apostatised from the religion of their fathers!

openly and to put themselves above all human considerations. And these are not vulgar, ignorant persons, but men of integrity, piety, of incontestable erudition; men who only entered into the pale of the Roman Church after having seriously studied Christian antiquity and being intimately convinced of the truth of the Catholic religion. These are certainly encouraging examples.

Monsignor Freppel has somewhere said most justly that 'the great obstacles to the conquests of faith are, that one ends by identifying oneself with error until one comes to look on the triumph of truth as a personal defeat.' And yet there cannot be a more humiliating defeat than that of being conquered by error, nor a more glorious victory than that which puts us in possession of truth.

My task is ended. If in the course of this book there has escaped me any expression capable of wounding any one's feelings, I would sincerely regret it, and I declare such to be against my intention. My aim has been to refute error, to explain the true doctrine, and not to indulge in any offensive recriminations. I beseech the divine Master to vouchsafe, in His infinite mercy, *to enlighten those who are sitting in darkness and in the shadow of death, and to direct them to the way of peace.* May the Saviour Jesus heal those born blind in heresy, and manifest Himself in His glory to those weak souls who are involved in the clouds of doubt! May all these unfortunate victims of error seek their salvation in Him, who is the Way, the Truth, and the Life, and in that only Church which

Conclusion. 247

He has instituted here below, the Catholic Apostolic Roman Church!

'Ipse est Petrus cui dixit: Tu es Petrus, et super hanc petram ædificabo Ecclesiam meam. Ubi ergo Petrus, ibi Ecclesia; ubi Ecclesia, ibi nulla mors, sed vita æterna.'—*St. Ambrose, Enarr. in Ps.* xi.

> 'Venite, fratres, si vultis ut inseremini in vite,
> Dolor est cum vos videmus præcisos ita jacere
> Numerate sacerdotes vel ab ipsa Petri sede,
> Et in ordine illo Patrum quis cui successit videte.'

'Ipsa est Petra, quam non vincunt superbæ inferorum portæ.'—*St. Augustine, Ps. contra partem Donati.*

'Alias oves habeo quæ non sunt ex hoc ovili; et illas oportet me adducere, et vocem meam audient, et fiet unum ovile et unus pastor.'—*Joan.* x. 16.

THE END.

LONDON:
ROBSON AND SONS, PRINTERS, PANCRAS ROAD, N.W.

BURNS AND OATES'S LIST.

LIBRARY OF RELIGIOUS BIOGRAPHY.
Edited by EDWARD HEALY THOMPSON, M.A.

Vol. I. *Life of St. Aloysius Gonzaga, S.J.* 5s. Second edition.

II. *Life of Marie-Eustelle Harpain, the Angel of the Eucharist.* 5s. Second edition.

III. *Life of St. Stanislas Kostka, S.J.* 5s.

IV. *Life of the Baron de Renty; or Perfection in the World exemplified.* 6s.

V. *Life of the Venerable Anna Maria Taigi, the Roman Matron* (1769-1837). With Portrait. Cloth, 6s.

VI. *Life and Revelations of Marie Lataste, Lay Sister of the Congregation of the Sacred Heart.*

Others in preparation.

Louise Lateau of Bois d'Haine: her Life, her Ecstasies, and her Stigmata. A Medical Study. By Dr. F. LEFEBVRE, Professor of General Pathology and Therapeutics in the Catholic University of Louvain, &c. Translated from the French. Edited by Rev. J. SPENCER NORTHCOTE, D.D. Full and complete edition. 3s. 6d.

Mental Prayer. By Père COURBON, S.J. Translated from the French, with Preface, by the Very Rev. Fr. GORDON, of the Oratory. Cloth, 2s. 6d.

Ecclesiastical Antiquities of London and its Suburbs. By ALEXANDER WOOD, M.A. Oxon., of the Somerset Archæological Society. 5s.

'O, who the ruins sees, whom wonder doth not fill
With our great fathers' pompe, devotion, and their skill.'

'Very seldom have we read a book entirely devoted to the metropolis with such pleasure. He has produced a book which from beginning to end is full of Catholic religious local lore of the highest interest.'—*Catholic Times.*

'Written by a very able and competent author, one who thoroughly appreciates his subject, and who treats it with the discrimination of a critic and the sound common sense of a practised writer.'—*Church Herald.*

The Early Martyrs. By Mrs. HOPE. New edition. 2s. 6d. and 3s.

Homeward: a Tale of Redemption. By the Rev. Fr. RAWES, O.S.C. Second edition. 3s. 6d.

'Full of holy thoughts and exquisite poetry.'—*Dublin Review.*

———o———

BURNS & OATES, 17 & 18 PORTMAN STREET, W.

The Prophet of Carmel: a Series of Practical Considerations upon the History of Elias in the Old Testament. With a supplementary Dissertation. By the Rev. CHARLES B. GARSIDE. Dedicated to the Very Rev. Dr. NEWMAN. 5s.
Contents: Chap. I. Introduction. II. The King and the Prophet. III. The Drought. IV. Sarephta. V. Mourning and Joy. VI. The Message of Mercy. VII. Troubling Israel. VIII. Necessary Antagonism. IX. Carmel. X. The Torrent of Cison. XI. Watching for Rain. XII. Fear and Flight. XIII. The Vision at Horeb. XIV. Breaking of the Clouds. XV. The Prophet's Mantle. XVI. The coveted Vineyard. XVII. The iniquitous Plot. XVIII. The unexpected Meeting. XIX. The Man of God. XX. The Parting and Ascension.
A Dissertation upon the following Questions: 1. The Condition and Abode of Elias after his Translation. 2. His Appearance on the Mount of Transfiguration. 3. His Return at the End of the World. 4. The Meaning of Luke i. 17; John i. 21, 25; Luke ix. 7, 8, 54-56; Matt. xxvii. 49.
'There is not a page in these sermons but commands our respect. They are Corban in the best sense; they belong to the sanctuary, and are marked as Divine property by a special cachet. Except the discourses of him to whom they are dedicated, Dr. Newman, we know of no better sermons in the language. They are simple without being trite, and poetical without being pretentious.'—*Westminster Gazette.*

Mary Magnifying God: May Sermons. By Rev. Fr. HUMPHREY, O.S.C. Cloth, 2s. 6d.
'Each sermon is a complete thesis, eminent for the strength of its logic, the soundness of its theology, the lucidness of its expression, and the force and beauty of its language.'—*Tablet.*

The Divine Teacher. By the same. 2s. 6d.
'The most excellent treatise we have ever read. It could not be clearer, and while really deep is perfectly intelligible to any person of the most ordinary education.'—*Tablet.*
'We cannot speak in terms too high of the matter contained in this most excellent and able pamphlet.'—*Westminster Gazette.*

God in His Works. A Course of Five Sermons. By the Rev. Fr. RAWES, O.S.C. Cloth, 2s. 6d.
Subjects: 1. God in Creation. 2. God in the Incarnation. 3. God in the Holy See. 4. God in the Heart. 5. God in the Resurrection.
'Full of striking imagery; and the beauty of the language cannot fail to make it valuable for spiritual reading.'—*Catholic Times.*

Fénélon's Reflections for every Day in the Month. Translated by the Rev. Dr. FLETCHER. Cloth, 1s.

Thoughts on some Passages of Holy Scripture. By a Layman. Translated from the French. Edited by JOHN EDWARD BOWDEN, Priest of the Oratory of St. Philip Neri. 2s. 6d.
'Contains some very devotional thoughts, and will be useful as a help to meditation.'—*Tablet.*

———o———

BURNS & OATES, 63 PATERNOSTER ROW, E.C.

Jesuits in Conflict; or Historic Facts illustrative of the Labours and Sufferings of the English Mission and Province of the Society of Jesus in the Times of Queen Elizabeth and her Successors. First Series. By a Member of the Society of Jesus. With illustrations in Photographed Etching. 1 vol. crown 8vo, 5s.

Life of Blessed Alphonsus Rodriguez, Lay Brother of the Society of Jesus. By the same. With Engraved Portrait. 1 vol. crown 8vo, 5s.

Lectures on certain Portions of the earlier Old Testament History. By PHILIP G. MUNRO. 3s. 6d.

'Sound, sober, and practical, and will be found extremely valuable.'—*Weekly Register.*

The Ritual of the New Testament: an Essay on the Principles and Origin of Catholic Ritual. By Rev. T. E. BRIDGETT, C.SS.R. Being the Second Edition of 'In Spirit and in Truth.' 5s.

'Written with singular force and simplicity. It goes to the root of the whole matter, discussing all the principles involved in a most exhaustive manner.'—*Tablet.*

The Question of Anglican Ordinations Discussed. By E. E. ESTCOURT, M.A. F.A.S., Canon of St. Chad's Cathedral, Birmingham. With an Appendix of Original Documents and Photographic Facsimiles. 14s.

'A valuable contribution to the theology of the sacrament of order.'—*Month.*

'Marks a very important epoch in the history of that question, and virtually disposes of it.'—*Messenger.*

'Will henceforth be an indispensable portion of every priest's library.'—*Tablet.*

'A work of very great value.'—*Catholic Opinion.*

'Superior both in literary method, tone, and mode of reasoning to the usual controversial books on this subject.'—*Church Herald.*

Count de Montalembert's Letters to a Schoolfellow: 1827-1830. Translated from the French by C. F. AUDLEY. With Portrait. 5s.

'Simple, easy, and unaffected in a degree, these letters form a really charming volume. The observations on men and manners, on books and politics, are simply wonderful, considering that when he wrote them he was only seventeen or eighteen years of age.'—*Weekly Register.*

Meditations for the Use of the Clergy for every Day in the Year, on the Gospels for the Sundays. From the Italian of Mgr. SCOTTI, Archbishop of Thessalonica. Revised and edited by the Oblates of St. Charles. Vols. i. ii. and iii., 4s. each.

'It is a sufficient recommendation to this book of meditations that our Archbishop has given them his own warm approval. . . . They are full of the language of the Scriptures, and are rich with unction of their Divine sense.'—*Weekly Register.*

'A manual of meditations for priests, to which we have seen nothing comparable.'—*Catholic World.*

'There is great beauty in the thoughts, the illustrations are striking, the learning shown in patristic quotation considerable, and the special applications to priests are very powerful. It is entirely a priest's book.'—*Church Review.*

———o———

BURNS AND OATES, 17 & 18 PORTMAN STREET, W.

Geology and Revelation; or the Ancient History of the Earth considered in the light of Geological Facts and Revealed Religion. With Illustrations. By the Rev. GERALD MOLLOY, D.D. Second edition, much enlarged and improved. 6s. 6d.

Art of always Rejoicing. By SARASA, S.J. 2s. 6d.

Bible History. By REEVE and CHALLONER. New and improved edition, 2s. Questions on ditto, 4d. Set of Illustrations for ditto, coloured, 12s.; larger size, 16s.

Manual of Church History. For Families and Schools. Compiled from the best sources. 12mo, cloth, 3s. (School edition, 2s.)

The Day Sanctified. Select Meditations and Spiritual Readings from Approved Writers. 3s. 6d.; red edges, 4s.

Sister Emmerich on the Passion. Full edition. 3s. 6d.

Fander: Catechism of the Christian Religion. Cloth, 2s.

Liguori (St. Alphonso). New and improved Translation of the Complete Works of St. Alphonso, edited by Father COFFIN:

Vol. I. The Christian Virtues, and the means for obtaining them. Cloth elegant, 4s. Or separately: 1. The Love of our Lord Jesus Christ, 1s. 4d. 2. Treatise on Prayer, 1s. 4d. (in the ordinary editions a great part of this work is omitted). 3. A Christian's Rule of Life, 1s.

Vol. II. The Mysteries of the Faith—the Incarnation; containing Meditations and Devotions on the Birth and Infancy of Jesus Christ, &c.; suited for Advent and Christmas. 3s. 6d.; cheap edition, 2s.

Vol. III. The Mysteries of the Faith—the Blessed Sacrament. 3s. 6d.; cheap edition, 2s.

Vol. IV. Eternal Truths—Preparation for Death. 3s. 6d.; cheap edition, 2s.

Vol. V. Treatises on the Passion: containing 'Jesus hath loved us,' &c. 3s.; cheap edition, 2s.

Vol. VI. Glories of Mary. New edition. 2s. 6d.; cloth, 3s. 6d.; with Frontispiece, cloth elegant, 4s. 6d.; also in better bindings.

'Jesus hath loved us,' separately, new and correct edition, 9d. cloth.

Visits to the Blessed Sacrament and to the Blessed Virgin Mary. An entirely new translation by the Redemptorist Fathers. 1s. cloth; bound roan, 1s. 6d.; French morocco, 2s. 6d.; calf, 4s. 6d.; morocco plain, 5s.; morocco gilt, 6s.

Month of Mary. 1s.; cloth, 1s. 6d.

Devotions to St. Joseph. 3d.; cloth, 4d.

Hymns and Verses on Spiritual Subjects. Cloth elegant, 1s.; cheap edition, 6d. Music, 1s.

Reflections on Spiritual Subjects, and on the Passion of our Lord. With Memoir and Frontispiece. Cloth, 2s. 6d.

BURNS AND OATES, 63 PATERNOSTER ROW, E.C.

THE THREE MISSION BOOKS,

Comprising all that is required for general use; the cheapest books ever issued.

1. *Complete Book of Devotions and Hymns: Path to Heaven*, 1000 pages, 2s. This Volume forms the Cheapest and most Complete Book of Devotions for Public or Private use ever issued. (33d Thousand.) Cloth, Two Shillings. Also in various bindings.
2. *Complete Choir Manual (Latin) for the Year*, 230 pieces. 10s. 6d.
3. *Complete Popular Hymn and Tune Book (English)*, 250 pieces. 10s. 6d. Melodies alone, 1s. Words, 3d.; cloth, 5d.

Prayers of SS. Gertrude and Mechtilde. Neat cloth, lettered, 1s. 6d.; Fr. morocco, red edges, 2s.; best calf, red edges, 4s. 6d.; best morocco, plain, 5s.; gilt, 6s. Also in various extra bindings. On thin *vellum paper* at the same prices.

Devotions for the 'Quarant' Ore,' or New Visits to the Blessed Sacrament. Edited by Cardinal Wiseman. 1s. 6d., or in cloth, gilt edges, 2s.; morocco, 5s.

Imitation of the Sacred Heart. By the Rev. Father ARNOLD, S.J. 12mo, 4s. 6d.; or in handsome cloth, red edges, 5s.; also in calf, 8s. 6d.; morocco, 9s. 6d.

Manual of the Sacred Heart. New edition, 2s.; red edges, 2s. 6d.; calf, 5s. 6d.; morocco, 6s. 6d.

The Spirit of St. Teresa. 2s.; red edges, with picture, 2s. 6d.

The Spirit of the Curé d'Ars. 2s. Ditto, ditto. 2s. 6d.

The Spirit of St. Gertrude. 2s. 6d.

Manna of the New Covenant: Devotions for Communion. Cloth, 2s.; bound, with red edges, 2s. 6d.

A' Kempis. The Following of Christ, in four books; a new translation, with borders, and illustrative engravings. Fcap. 8vo, cloth, 3s. 6d.; calf, 7s.; morocco, 8s. 6d.; gilt, 11s. The same, pocket edition. Cloth, 1s.; bound, roan, 1s. 6d.; calf, 4s. 6d.; morocco, 5s.

Spiritual Combat; a new translation. 18mo, cloth, 3s.; calf, 6s. 6d.; morocco, 7s. 6d. The same, pocket size. Cloth, 1s.; calf, neat, 4s. 6d.; morocco, 5s.

———o———

BURNS AND OATES, 17 & 18 PORTMAN STREET, W.

Missal. New and Complete Pocket Missal, in Latin and English, with all the new Offices and the Proper of Ireland, Scotland, and the Jesuits. Roan, embossed gilt edges, 5s.; calf flexible, red edges, 8s. 6d.; morocco, gilt edges, 9s. 6d.; ditto, gilt, 11s.

Epistles and Gospels for the whole Year. 1s. 6d.

Vesper Book for the Laity. This Volume contains the Office of Vespers (including Compline and Benediction), complete for *every day in the year.* Roan, 3s. 6d.; calf, 6s.; morocco, 7s.; gilt, 8s.

The Golden Manual; or Complete Guide to Devotion, Public or Private. New edition, enlarged and improved, 800 pp. Embossed, gilt edges, 6s.; calf flexible back, very neat and durable, 8s. 6d.; morocco plain, 9s. 6d.; gilt, 11s. Also bound for presents in elegant bindings, with antique boards and edges, clasps, corners, &c., 21s. and upwards; ivory, beautifully ornamented, 42s.; velvet rims and clasp, very elegant, 24s.

    Also an edition on fine thin satin paper, *one inch thick.* Calf, 8s. 6d.; morocco, 9s. 6d.; gilt, 11s.; limp morocco, edges turned over, 12s.

    The same, with *Epistles and Gospels,* 1s. extra.

Golden Manual and Missal in one. Calf, 15s.; morocco plain, 17s.; gilt, 18s. Also in various antique bindings.

Holy Communion, Books on the, &c.:
    Sacramental Companion. [Manna of the New Covenant.] New edition, 2s. 6d.
    Eucharistic Month. 6d.; cloth, 1s.
    Père Boone on Frequent Communion. Cloth, 6d.
    Devotions for Confession and Communion (Oratory). Covers, 6d.
    Liguori, St., on the Holy Eucharist. 3s. 6d.; cheap edition, 2s.
      ,,   Visits to the Most Blessed Sacrament. 1s.
    New Visits. Preface by Cardinal WISEMAN. 1s. 6d.; cloth, 2s.
    First Communion, Letters on. 1s.
    Reflections and Prayers for Holy Communion. From the French. Cloth, 4s. 6d.; do., red edges, 5s.; calf, 9s.; morocco, 10s.

Considerations for a Three Days' Preparation for Communion. Taken chiefly from the French of St. JURE, S.J. By CECILIE MARIE CADDELL. 8d.

Day Hours of the Church. Cloth, 1s. Also, separately, The Offices of Prime and Compline, 8d.; The Offices of Tierce, Sext, and None, 3d.

———o———

BURNS AND OATES, 63 PATERNOSTER ROW, E.C.

The Words of Jesus. Edited by the Rev. F. CASWALL. Cloth, 2s.

Lyra Liturgica: Verses for the Ecclesiastical Seasons. By Canon OAKELEY. 3s. 6d.

Select Sacred Poetry. 1s.

Instructions in Christian Doctrine. 3s.

New Testament Narrative for Schools and Families. 2s. 6d.

Letters on First Communion. 1s.

Flowers of St. Francis of Assisi. 3s.

Manual of Practical Piety. By St. FRANCIS DE SALES. 3s. 6d.

Manresa; or the Spiritual Exercises of St. Ignatius. 3s.

The Christian Virtues. By St. ALPHONSUS. 4s.

Eternal Truths. By the same. 3s. 6d.

On the Passion. By the same. 3s.

Jesus hath loved us. By the same. 9d.

Reflections on Spiritual Subjects. By the same. 2s. 6d.

Glories of Mary. By the same. New edition. 3s. 6d.

The Raccolta of Indulgenced Prayers. 3s.

Rodriguez on Christian Perfection. Two vols. 6s.

Stolberg's Little Book of the Love of God. 2s.

The Hidden Life of Jesus: a Lesson and Model to Christians. Translated from the French of HENRI-MARIE BOUDON, Archdeacon of Evreux, by EDWARD HEALY THOMPSON, M.A. 3s.

Devotion to the Nine Choirs of Holy Angels, and especially to the Angel-Guardians. Translated from the French of HENRI-MARIE BOUDON, Archdeacon of Evreux, by EDWARD HEALY THOMPSON, M.A. 3s.

Family Devotions for every Day in the Week, with occasional Prayers. Selected from Catholic Manuals, ancient and modern. Foolscap, limp cloth, red edges, very neat, 2s.

Aids to Choirmasters in the Performance of Solemn Mass, Vespers, Compline, and the various Popular Services in General Use. 2d.

P.S. Messrs. B. & O. will be happy to send any of the above books on inspection.

A large allowance to the Clergy.

———o———

BURNS & OATES, 17 & 18 PORTMAN STREET, W.

RELIGIOUS BIOGRAPHY AND HISTORY.

St. Aloysius Gonzaga. 5s.
St. Stanislas Kostka. 5s.
St. Paula. 2s.
Marie-Eustelle Harpain. 5s.
St. Charles Borromeo. 3s. 6d.
St. Vincent de Paul. 3s.
St. Francis de Sales. 3s.
The Curé d'Ars. 4s.
St. Thomas of Canterbury. 4s. 6d.
Wykeham, Waynflete, & More. 4s.
The Blessed Henry Suso. 4s.
M. Olier of Saint Sulpice. 4s.
The Early Martyrs. 2s. 6d.
St. Dominic and the Dominican Order. 3s. 6d.
Madame Swetchine. 7s. 6d.
The Sainted Queens. 3s.
Blessed John Berchmans. 2s.
St. Francis Xavier. 2s.
St. Philip Neri. 3s.
St. Frances of Rome. 2s. 6d.
Heroines of Charity. 2s. 6d.
Saints of the Working Classes. 1s. 4d.
Sœur Rosalie and Mdlle. Lamourous. 1s.
St. Francis and St. Clare. 1s.
Lives of Pious Youth. 2s.
Modern Missions in the East and West. 3s.
Missions in Japan and Paraguay. 3s.
The Knights of St. John. 3s. 6d.
Anecdotes and Incidents. 2s. 6d.
Remarkable Conversions. 2s. 6d.
Pictures of Christian Heroism. 3s.
Lives of the Roman Pontiffs. By DE MONTOR. 2 vols. 58s. (cash, 48s.).
Darras' History of the Church. 4 vols. 2l. 8s. (cash, 2l.).
Mary Ann of Jesus, the Lily of Quito. 3s. 6d.
A Noble Lady. 2s. 6d.
Mme. de Soyecourt. 3s.
St. Ignatius. By BARTOLI. 2 vols. 14s.—Ditto, small size, 2s.

St. Ignatius and his Companions. 4s.
Abulchar Bisciarah. 2 vols. 3s. 6d.
St. Angela Merici. 3s. 6d.
St. Margaret of Cortona. 3s. 6d.
Princess Borghese. 2s.
F. Maria Ephraim. 5s.
Mrs. Seton. 8s. 6d.
Mme. de la Peltrie. 2s.
F. Felix d'Andreis. 4s. 6d.
St. Philomena. 2s. 6d.
St. Cecilia. By GUERANGER. 6s.
Fathers of the Desert. 4s. 6d.
Pius VI. 3s.
St. Bridget. 2s. 6d.
St. Mary Magdalen. 2s. 6d.
St. Zita. 3s.
St. Francis of Assisi. 2s.
St. Catherine of Sienna. 5s.
Bishop Flaget. 4s. 6d.
Dr. Maginn. 4s. 6d.
Cath. M'Auley. Foundress of the Sisters of Mercy. 10s. 6d.

EDITED BY LADY G. FULLERTON.
Mary Fitzgerald, a Child of the Sacred Heart. 2s.
The Honourable F. Dormer, late of the 60th Rifles. 2s.

The Apostle of Abyssinia. By Lady HERBERT of Lea. Post 8vo, cloth, 6s.; cheap edition, 3s.

The Corean Martyrs. 2s.

FOREIGN MISSIONARY SERIES.
1. Henry Dorié, Martyr. Translated by Lady HERBERT. Cloth, 2s.
2. Théophane Vénard, Martyr in Tonquin. Cloth, 3s.
3. Bishop Bruté. Cloth, 3s.
4. Monseigneur Berneux, Bishop and Martyr. Cloth, 3s.

———o———

BURNS & OATES, 63 PATERNOSTER ROW, E.C.

www.ingramcontent.com/pod-product-compliance
Lightning Source LLC
Chambersburg PA
CBHW031951230426
43672CB00010B/2127